Musical Modernism at the Turn of the Twenty-First Century

Providing a new approach to developments in recent modernist music – from 1980 to the present day – this study also presents an original perspective on the larger history of modernism. Far from being supplanted by a postmodern period, argues David Metzer, modernist idioms remain vital in the contemporary scene. The vitality comes from the ways in which those idioms have extended impulses of modernist styles from the early twentieth century. Since that time, works have participated in lines of inquiry into various compositional and aesthetic topics, particularly the explorations of how to build pieces around such aesthetic ideals as purity and silence and how to deliver and manipulate expressive utterances. Metzer shows how these inquiries have played crucial roles in defining directions taken since 1980, and how, through the inquiries, we can gain a clearer idea of what makes the decades after 1980 a distinct period in the history of modernism.

DAVID METZER is Professor of Music at the University of British Columbia. He is the author of *Quotation and Cultural Meaning in Twentieth-Century Music* (Cambridge 2003), and has contributed to numerous journals, including *Journal of the American Musicological Society*, *Modernism/Modernity*, and *Journal of Musicology*.

Music in the Twentieth Century

GENERAL EDITOR Arnold Whittall

This series offers a wide perspective on music and musical life in the twentieth century. Books included range from historical and biographical studies concentrating particularly on the context and circumstances in which composers were writing, to analytical and critical studies concerned with the nature of musical language and questions of compositional process. The importance given to context will also be reflected in studies dealing with, for example, the patronage, publishing, and promotion of new music, and in accounts of the musical life of particular countries.

Musical Modernism at the Turn of the Twenty-First Century

David Metzer

CAMBRIDGE
UNIVERSITY PRESS

CAMBRIDGE UNIVERSITY PRESS
Cambridge, New York, Melbourne, Madrid, Cape Town, Singapore, São Paulo, Delhi

Cambridge University Press
The Edinburgh Building, Cambridge CB2 8RU, UK

Published in the United States of America by Cambridge University Press, New York

www.cambridge.org
Information on this title: www.cambridge.org/9780521517799

First published 2009

Printed in the United Kingdom at the University Press, Cambridge

A catalogue record for this publication is available from the British Library

Library of Congress Cataloguing in Publication data
Metzer, David Joel, 1965–
Musical modernism at the turn of the twenty-first century / David Metzer.
    p.   cm. – (Music in the twentieth century)
Includes bibliographical references and index.
ISBN 978-0-521-51779-9 (harback)
1. Modernism (Music)   2. Music – 20th century – Philosophy and aesthetics.
3. Music – 21st century – Philosophy and aesthetics.
I. Title.   II. Series.
ML3845.M44   2009
780.9′05 – dc22   2009025309

ISBN 978-0-521-51779-9 Hardback

Contents

Music examples and figures

Music examples

Figures

Acknowledgements

I was drawn to the "Music in the Twentieth Century" series by the prospect of working with the series editor Arnold Whittall. As I had hoped, Professor Whittall had much to say during the production of the manuscript. Another voice is always welcome in the solitude of scholarly writing. It is especially so when the book, like this one, ventures new views on well-covered topics, no better example being the history and nature of musical modernism. Such boldness needs to be challenged and encouraged. Prof. Whittall did both in his comments on chapter drafts. To have been engaged in an ongoing and spirited conversation with an elite scholar in the field has been a rare opportunity for which I am grateful. I am also pleased to continue the rewarding relationship with Cambridge University Press that began with my first book, *Quotation and Cultural Meaning in Twentieth-Century Music*. Vicki Cooper has championed this project since the earliest stages. Rebecca Jones has patiently answered my many questions and unfailingly steered me in the right directions.

Throughout the writing of the book, I have benefited from the assistance of friends and colleagues. They have provided so much of what a scholar requires, including encouragement, lodging, bibliographic suggestions, incisive criticism, and humor. Each has made a personal contribution, which I unfortunately do not have the time to describe here. I hope that they do not mind being lined up in an alphabetical list of thanks: Arved Ashby, Amy Bauer, Sally Bick, Dániel Péter Biró, Greg Butler, Alan Dodson, Eric Drott, Alex Fisher, Jonathan Goldman, Jim Grier, Matthew Head, Rachel Iwaasa, Richard Kurth, Sherry Lee, Trent Leipert, Richard Leppert, Vera Micznik, Greg Miller, Greg Newsome, David Paul, and Rodney Sharman. I would also like to thank my parents for their undying support. Gordon Paslawski provided invaluable assistance with the musical examples, not any easy task with scores abounding with intricate and idiosyncratic notation.

I completed the manuscript during a sabbatical stay at Peterhouse at Cambridge University. The college was generous in allowing me to use its academic and computer resources. I especially enjoyed the wonderful scholarly company. My deepest thanks to Richard Grigson for making those memorable months possible.

This project was supported by grants from the Social Sciences and Humanities Research Council of Canada.

Sections of Chapter 1 appeared previously in "The Paths from and to Abstraction in Stockhausen's *Gesang der Jünglinge*," *Modernism/Modernity* 11 (2004), 695–721. Sections of Chapter 2 were originally published in "Modern Silence," *Journal of Musicology* 23 (2006), 331–74.

Introduction

Musical Modernism at the Turn of the Twenty-First Century. Some readers may float a question mark at the end of the title. After all, modernism has supposedly been succeeded by the bluntly named postmodernism. Surely by the dawn of this new century all that is left of modernism are vestiges and memories. This study hopes to delete any such mental question marks. Modernism, as argued here, remains vital. It has not been supplanted. It draws upon a wealth of ideals and precedents and is fueled by continuing impulses. With such resources, it has crossed over into the twenty-first century.

In making such claims, this book joins a group of studies that have reassessed the position of both modernism and postmodernism in recent decades. Even some of the scholars who theorized the rise of the latter, notably Fredric Jameson and Charles Jencks, have had to acknowledge the obstinacy of modernism.[1] So resilient has it proven to be that Jencks has identified two streams in contemporary architecture: neo- and late modernism. The former "plays with" established forms, creating what amounts to "a new baroque elaboration of the language synthesized in the twenties."[2] The latter exaggerates and complicates elements of 1950s–60s high modernism. The result in both cases is architecture of stylistic extremes and little ethical relevance. The emptiness of the two gives Jencks confidence to proclaim, once again, that modernism has a "limited future," and to go as far as to predict its demise in fifty or sixty years.[3]

Where some see a slowly dying modernism, others perceive renewal. Marjorie Perloff has described how contemporary poets have rekindled the dynamics of classic early twentieth-century works to create a "twenty-first century modernism," the beginnings of "a 'new' poetics." If anything, postmodernism "seems to have lost momentum" at the turn of the new century, whereas the "modernist challenge" from the beginning of the last century "remains open."[4] Claus-Steffen Mahnkopf has made an equally bold

---

[1] See Fredric Jameson, *Postmodernism or the Cultural Logic of Late Capitalism* (Durham: Duke University Press, 1991) and *A Singular Modernity: Essay on the Ontology of the Present* (London and New York: Verso, 2002). Also Charles Jencks, *What is Postmodernism?* (New York and London: St. Martin's Press, 1986) and *The New Moderns: From Late to Neo-Modernism* (London: Academy Editions, 1990).

[2] Jencks, *The New Moderns*, 17.   [3] Jencks, *The New Moderns*, 10.

[4] Marjorie Perloff, *21st-century Modernism: The "New" Poetics* (Oxford: Blackwell, 2002), 2, 164.

statement about concert music. According to him, a "second modernism" emerged around 1980. Claims of a postmodernist movement have proven to be shortsighted and rash. Whereas theories of postmodernism bandy about ideas like pluralism, heterogeneity, and the multifacetedness of the contemporary subject, second modernist works realize them through such means as complex polyphony, intricate rhythms, disconnected structures, microtonality, and conceptions of the work that have outgrown the opposition between open and closed. The leaders of this new period are three composers discussed here: Ligeti, Ferneyhough, and Lachenmann.[5]

In lieu of moribundity and rebirth, some scholars have described a modernism that simply carries on. It extends, sometimes brilliantly, sometimes laboriously, the impetuses of the early period while all the time changing in response to new inspirations and pressures. Alastair Williams argues that the 1970s produced a "transformed" modernism.[6] He considers postmodernism more as a critical revision of modernism than as a successor.[7] In particular, the semantic breadth of modernism expanded as it reached out to a host of styles and discourses even as it continued the characteristic self-contained explorations of material and structure.[8] Concluding an insightful account of different topics across a range of twentieth-century works, Arnold Whittall arrives at this century with both concerns over the vicissitudes confronting modernism and optimism about the future of the music. He holds up a group of recent pieces by Carter, Boulez, Berio, and Ligeti and reveals how they build upon previous developments and betoken a music that "could acquire new contexts, new perspectives."[9] Such pieces reveal modernism to be, as Whittall has said elsewhere, "an aesthetic more than capable of survival, and indeed further evolution, within the ultra-heterodox climate of the new century."[10]

This study seconds many of the points raised by the above authors, except for Jencks's death writ. As to the divide between modernism and postmodernism, there has been, as mentioned at the outset, no such split. This is

---

[5] Claus-Steffen Mahnkopf, "Neue Musik am Beginn der Zweiten Moderne," *Merkur* 594/595 (1998), 873–75. The ideas in this essay have been explored further in a collection of essays: *Facets of the Second Modernity*, ed. Claus-Steffen Mahnkopf, Frank Cox, and Wolfram Schurig (Hofheim: Wolke Verlag, 2008).

[6] Alastair Williams, "Ageing of the New: The Museum of Musical Modernism," in *The Cambridge History of Twentieth-century Music*, ed. Nicholas Cook and Anthony Pople (Cambridge University Press, 2004). 523, 535.

[7] Alastair Williams, *New Music and the Claims of Modernity* (Hants: Ashgate, 1997), 148.

[8] Williams, "Ageing of the New," 526.

[9] Arnold Whittall, *Exploring Twentieth-century Music: Tradition and Innovation* (Cambridge University Press, 2003), 207.

[10] This quotation is taken from an interview in John Palmer, *Jonathan Harvey's "Bhakti" for Chamber Ensemble and Electronics: Serialism, Electronics and Spirituality* (Leviston: Edwin Mellen Press, 2001), 153.

not to suggest that modernism is a dominant movement that encompasses the diversity of recent cultural production. No "ism," as to be discussed in the Conclusion, has the amplitude to do so, nor is it clear that modernism ever played such a magisterial role in the past. Modernism at this point in time is indeed one part of an "ultra-heterodox climate." Moreover, at this point in time, we are experiencing one particular period in the history of modernism. This study identifies the years from roughly 1980 to the present as such a period, which, to add to all the temporal qualifications attached to the ephemeral "modern," will be referred to as late modernism (yes, there will undoubtedly be later modernisms to come). The chronology loosely accords with the divisions proposed by Williams and Mahnkopf, the "transformed modernism" of the former and the "second modernism" of the latter. Such shifts obviously cannot be pinpointed but what can be observed is that modernist idioms during this time changed in ways that departed from the ideals of the decades following World War Two, departures striking enough to inaugurate a new period of modernist music.

Before discussing those changes, a general conception of modernism needs to be established. Modernism is used here in the widely accepted notion of the term, that of the significant departures in musical language that occurred around the turn of the twentieth century.[11] The departures created new understandings of the harmonic, melodic, sonic, and rhythmic realms of composition. Needless to say, the nature of the departures, their significance, and their scope have been the stuff of critical scrutiny and debate. Some recent scholarship has aimed to expand the idea of modernism beyond the focus on compositional innovation by staking out modernist ideals in popular culture or in more traditional composers.[12] This study holds to the more established notion of modernism, a notion truer to the types of works discussed here. Yet, like those other approaches, it creates new perspectives by viewing early modernism from afar, not from the realms of popular culture or traditional idioms but rather from a later period, that from the 1980s to the present. In particular, the ideals and behavior of late modernist styles can be spotted in earlier styles. Projecting those qualities upon the initial styles offers alternative ways to appreciate the latter.

Most changed is our understanding of how modernism acts, particularly the action most associated with it, that of innovation. The idea of

---

[11] There have been attempts to situate the origins of modernism further back in the nineteenth century. J. Peter Burkholder sees modernism as extending the historicist tendency in nineteenth-century music. Burkholder, "Museum Pieces: The Historicist Mainstream in Music of the Last Hundred Years," *Journal of Musicology* 2 (1983), 115–34.

[12] Two studies pursuing these directions include Alfred Appel, Jr., *Jazz Modernism From Ellington and Armstrong to Matisse and Joyce* (New York: Alfred A. Knopf, 2002) and J. P. E. Harper-Scott, *Edward Elgar, Modernist* (Cambridge University Press, 2006).

modernism acting, let alone the action of innovation, requires explanation. In many evocations of the concept, modernism – called the new, modern art, a new spirit, or some other characteristic name – assumes the position of a subject that does something, like, as Ezra Pound memorably remarked, "make it new." Innovation, the breaking away from the conventional, is one role typically assigned to modernism. In his *Aesthetic Theory*, Adorno whips up a frenetic energy called "the new." As he describes it, the new "seeks," "explodes," "negates," and commits "violence," all things done to the secure and staid.[13] Adorno also presents modernism as tracking "advanced material," the most challenging conceptions of form and expression at a given time.[14]

Modernism has acted out the role of innovation on many of the historiographical stages set for it. This assigned part, though, is rather limited, as the advances made have been confined to areas of compositional technique, a focus that neglects the jarring effects modernist idioms have had on the larger cultural arena and modes of expression. Carl Dahlhaus traces this narrow focus back to the decades after World War Two. At that time, composers and critics, emulating the scientific ethos of the Cold War period, emphasized "compositional-technical discoveries and hypotheses" in surveying both the present and immediate past. They unfolded a "problem history," in which a work responds to and solves the compositional problems raised by previous pieces. Each solution yields not only new approaches but also fresh problems to be tackled by future works.[15] By perpetuating the new, the solutions consign previous works, some still rather new, to the pile of past and no longer relevant results. Most textbooks of twentieth-century music reinforce the bias toward innovation.[16] The result is a chronological log of compositional advances.

Innovation is, however, a hard act to keep up, for both modernist works and the historical narratives built around them. The strain is particularly great for the latter, which are so invested in the idea of compositional progress. The narratives typically flag when they hit the 1960s and 1970s, if not earlier. At this point, newness, especially the wholesale kind achieved at the beginning of the century, is hard to be had, as it seems that everything

[13] Theodor Adorno, *Aesthetic Theory*, trans. and ed. Robert Hullot-Kentor (Minneapolis: University of Minnesota Press, 1997), 19–24.

[14] Adorno, *Philosophy of New Music*, trans. and ed. Robert Hullot-Kentor (Minneapolis: University of Minnesota Press, 2006), 31–34. Max Paddison, *Adorno's Aesthetics of Music* (Cambridge University Press, 1993), 85–89.

[15] Carl Dahlhaus, "Progress and the Avant Garde," in his *Schoenberg and the New Music: Essays*, trans. Derrick Puffett and Alfred Clayton (Cambridge University Press, 1987), 20.

[16] As Christopher A. Williams has remarked, these "ingrained patterns of thinking" have been "replicated" in "book after book." Williams, "Of Canons and Context: Towards a Historiography of Twentieth-century Music," *repercussions* 2 (1993), 37.

has already been done. For Adorno, the quandary was not a sign of defeat but
rather a defining characteristic of the new. Instead of the intrepid composer,
he personifies the quest for the new in the figure of a child at the piano
trying to find a chord that he or she has not hit before. Of course, there
are only so many possible chords, but it is the determination not the results
that is important.[17] As Adorno concludes, "the new is the longing for the
new, not the new itself."[18] "The cult of the new," he adds, "is a rebellion
against the fact that there is no longer anything new," a fact reinforced
by the mass-produced sameness issued by factories.[19] Even the seemingly
endless development of "advanced material" reaches an end. In a 1954 talk
on the "aging" of new music, he mentioned how the "expansion of musical
materials" had come to a remote, "extreme point" and that the possibilities
of sound within the equal-temperament system had been exhausted.[20] A
few years later, writing on Berg, he stated that the "pure evolution of the
materials of music had reached a certain threshold."[21]

At this point, textbook histories typically shift narratives from tales of
innovation to repeated notices about pluralism.[22] Instead of looking at the
singular advances of the individual work, we now consider the place of
the lone work, radical or conservative, within an all-encompassing stylistic
diversity. Everything belongs to the stylistic mass, which is presented as a
feature of contemporary musical life and one that will continue to be a
feature for the foreseeable future. Unlike Adorno's material, the mass never

[17] Perhaps it was only a matter of time before the intrepid composer and curious child met. In his *Chord Catalogue* (1986), Tom Johnson states every chord that can be formulated within the span of an octave. That makes for 8,178. The work is for any keyboard instrument. A few years later he wrote *Music for 88* (1988), a piece that involves all the keys of the piano.

[18] Adorno, *Aesthetic Theory*, 32.

[19] Theodor Adorno, *Minima Moralia: Reflections from a Damaged Life*, trans. E. F. N. Jephcott (London: NLB, 1974), 235. For a discussion of Adorno's concepts of the "new" and modernity, see Daniel Chua, "Drifting: The Dialectics of Adorno's *Philosophy of New Music*," in *Apparitions: New Perspectives on Adorno and Twentieth-century Music*, ed. Berthold Hoeckner (New York: Routledge, 2006), 1–17.

[20] Theodor Adorno, "The Aging of the New Music," in his *Essays on Music*, ed. Richard Leppert (Berkeley: University of California Press, 2002), 190. Here I depart from the translation by Robert Hullot-Kentor and Fredric Will published in the Leppert collection. The original German (Zugleich jedoch ist die Expansion des musikalischen Materials selbst bis zu einem Äußersten vorgestossen) states that the expansion has reached an extreme point. According to the translation by Hullot-Kentor and Fredric Will, the expansion "has gone ahead limitlessly," a phrase that implies endless expansion and not the possibility of the remote terminus suggested by an extreme. For the original German, see "Das Altern der neuen Musik," in Adorno's *Dissonanzen: Musik in der verwalteten Welt* (Göttingen: Vandenhoeck & Ruprecht, 1963), 147.

[21] Adorno, "Berg's Discoveries in Compositional Technique," in *Quasi una Fantasia: Essays on Modern Music*, trans. Rodney Livingstone (London and New York: Verso, 1992), 192. The limits reached by Adorno's ideas of advanced material are discussed in Günter Seubold, "Some Reflections on Th. W. Adorno's Music Aesthetics," *Canadian Aesthetics Journal/Revue canadienne d'esthétique* 6 (Fall 2001) (www.uqtr.ca/AE/Vol_6/articles/seubol.html).

[22] See Robert Morgan, *Twentieth-century Music: A History of Musical Style in Modern Europe and America* (New York: W. W. Norton, 1991), 407–22, 484–86.

moves, either forwards or backwards. The individual work remains part of a static diversity. Things, though, are not so static. Within the mass, there are all sorts of relationships between pieces, from confrontation to collaboration. As called for here, we must reckon with this diversity rather than repeat cant about an unprecedented pluralism. One way of doing so is to reveal the antinomies and convergences within the mass.

This study will build a historical narrative around the mode of inquiry, another characteristic way in which modernism "acts." Inquiry is used here in the general sense of the term, an investigation into points of interest. In this case, the investigation is made through and sustained by musical works. The points of interest explored by the pieces include aesthetic ideals, compositional material, and facets of expression. Throughout the history of modernism, works have taken up such points. Aware of these repeated explorations, we can perceive long-standing lines of inquiry. For example, pieces by Debussy, Webern, Boulez, and Kurtág have scrutinized the properties of the fragment. There may or may not be specific ties between their works, but the compositions do share an interest in fragmentary states. That interest is enough to bring them together. Linked with one another, the pieces can be seen as forming a single line of inquiry, one that has stretched across the twentieth century.

With this in mind, we can begin to perceive the differences between historical accounts premised upon innovation and an account based on lines of inquiry. To make the point, two late twentieth-century idioms will be discussed: spectralism and the new complexity. The two are often viewed as being among the "newer" developments during the 1970s and 1980s, as attested to by the name coined for the latter. The following discussion provides a different way of viewing them than that of sheer innovation, a way that accords more with the dynamics of late modernism. To be blunt, neither idiom was so new after all. They had precedents, or, as Fredric Jameson has put it, they had a "place" established for them. Writing on obdurate modernist styles that endure in the face of postmodernism, he shows how more recent styles (which in his example only go as far as Nabokov and Beckett) have settled into the place made for them by earlier styles. The "codification" of earlier innovations has provided them with a "theoretical certainty" and "models" upon which to draw.[23] Spectralism may have changed conceptions of the nature and construction of the sonic object, but it was still working within a specific model, that of the independent and volatile realm of sound opened up by Varèse, Cage, Ligeti, and others. The complexity at the heart of the new complexity had already been attained in works by integral serialist composers and Xenakis (for

---

[23] Jameson, *A Singular Modernity*, 197–200.

example, *Eonta*). The composers in the movement ratcheted up both the level of intricacy found in such pieces and the virtuosic strain placed on performers.

In lieu of innovation, both spectralism and the new complexity can be heard as partaking in a mode of inquiry. Studies of modernism have failed to isolate this modus operandi, let alone explain it in any detail. To observe it at work, we need once again to recast the notion of innovation central to modernism. The compositional departures of early modernism can be considered as possibilities. With these developments, composers immeasurably broadened the musical world, opening up whole new tonal, rhythmic, and sonic frontiers. A history of modernism could be written around the explorations of those possibilities, a search of the frontiers. So vast has the new musical world proven that the explorations have continued on through the twentieth century and into the next. The investigations have resulted in a range of new styles, sounds, and organizational approaches. To return to the above two examples, spectralism and the new complexity have furthered inquiries that have long been under way. The former, along with works of Varèse, Cage, and Ligeti, grows out of the isolation and cultivation of sound that began with the unprecedented emphasis placed on timbre in the works of Debussy and the Second Viennese School. The latter probes the limits of compositional density, asking what happens when there is "too much."[24] The multilayered works of Ives and early Stravinsky were among the first to accumulate such a surplus of detail.

Inquiry gets at the restless curiosity driving modernism. Rather than fixating on the new, the rare quantity of that which is "not already used-up," modernist idioms return to specific ideas and materials and never manage to use them up.[25] Modernism has a strong awareness of its own precedents and builds upon them. Constantly reworking established elements, modernist idioms strengthen connections with past explorations, thereby creating the surprising result of modernism solidifying the past, its own past. At the same time, the involvement with previous explorations can yield the new, not so much the shocking gesture as the different ways in which an idea has been treated. The mode of modernist inquiry is not unlike that in science, one in which an experiment cites and departs from previous research in the hope of reaching new insights.[26]

---

[24] Brian Ferneyhough, *Collected Writings*, ed. James Boros and Richard Toop (Amsterdam: Harwood, 1995), 117.

[25] Adorno, *Aesthetic Theory*, 26.

[26] The mode of inquiry is different from the self-amputating scientific models that influenced accounts of compositional method in post–World War Two repertoires mentioned above. In his discussion of the emphasis on "discovery" in that literature, Dahlhaus makes a similar point: "Modern physics includes classical physics; yet it would be a gross overstatement to say the same about modern compositional technique." Dahlhaus, "Progress and the Avant Garde," 20.

The prolongation of lines of inquiry may suggest that the history of modernism has been one of smooth continuity. This is obviously not the case. It is a history marked by both continuity and disruption. This study chronicles a particular break, that occurring around 1980. The break, as will be discussed, was made largely along the lines of construction and expression. Late modernist works departed from previous approaches to those two areas, but they also extended other approaches. To capture these contrary tendencies, this study adopts a dual historical focus, one split between discontinuity and continuity. A model of inquiry demands such a focus, as individual lines typically cite and take further explorations begun in earlier pieces while changing directions. Such is the case with the two inquiries described here: those into compositional states and the act of expression.

Compositional states have played a prominent role in musical modernism. Surprisingly, this role has received little attention, let alone been identified as an ongoing point of exploration. A compositional state involves the shaping of the musical language in a work so as to emulate a specific ideal. The ideals can be sonic in nature, such as silence and the mutability of sound, or conceptual, such as purity, complexity, and the fragmentary. An ideal governs a piece. It provides sounds, behaviors, and structural patterns to which the musical language adheres. The sounds are approximated, the behaviors are followed, and the patterns are erected. Through this diligence, the music aims to become the ideal, or, more accurately, it aims to become a manifestation of the ideal – flecks in the fragmentary, a facet of the pure, or a spell of silence.

Works involved with compositional states do not merely mimic a specific condition; rather, they engage an ideal so as to delve into its unique associations and properties. A musical exploration of silence, for instance, can lead to suggestions of absence, death, and mystery. Purity holds out ascetic notions of wholeness and integrity. The scrutiny of these ideals also offers intriguing musical inquiries that go beyond those required to evoke a state. Entering the fragmentary, composers can challenge notions of unity and form; drawing upon the flux of sound, they can probe thresholds of transformation. As these examples make clear, there is no such thing as a single inquiry into a compositional state. The exploration of a compositional state fans out into many directions: how the material can be molded to fit an ideal, the associations of the ideal, and the formal and sonic explorations spurred on by a state. This study concentrates on four states, each of which sustains multi-level inquiries. The four are purity, silence, the fragmentary, and the flux of sound.

The idea of compositional elements inhering in larger musical or aesthetic entities calls to mind Adorno's concept of "musical material," which includes the advanced type pursued by modernism. A comparison of material and states reveals differences and similarities between the two and puts into sharper relief defining characteristics of the latter. As Dahlhaus has argued, the notion of advanced material epitomizes Adorno's idea of the historical properties of tones.[27] Musical material stores precedents and conventions and, driven by a tendency to change, it pushes toward new possibilities. Consistent with the expansive critical forum in which Adorno places works, the historical is just one aspect of musical material, which also possesses compositional/technical, aesthetic, philosophical, and sociological dimensions. The broad scope makes clear that Adorno's material is far from the natural resource that past theorists considered pitches and harmonies to be. It is not raw clay that composers can mold as they like. On the contrary, they must submit to its exigencies. Most unwieldy of all is advanced material. The rarefied compound holds the most demanding technical and expressive means of a particular historical moment. It is highly independent, driven by its own tendencies and beholden to no work or outside ideal. Pieces tap into the elite stuff, capturing bits, not all, of its newness.[28]

Compositional states may seem to involve the kind of sculpted material dismissed by Adorno. As outlined earlier, the "material" of a state is handled in ways to evoke an ideal, but it is not just the notes that are being shaped, so too is the ideal. Ideals, like the fragmentary or purity, are just that – ideals. They exist as abstractions. To become the stuff of art, they have to be realized in material terms. Works engaged with states perform this transubstantiation. In doing so, each arrives at one of the many different guises that the ideals can assume. For example, the fragmentary, fitting for an ideal about strewn pieces, can take myriad individual shapes. Compositions create their own version of the state by concentrating on the crucial relationship between part and whole. Some works set the fragments in oblique orbits around a whole, whereas others attempt to annul the possibility of coherence. If states are to be considered as sculpting, then the sculpting creates a far more interesting compositional scenario than any kind of utilitarian molding. In this case, the sculpting of the material, how the pitches and sounds are used, is just as important as the appearance of the final sculpture, the evocation of the ideal.

---

[27] The following observations about advanced material draw upon Dahlhaus's discussion of the concept. Dahlhaus, "Adornos Begriff des musikalischen Materials," in *Schönberg und andere* (Mainz: Schott, 1978), 336–39. See also Adorno, *Philosophy of New Music*, 31–34.

[28] Paddison, *Adorno's Aesthetics of Music*, 88–89, 149.

Adorno's advanced material and compositional states occupy separate historical dimensions. Aloof and willful, the former flows within a self-contained historical stream, apart from the pieces that dip into it. Compositional states are not so removed. They commit to large aesthetic ideals that exist outside of both the material and the piece. If anything, it is the ideals that form a historical stream, which is sustained by the ongoing inquiry into states. Adorno's own theoretical discussions of the fragment in musical works, for example, added to the inquiry into the state of the fragmentary. The continuity of the ideals brings up another difference from Adorno's model. As he admitted, advanced material had run its course, succumbing to the depletion of the new. No such terminus has arisen for the ideals taken up in states, which have figured prominently throughout the history of modernism. The interest in them has not dimmed, as seen in the works considered here. As long as the ideals remain vibrant, so too will the inquiry into states.

A broader understanding of states can be gained by changing emphasis from material to compositional focus. Whereas the former concept details the types of sounds selected by a composer and the shapes they take in a work, the latter emphasizes how the ideals of a state influence aspects of compositional method and structure. The dynamics and patterns intrinsic to an ideal serve to construct a logic for the composer to follow. Consistency with those properties can assure consistency within a piece. For example, purity, as to be expected, enforces a severe compositional logic. Only sounds recognized as pure are to be chosen and they must be handled in certain ways, typically through means of refinement or reduction. Through such steps, purity serves as both an inspiration and a means by which the composer can conceive of and organize a piece. The ideals in a state also play a role in terms of reception. In regard to purity, listeners can comprehend the piece in relation to conceptions of the pure. The sparse materials can be heard as manifestations of the restrictions dictated by the ideal, and the winnowing down of sounds can be perceived as the workings of the process of reduction used to attain an essence.

The role of states as a point of compositional focus is pertinent to modernist music since 1980. To understand how and why, we need to adopt the dual historical perspective described above. Given that the inquiry into states has been active since the early years of modernism, it is safe to assume that the ideals in states have long served in such a role. Chapters 1 and 2 make that point by examining the cultivation of purity in Stockhausen's *Gesang der Jünglinge* and silence in Webern's Five Pieces for Orchestra (op. 10).[29]

---

[29] Chapter 4 discusses a non-musical example, looking at how Thomas Mann's *Doctor Faustus* extends the modernist interest in the genre of the lament.

Both chapters reveal how works composed later in the twentieth century extend points taken up by the two earlier pieces, particularly the use of purity and silence as means of compositional focus. When looking at those works alongside other late modernist pieces, we can begin to get an idea of the strong emphasis placed on the structural and aesthetic inspiration offered by states in music written since 1980. The analyses pursued here are the only evidence in support of such a claim. There are no numbers to back it up, say a count of pieces using states in this manner before and after 1980. How could there be when this book is the first to identify the inquiry into states? The argument instead rests upon observations made from an in-depth study of recent works and a broad knowledge of twentieth-century music. Much more needs to be done in refining our understanding of states. The above position is a start.

An important first step is to ask why compositional states play such a prominent structural role in late modernist pieces. An answer can be found in what Williams has called "the general softening of structural obsessions since the 1950s."[30] By 1980, the obsessions had softened quite a bit, as serialism and other systematic approaches no longer held the sway that they once did. There are, of course, notable exceptions, such as the music of Ferneyhough mentioned by Williams. There is still, however, a pronounced shift away from the precompositional rigor of the 1950s and 1960s. Even some composers who used, or who continue to rely upon, systematic methods have made such a move. Boulez, for example, has long ago backed off from the strictness of works such as *Structures I*, allowing room for "accidents," the digressions from the governing system, and more intuitive moments. In the 1980s, he questioned more seriously the assumptions of post–World War Two serialism.[31] A 1986 article goes so far as to admit that integral serial methods "raised a formalist utopia without direct effectiveness."[32]

The structural potential of states can be seen as a response to the decline of serialism and other systematic methods. States filled some of the receding space left by those approaches. They have provided an alternative point of compositional focus. To turn Williams's phrase, it is a "soft" focus, which may be part of the appeal. The ideal of a state is specific enough to generate ideas as to how to structure a work and handle the materials, but it is also flexible and open to contrasting interpretations. As we will see, there are

[30] Williams, "Ageing of the New," 527.
[31] On these developments within Boulez's thought and practice, see Jonathan Goldman, "Exploding/Fixed: Form as Opposition in the Writings and Late Works of Pierre Boulez," Ph.D. thesis (Université de Montréal, 2006), 84–90.
[32] Boulez, "Le système et l'idée," in *Points de repère III: Leçons de musique*, ed. Jean-Jacques Nattiez and Jonathan Goldman (Paris: Christian Bourgois, 2005), 363.

different ways to evoke silence yet all of them must operate within and adhere to an ideal of silence.

A historiographical postscript to this discussion of compositional states is in order. For some readers, a question has hovered in the air: have not works in earlier periods pursued these ideals? Of course they have. Beethoven's late pieces and some compositions by Schumann gather up fragments. Composers have long exploited silence in capacious, tense rests. Purity serves as an acoustic and spiritual ideal in medieval and Renaissance music. As for the fourth state discussed here, the flux of sound, it does not appear prominently, if at all, in earlier periods. The reasons for its relative absence have much to do with the fact that sound had not been set aside and explored as a compositional realm until the twentieth century. The rise of non-tonal idioms and electronic technologies created, or responded to, the interest in tapping into the power of sound. The case of sonic flux raises a larger point about the strong interest in states held by modernist works. From early on, such pieces have had the resources to engage the ideals of states to an unprecedented degree. The harmonic, textural, and sonic liberties won by modernism could be used to generate mutable, unstable sounds. They could also be employed to create more scattered and disparate collections of fragments than composers ever dreamed of in the nineteenth century, to sustain music at the edge of silence for an entire thirty-minute piece rather than for a long rest, and to satisfy the severe restrictions of sonic material mandated by purity. The idioms of modernism not only provided the means to realize such striking visions of these ideals, but they also created a need for the ideals. As mentioned above, states can provide points of compositional focus. During the early years of modernism, such points were needed as the structural conventions of the tonal system waned, and they were again needed with the decline of serialism. Throughout the history of modernism, the workings of fragments, silence, purity, and sound have provided new ways of conceiving and organizing pieces. Although the ideals of compositional states have been explored prior to the twentieth century, it is the centrality of the ideals to the languages and aesthetics of modernism that has made the lines of inquiry into those ideals so crucial to that music.

The second inquiry examined in this study deals with the act of expression. The discussion takes a different course from that followed in the account of compositional states. Whereas the latter started with the general, the terms of the inquiry, and moved on to the particular, how those terms have played out in music since 1980, the former begins with the particular, expressive qualities of recent works, segues to general aspects of both the inquiry and the topic of expression, and then swings back to specific issues in the contemporary scene. The U turn provides a clearer understanding of the expressive currents in new styles and how they have both extended and departed from impulses in previous periods of modernism.

The expressive tendencies of recent works have caught the attention of several scholars. The topic returns frequently in the writings of Hermann Danuser. In his history of twentieth-century music, Danuser, like most scholars undertaking the task, concluded by attempting to divine incipient and ultimately historically significant developments within the spread of contemporary styles. Writing in the early 1980s, he picked out the music of Wolfgang Rihm and other young West German composers, a group central to what would become known as neo-Romanticism. According to Danuser, they no longer felt bound to the ruling modernist "aesthetic of negativity," which critiqued and disrupted the communication of supposedly problem-free aesthetic and expressive ideals in an effort to liberate the human subject by awakening its critical consciousness. Drawing upon nineteenth- and early twentieth-century idioms, the neo-Romantic composers sought more immediate means of communication and embraced such older ideals. Like strands of German literature of the time, neo-Romantic idioms invoked categories such as freedom, subjectivity, privacy, and interiority. For Danuser, the recourse to historical materials and ideals was one way out of the difficulties of expression facing young composers, for whom there was no longer the possibility of partaking in the kinds of free, spontaneous subjectivity that emerged in previous styles, like that of the *Sturm und Drang*. The only way to come close to such immediacy was by tapping into those older styles.[33]

In a later essay, Danuser describes what he calls the "Neue Innerlichkeit."[34] The movement arises from a contemporary connection with Hegelian notions of interiority, a concept that encompasses the totality of the capacity of the feeling, desiring, thinking subject. Ideas of interiority were crucial to nineteenth-century aesthetics, which held that inner experiences could be manifested in and expressed through musical works. Such notions were vanquished by a sequence of modernist developments, particularly the objectivity of neoclassicism and the emphasis on method in serial and chance procedures. Late twentieth-century reincarnations of the ideals of interiority took different guises, among them the oscillation between expressionistic eruptions and peaceful quiet in Rihm's Third String Quartet (*Im Innersten*),

---

[33] Hermann Danuser, *Die Musik des 20. Jahrhunderts* (Laaber: Laaber-Verlag, 1984), 400–403.
[34] Danuser, "Innerlichkeit und Äußerlichkeit in der Musikästhetik der Gegenwart," in *Die Musik der achtziger Jahre*, ed. Ekkehard Jost (Mainz: Schott, 1990), 17–29. Danuser also discusses another approach to interiority in avant-garde (Cage) and meditation-based styles, both of which are opposed to the nineteenth-century ideal.

the appeal to "inner songs" in Nono's string quartet *Fragmente-Stille, An Diotima*, and the use of the sweeping emotionality of grand Romantic idioms in works by Penderecki (Second Symphony) and del Tredici.

Alastair Williams similarly places Rihm's works amid widening changes in the aesthetics of expression under way in the last decades of the twentieth century. He discerns a movement from the structural obsessions of the post–World War Two period toward a "renewed emphasis on subjectivity."[35] The latter involved a return to nineteenth-century precedents, particularly the ideal of musical works conveying inner emotions. A modernist consciousness, though, bears down upon the pieces and prevents the naïve use of past materials and ideals. Faithful to principles of distance and objectivity, the works do not so much borrow as construct the materials used to communicate inner experiences and, in remaking the materials, they critique both the materials and the promise of such types of communication.[36]

Mahnkopf too focuses on shifts in the expressive modes of recent idioms, but he points to different means and styles than Danuser and Williams. The changes are part of the second modernism that he has announced and are manifested in the new complexity works characteristic of that dawning period. Complexism, his term for a larger idiom including new complexity and related pieces, has stirred "expressivist expressionism," a reborn and enhanced version of the early twentieth-century movement. As defined by Mahnkopf, the new version, like the original, yields works of forceful expressive communication and impact. The music "strives out" from the artistic subject and bonds with the recipient.[37] Danuser and Williams describe a similar immediacy in neo-Romantic works, but the means used by the two types of pieces are antithetical. There is no "regression" to past styles in second modernist compositions but rather a wrestling with the most challenging idioms of the day. Akin to Adorno's idea of advanced material, the works yield powerful expressive effects by engaging complexity idioms in unique and self-aware ways.[38]

For additional observations on expressive currents in music since 1980, we can turn to pieces by three composers who figure prominently in this study: Ligeti, Lachenmann, and Nono. Around 1980, the expressive means and tenor of their music begin to take new forms, changes indicative of the shift between the post–World War Two and late modernist periods. During

[35] Alastair Williams, "Swaying with Schumann: Subjectivity and Tradition in Wolfgang Rihm's 'Fremde Szenen' I–III and Related Scores," *Music and Letters* 87 (2006), 384.

[36] Williams, "Swaying with Schumann," 396–97.

[37] Claus-Steffen Mahnkopf, "Complex Music: An Attempt at a Definition," in *Polyphony and Complexity*, ed. Claus-Steffen Mahnkopf, Frank Cox, and Wolfram Schurig (Hofheim: Wolke Verlag, 2002), 62–63.

[38] Mahnkopf, "Neue Musik am Beginn der Zweiten Moderne," 873–75.

the 1960s, such pieces by Ligeti as *Aventures*, the Requiem, and the Second String Quartet display a range of expressive gestures and sensations, notably the "cooled expressionism" created by paralyzing normally demonstrative gestures.[39] A series of laments in the 1980s, in contrast, kindle emotional heat. For Ligeti, the lament was a touchstone of expression, an age-old genre capturing raw voices of grief. He adds his own voice to the genre, one characterized by lyrical breadth, touches of tonality, and propulsive expressive momentum. For some critics, the laments attain emotional depths unheard in Ligeti's previous works.[40] As Lachenmann has recalled, he tried in his earliest pieces to "refuse" expression, a statement that could serve as a platform for the "aesthetics of negativity" that Danuser considered his music to exemplify.[41] How surprising then for a composer who subverted conventional genres, sounds, and modes of expression to write an opera. *Das Mädchen mit den Schwefelhölzern* (1997) continues Lachenmann's interrogation of the conventional but at the same time it takes command of the lyrical and dramatic powers of the genre. Lachenmann employs these forces to build sympathy for and outrage over the plight of the girl in the Hans Christian Andersen story upon which the work is based. With the string quartet *Fragmente-Stille, An Diotima* (1980), Nono moved from the political stage of earlier pieces to the private world of chamber music. Fittingly, the move corresponds with a change from public commentary to, as mentioned earlier, personal inwardness. The key to the latter is a score direction taken from Beethoven: "mit innigster Empfindung." It captures the internal depths of emotion that Nono attempts to reach. The composer pushes the piece to the edge of silence, which is perhaps the only spot, the string quartet argues, that such intense feelings can still be voiced. The danger of being annulled by silence makes the voicing of those feelings all the more expressive.

The above discussion has canvassed a mix of idioms, including two – neo-Romanticism and new complexity – that are considered to be antipodes and the singular languages of three elder modernist composers. Even within such variety, a consensus emerges: the turn to more directly expressive styles around 1980. The statement demands clarification. The first step is to admit the difficulties in doing so. Expression, it goes without saying, is a broad concept that resists encapsulation, especially when we are contemplating a larger change in approaches to expression across a broad range of styles. Caveat made, the above examples offer enough ideas to get at what this new

---

[39] Ligeti, *György Ligeti in Conversation* (London: Eulenburg Books, 1983), 15–19.
[40] Chapter 4 will present such views of the laments.
[41] David Ryan, "Composer in Interview, Helmut Lachenmann," *Tempo* 210 (October 1999), 22. Danuser, *Die Musik des 20. Jahrhunderts*, 400.

directness involves. In his discussion of neo-Romanticism, Williams too recognizes directness as a characteristic of such works. He describes how that music "seeks" and "yearns for" "directness," which, as he employs it, refers to an immediate expressive effect.[42] As used here, directness captures such immediacy as well as a forthrightness and pointedness in both the means and the modes of expression.

For means, many composers have turned to the past. Neo-Romantic composers relied upon the rather obvious source of nineteenth- and early twentieth-century idioms, music that, on the one hand, had created emphatic expressive means and, on the other, has become a sign of ardent emotionality for present-day listeners. Composers have also gone back to the genres of the eighteenth and nineteenth centuries. Danuser considers the use, albeit a rather free use, of traditional genres as a characteristic element of the new types of musical subjectivity created by Rihm and other neo-Romantics.[43] Just as noteworthy is the turn to the string quartet and opera by Nono and Lachenmann, respectively. The two draw upon the genres, if not the traditional languages that once filled them. Whether it be the neo-Romantics or Nono and Lachenmann, the choice of conventional genres abets an expressive directness. The genres possess strong expectations of the types of expressive statements that can be made through them, expectations that can be heightened by playing up the conventional elements, as in neo-Romantic works, or through the radical transformations of Nono and Lachenmann. Some composers have looked well beyond the common practice era for expressive means and have disinterred the lament, as seen in the strong interest in this archaic genre on the part of Ligeti and others since 1980. The title alone asserts overwhelming emotions, a billing that inspires the anguished music coiled in their works.

Composers have not only found potent expressive means in past repertoires; they have also cultivated such means in the more innovative idioms of the contemporary scene. The ripping dissonances and frantic rhythms of new complexity pieces, for instance, practically overload in creating sensations of extreme intensity. In a contortion of nineteenth-century virtuosity, the physical frenzy and depletion involved in performing the works compound the effect. Additional expressive means have been found in the expressive potential of sound. As discussed in Chapter 5, works exploit the relationship between sound and voice. The two form a basic opposition in which the former typically resides in masses and mixes, whereas the latter is a single line, be it vocal or instrumental. Some pieces imperil the lone

[42] Williams, "Ageing of the New," 532, and *New Music and the Claims of Modernity*, 532.
[43] Danuser, *Die Musik des 20. Jahrhunderts*, 400.

voice within crowded, mutating sonorities, dangers that conjure feelings of loss and alienation, among possible effects. Other compositions turn sound into a voice by crafting single concentrated lines, such as a glissando or an open-ended crescendo. Merged together, sound and voice form powerful gestures, gestures that combine the force and variety of sound with the capacity of voice to speak of or to some expressive quality.

Despite the differences in means, the works discussed here share a similar mode of expression. It is premised upon a line of communication between the work and listener in which the clarity and force of the expressive gestures have the music strike the listener in immediate and absorbing ways. The pieces reviving nineteenth-century models of interiority, for example, hold out that some inner personal conception can be rendered in a manner that allows another individual to experience it. Mahnkopf sees new complexity works building an expressive momentum that pushes out from the work and inhabits the listener. Even sound, which can be a blunt and unwieldy resource, has been fitted for such a role. By melding sound and voice, composers have turned something as abstract as a glissando, as illustrated in an example from Olga Neuwirth's *Lost Highway* described below, into the voice of a character.

The expressive qualities of post-1980s music can also be approached through the concept of subjectivity. Danuser, Williams, and Mahnkopf all elaborate upon this idea. The analyses in the following chapters will pick up on it as well, but for now it is enough to note that subjectivity offers a way of appreciating the expressive directness of such music. The emotional and physical sensations coursing through recent works create the impression of a subjective presence. It is difficult to think of such sensations as floating independently and existing on their own. There is a tendency either to identify with them ourselves, and thereby occupy a foreign subject position created in the music, or to assign them to some sort of removed subjectivity.[44] Some works suggest a subject position, such as the inwardness plumbed by pieces taking up notions of interiority. The presence can be just that, an amorphous emotional density, or, as explored here, it can be assigned to a specific persona in a work, including a character, performer, or the anonymous social subject populating Adorno's criticism. Subjectivity is not just the byproduct of the types of direct expression appearing in late modernist music, it is also a quality that enhances such forthrightness. When connected to a subjective presence, the expressive currents come across as focused, sensations that inhere within and emerge from a particular

---

[44] Williams, "Swaying with Schumann," 395–97; Lawrence Kramer, "The Mysteries of Animation: History, Analysis, and Musical Subjectivity," *Music Analysis* 20 (2001), 153–78.

source. Concentrated in a presence, the currents become more forceful and pointed.

These are some of the characteristics of the types of direct expression that modernist idioms turned to around 1980. If that is what they turned to, then what did they turn away from? In a discussion of neo-Romantic composers, Williams describes not so much a pivot as rather a "push beyond the constraints of constructivist composition towards a music more aware of its own subjectivity."[45] The observation is helpful in that it sets the stage for the following discussion, but before we get to the historical turn we need to arrange the figures on the historical stage. Williams and Danuser place neo-Romantic composers at the front of the stage, seeing their works as most indicative of the larger change in expressive means. The two, though, do not etch a firm line between neo-Romanticism and modernism, as evident in their emphasis on the polyglot Rihm, whose music draws upon both nineteenth-century and modernist idioms. This study, in contrast, sees a range of pieces involved in the move toward more directly expressive idioms. The reach for such idioms was made not just through an appeal to nineteenth-century precedents but also through a variety of modernist styles. The shared reach revises the historiographical picture by revealing both neo-Romantic and modernist styles participating in the broader historical turn. The two are not as far apart as they have often been made out to be; rather, there is overlap, even cooperation.

Williams's split between "construction" and "subjectivity" is one way to draw a line between post–World War Two and late modernist works. The terms, though, easily play into a historical simplification, something that Williams avoids. On the one hand, there is serial rigidity and sterility, while, on the other hand, there is a reanimated Romanticism. Both views miss the mark. The idea of a return to Romanticism can be quickly dismissed by pointing to the continuing vitality of modernist styles, which have fostered a variety of compelling expressive means. As for serial idioms, a few words about the period following World War Two are in order. So hardened have views of that period become that "rigid" and "sterile" may not seem to be a simplification. To be sure, the adjectives have earned their keep in describing some works, but the expressive currents in serial styles are too varied to be dismissed as cerebral antiseptic. The Darmstadt scene did, as Adorno mentioned, have an "allergy" toward expression, evident in the neglect of the topic in its in-house journal *Die Reihe*.[46] Moreover, the aleatoric approaches created by Cage and adapted by Darmstadt composers attempted to bypass expression, along with any type of creative volition on the part of the

---

[45] Williams, "Swaying with Schumann," 385.   [46] Adorno, "The Aging of the New Music," 191.

composer.[47] Yet this is not to say that the music does not possess expressive force. Even the bogeyman of 1950s serialism, Boulez's *Structures*, generates diverse expressive effects, including kaleidoscopic shifts, tension created in extreme ranges, and softer, pensive passages.[48] Much more work needs to be done before we can appreciate the range of expressive positions in post–World War Two music and get beyond preconceived ideas of coldness and mechanism.

Much more work, of course, needs to be done to identify the expressive directions taken in music written since 1980, especially given that little has been done to identify the period as such. This study is devoted to both tasks. One of the first steps is to show the larger ways in which pieces from the late modernist period contrast with those from the decades immediately after World War Two in terms of expression. The former have been driven by an interest in the force, range, and communicative power of the expressive impulse. This interest could be seen as a reaction against the structural "constraints" of the earlier period. The forceful expressive gestures fostered in works since 1980 have provided an escape from such controls. The gestures have their own independence and drive, anathema to the equalizing and conforming logic of integral serial designs. The willfulness of the gestures is so strong that they would disrupt, if not tear apart, those schemes. Moreover, the turn to older means and expressive ideals is also an affront to the newness mandated in 1950s–60s idioms.

The result is music of expressive candor and immediacy, achieved through the prominent, graspable means of expression, evocations of subjectivity, modes of direct communication, and forceful gestures discussed above. It is not that these means and modes are altogether unknown in the post–World War Two period or that the music of that time lacks in directness. On the contrary, such works make an expressive impact, but they do it through a largely different set of means and modes, which again need to be identified through further studies of the expressive resources of that music. The key difference between the two periods is the consistency of the above features across late modernist works. The result is an expressive landscape strikingly different from that in music of the previous decades. In

---

[47] Cage turned to chance procedures in *Music of Changes* as a way out of what he took to be the morass of personal expression. As he would later describe, the negative reception of *The Perilous Night* inspired this realization. Cage had loaded the work with the woes surrounding the divorce from his wife, a sorrow that the critics failed to detect. David Revill, *The Roaring Silence: John Cage, A Life* (London: Bloomsbury, 1992), 88–89.

[48] Ben Parsons has provided additional contexts besides those of rigid precompositional planning in which to hear *Structures 1a*. He discusses the historical, political, aesthetic, and expressive contexts of the work. Parsons, "Sets and the City: Serial Analysis, Parisian Reception, and Pierre Boulez's *Structures 1a*," *Current Musicology* 76 (2003), 53–79.

this new landscape, we come across expressive moments rarely encountered, if not unimaginable, in the post–World War Two period, such as the crowd of wrenching laments arising from the renewed interest in the genre, the intense quiet patches formed by the linkage between silence and interiority, and the thwarted cry of the operatic subject in a realm of sonic flux. Moving back from the individual details to the larger scene, we can perceive a range of richly expressive idioms, the vibrancy of which emerges from a fascination with the immediacy and communicative force of that expressive moment.

The turn to more directly expressive idioms in post-1980 works must be considered within the larger history of modernism. As argued here, the shift fits into an ongoing modernist inquiry, or, more to the point, inquiries, into expression. The interest in the dynamics and dimensions of expression began during the initial decades of modernism.[49] Perhaps inevitable for a music emerging in the wake of Romanticism, modernism concentrated on aspects of expression, scrutinizing the expressive models of the preceding period and seeking alternatives in an attempt to break away from them. In particular, early modernist styles took on the expressive abundance of Romantic works, especially the ideal, realized in the operas of Wagner, that music could unleash an ecstatic, overwhelming emotional current.[50]

The modernist inquiry began by focusing on the intensity of that current, finding different ways to gauge it. Two different measurements were calculated in Expressionism and neoclassicism. The former escalated the expressive flow established by Romanticism, feeding it to the point that it could not be held by either conventional forms or tonal languages. The latter regulated the flow within "old" forms and arch tonal idioms. Besides intensity, the initial stages of the inquiry increasingly drew attention to expression as an act. Operas in both styles figure expression in such a way. Schoenberg's *Erwartung* removes all sorts of hindrances surrounding its anonymous female character, those of name, background, traditional plot development, interaction with other characters, conventional vocal

---

[49] The self-consciousness about expression described here, it should be acknowledged, has nineteenth-century precedents. Some Romantic pieces show an awareness of the limits of the expressive voice. As mentioned in chapters 2 and 3, Beethoven's late string quartets feature both extended lyrical moments and fragmentary sections that cut off such lyricism and the promise of the spontaneous, flowing expressive voice held in those moments. The difference between the nineteenth and twentieth centuries can be formulated as that between awareness and analysis. Modernist pieces, as we will see, expose the act of expression so that it can be scrutinized, or, as in some late modernist compositions, dissected.

[50] The expressive power of Wagner's music became the object of theories that viewed heightened expression as the essence of music. On those theories and opposing views, see Stephen McClatchie, *Analyzing Wagner's Operas: Alfred Lorenz and German National Ideology* (Rochester, NY: University of Rochester Press, 1998), 27–42.

melodies and forms, and the underpinnings of tonality. The result is what expression might sound like if it was left unfettered: a series of outbursts, no two alike, each just as wild as the others. Stravinsky's *Oedipus Rex* encumbers characters with restraints, singing in a dead language, wearing masks, standing motionless on stage, and standing motionless in a plot that is not shaped by the stage actions of the characters but rather narrated by an emcee. The effect, consistent with the composer's original conception of the staging, is what it would be like if statues were to express emotions.[51] The characters may be physically immobile, but they are not emotionally so. Strong feelings – fear, rage, loss, and resignation – shake them. The dramatic power of the work comes not just from those emotions but also from the tensions created by them rattling the restraints imposed upon the characters.[52]

The interest in the act of expression in *Erwartung* and *Oedipus Rex* deepened in subsequent modernist works, so much so that it branched off into a separate line within the larger inquiry into expression. This study follows that line, one crucial to late modernist works. As presented in compositions involved in the inquiry, the act of expression breaks down into distinct components: the inception of an emotion or idea, the rendering of it into some distinct form, often referred to here as a voice, and the projection of the mediated emotion or idea, which is taken in by a recipient. The concept of voice is being used in a broad and sometimes conventional way. The voice functions as the bearer of an expressive utterance.[53] It is also associated with aspects of individuality, particularly the single line or gesture in which it usually inheres or the lone figure, such as a character or the anonymous subject, whose means of expression it becomes. This description runs the risk of reducing the act of expression to simplistic extremes. The reduction, though, is necessary to accommodate all the different ways in which works have displayed that act. As we will see, the basic structure allows composers to manipulate the act by concentrating on one or more of the components.

Having identified the mechanics of the act of expression, it is now time to situate the modernist inquiry within the context of other models and theories of expression. The inquiry overlaps with some of those views, but it ultimately remains distinct. At first, it might appear that modernist

---

[51] Igor Stravinsky, *Oedipus Rex* (reduction for voice and piano by the composer) (New York: Boosey & Hawkes, 1949).

[52] On such tensions, see Arnold Whittall, "Stravinsky in Context," in *The Cambridge Companion to Stravinsky*, ed. Jonathan Cross (Cambridge University Press, 2003), 44–46.

[53] This conventional understanding of the voice is treated in Mladen Dolar, *A Voice and Nothing More* (Cambridge, MA: MIT Press, 2006), 14.

forms of expression did not so much break away from nineteenth-century Romantic ideals as cooperate with them. The above depiction of the act of expression calls to mind Romantic models of interiority in which the artist taps into an emotional interior to create an artwork that arouses feelings in the recipient similar to those experienced by the artist. John Hospers placed this model and later ones in a particular category that he labels the "expressive process." As he shows, adherents to this view have brought out different sides of the "process," including the mind of the creator (Croce, Collingwood), the involvement with the aesthetic medium (Dewey), and the emotional response of the recipient (Tolstoy).[54] The expressive act probed by modernism can be considered a process in that the utterance initiates a chain of events. The crucial difference is how the process plays out. In the various Romantic models and theories presented by Hospers, it remains more or less spontaneous and unhindered, proceeding smoothly from creator to recipient. Modernist works set up the act of expression only to tinker with it. Interruptions and obstructions rob the act of its naturalness, allowing for a clearer idea of how expression unfolds and what can be made of the act itself.

In a recent book, the philosopher Stephen Davies summarizes and responds to three broad theories of musical expression.[55] He first presents the "expression theory," which is analogous to Hospers's "process," and then quickly dismisses it as "empirically false," since "not all expressive music is written by composers who feel emotions and try to express them." The "arousal theory," that which finds the expressive aspects of music in the ability to evoke a corresponding emotion in a listener, also meets doubt. Davies argues that the correspondence between a listener attributing to a piece qualities of sadness and their experiencing of that piece as sad is not "sufficient enough to make the arousal theory plausible." The third approach is the "contour theory," which has been strongly championed by Peter Kivy.[56] It proposes that music can be expressive of a feeling by resembling characteristics of that emotion established through conventions, such as figural shapes. Among other objections, Davies finds such resemblances to be "insufficient" to explain why we can experience music as being deeply emotional. One account of expression put forth by a musicologist is that of Anthony Newcomb; in a response to Kivy, Newcomb emphasizes the

---

[54] The authors cited above all have essays in an edited collection by John Hospers: *Artistic Expression* (New York: Meredith Corporation, 1971), 3–94.

[55] The following discussion draws upon Stephen Davies, *Themes in the Philosophy of Music* (Oxford University Press, 2003), 177–85.

[56] Peter Kivy, *Sound Sentiment: An Essay on the Musical Emotions (Including the Complete Text of "The Corded Shell")* (Philadelphia: Temple University Press, 1989).

importance of the structure of a musical work, a feature, as he mentions, typically overlooked by philosophers. Structure, along with other "intrinsic properties" of a piece, is an important part of his understanding of expression as "interpretation," the mediation by the recipient of the "properties that an object possesses and properties outside of the object itself."[57]

The modernist inquiry into the act of expression does not fit into any of these theories. It is too broad, focusing on all the stages in the act, some of which, notably the role of the initiator of the act, have been downplayed to the point of omission in many of the above views, particularly the arousal and contour theories. It is also too narrow, at times more interested in following the course of the act than in analyzing "properties" inside or outside of the artistic work, including structure. The difference is not so much one of breadth as one of function. The modernist inquiry is not a theory. Like a theory, it scrutinizes its object, but the goal of the scrutiny is not to offer an explanatory model. It instead analyzes the act in order to create expressive effects. The inquiry into the act of expression by modernist works is ultimately a means of expression.

To reveal how the inquiry can be expressive we need to refine our understanding of the act of expression. One of the first points to discuss is the figures involved, particularly those who initiate the act. Unlike in the "expressive process" models, the composer does not play a role. He or she is not the figure starting the act, or the figure scrutinized in the study of it. If anything he or she is the one studying the act from a creative distance. But if the composer is not involved, who is? Recent studies in aesthetics and music theory put forward some candidates. The philosopher Jerrold Levinson argues that music can be considered expressive if the expression of an emotion can be assigned to an imaginary figure or persona.[58] Edward T. Cone identifies specific personas that play expressive roles in the world of song. They include the "vocal" (the characters depicted in a work), the "instrumental" (a persona suggested by the accompaniment), and the "(complete) musical" (a figure created by the interaction of the above two parts and which can be taken as "*a* persona of the composer" and not "*the* persona of the composer").[59]

This study follows Cone's lead in that it brings together a group of expressive figures. These personas, though, are not so much expressive presences as people who undertake the act of expression. Within a piece, we can hear the act being carried out by a range of figures. The most conspicuous

[57]   Anthony Newcomb, "Sound and Feeling," *Critical Inquiry* 10 (1984), 624–26.
[58]   Jerrold Levinson, *The Pleasures of Aesthetics* (Ithaca: Cornell University Press, 1996), 90–125.
[59]   Edward T. Cone, *The Composer's Voice* (Berkeley: University of California Press, 1974), 17–18.

are characters in a song or dramatic work. Not just any character fills this role – say a Pelléas or Wozzeck – rather it must be a character who executes the act of expression in an observable way. A striking example can be found in Sister Maria Maddalena de' Pazzi from Salvatore Sciarrino's *Infinito nero* (see Chapter 2). Her religious visions traverse the entire act, emerging in some sort of inner communion, erupting through silence, and taking forms that bewildered her original sixteenth-century listeners and now us. Performers also can bring out the act of expression. Performance by itself would seem to do so, but some modernist works have placed demands on the musicians that have them fulfill the act in ways that go beyond the notes they play or sing. The quartet members in Nono's *Fragmente-Stille, An Diotima*, for instance, are called upon to sing "inner songs," melodies that never leave the interior worlds of the musicians but that in some enigmatic way inflect the music they play.

Adorno has inspired my use of another expressive persona – the subject. In his criticism, the figure, drawn from philosophical discourse, plays many parts, from a creative presence shaping and working within the language of a composition to a social presence, the anonymous bourgeois individual whose situation is captured in the form of a piece, like the fragmented subject in a fragmentary work.[60] This book presents the subject in similar roles, but, unlike Adorno, it emphasizes how the figure executes the different parts of the act of expression. Finally, the act of expression can stand by itself, not necessarily assigned to any specific persona. Such independence can be found in works that draw upon a particular model of expression. It involves the taking up of a voice that lays out musical patterns of behavior and is rich in established emotional associations. The lament is an age-old version of the model. As seen in the modernist revival of the genre, the person who raises the ritual voice, be it the composer or a character, does not demand as much attention as what happens to the voice. In particular, how is the lament voice raised, what directions does it take, what emotional points does it reach? These questions show that once evoked the lament voice takes on a life of its own, one that carries out the act of expression.

The works discussed in this study all approach the act of expression in a similar manner. One way to scrutinize something that appears to be inherent in a piece is to bring it to the surface. Compositions can expose the dynamics of expression by calling attention to one or more parts of the act, for instance the inner realms in which an emotion is born or the gesture of raising of a voice. Once a single component is materialized, the whole chain usually comes into view. Such exposure fits into the technique

---

[60] For a discussion of Adorno's conception of the subject, see Paddison, *Adorno's Aesthetics of Music*, 115, 118.

of "defamiliarization" described by Viktor Shklovsky.[61] It has proven incisive when it comes to expression. Bertolt Brecht's "alienation effect," to cite a celebrated example, used this general approach to undermine traditional conceptions of dramatic expression in theater. Through gestures and staging, the emotional displays of characters can be rendered in artificial, strange ways that denaturalize expression and forestall the empathy traditionally sought in dramatic scenes. With its singing statues, Stravinsky's original conception of the staging of *Oedipus Rex* works along lines similar to Brecht's concept.

Once a composition has exteriorized the act, the inquiry can begin. To proceed, a work must further manipulate individual components, going beyond what is necessary to reveal the act in the first place. The alterations can be employed to bring out different properties and dynamics. Relying on this strategy, the pieces discussed below consider numerous facets of expression: the boundaries between inner emotion and outer statement; the intensity of expression; the various outcomes of the expressive utterance; the transformation of a voice once the act of expression has begun; and the possible erasure of that voice.

Another tactic used to probe the act of expression is to place it under adverse conditions. This approach brings together the two chief topics of this study: expression and compositional states. The latter can create a withering environment. Silence, for instance, can be inimical to expression, as it can prevent an utterance from ever emerging or sink it into nothingness. The fragment is equally treacherous, for its narrow confines could crush an utterance. Compositional states provide new ground on which to conduct the inquiry into expression. Once there, additional questions arise: How will the act fare under such terms? Indeed, will it survive there and, if so, what forms will it take?

The manipulations of the act of expression are not so much analytical as expressive. Works taking up the inquiry produce rich expressive effects. They do so by reconceiving a traditional conception of expression. As frequently described in aesthetics, the raw act by itself, say a frightened child screaming, is not expressive, at least not in any rewarding artistic sense. Artistic and expressive enjoyment can be gained when the emotional impetus is mediated in some way, like being subjected to the rigor of a prescribed form. Adorno described expression as an "interference phenomenon" that emerges between aspects of expression, especially its mimetic components

---

[61] As made clear in Shklovsky's references to eighteenth- and nineteenth-century literature, the technique is not confined to the modernist period. Shklovsky, "Art as Technique," in *Russian Formalist Criticism*, ed. and trans. Lee T. Lemon and Marion J. Reis (Lincoln: University of Nebraska Press, 1965), 3–24.

and the structure of a piece.[62] The works inquiring into the act of expression, as discussed below, generate a lot of "interference," but the sources of those clashes are different than those formulated by Adorno or more conventional theories of expression. Instead of mimetic affinities, there are the stages of the act. Structure is a powerful controlling force but so too are the conditions of compositional states. In this model, expressive effects come not from shaping the utterance through an established form but rather by placing it in constant danger.

What types of expressive effects are they? The tensions created by hindrances to the act of expression often translate into sensations of intensity. It should be acknowledged that intensity is hardly a new sensation for modernist music. Some critics of modernism have claimed that it is one of the few effects created by the music, so limited is its expressive palette.[63] Intensity, though, can offer a rich palette, one full of different effects and gradations. The works discussed below provide us with opportunities to hear the many ways in which charged sensations can be created and the various forms that they can assume. The pieces also give the lie to the assertion that modernism is addicted to intensity. A range of other emotions and effects emerge in these pieces, including cold and warmth (Lachenmann), imposing weight (Saariaho), lyricism (Ligeti and Nono), emptiness (Lachenmann), loss (Nono), madness (Sciarrino), repose (Harvey), and sensuality (Neuwirth).

A sampling of expressive streaks in recent works swings us back to where we began, the turn to more directly expressive idioms in music since 1980. The inquiry into the act of expression has served composers well in achieving that directness. In particular, the strain created by the act unfolding under extreme conditions generates expressive effects that seize the listener. The expressive utterance becomes so much more expressive when it is severely contorted or possibly even extinguished. The works discussed below raise the stakes to that point. They offer stark depictions of emotional conditions, such as passion and loneliness, and heighten them by dooming the expression of those feelings. We will encounter, for example, voices of lust smothered by indifferent silence, repeated desperate cries of "I" sucked into churning sound, and the deluded attempts to connect with another person crushed.

The three scenes capture the galvanizing types of expression characteristic of late modernism. As mentioned above, composers have relied on other approaches than the inquiry into the act of expression to produce such force. The revival of past styles in neo-Romanticism and the overwhelming

---

[62] Adorno, *Aesthetic Theory*, 114.
[63] George Rochberg, *The Aesthetics of Survival: A Composer's View of Twentieth-century Music*, ed. William Bolcolm (Ann Arbor: University of Michigan Press, 1984), 239.

intricacy of new complexity idioms have proven to be potent expressive idioms. The inquiry, it should be mentioned, is not completely separate from those two styles. It is an approach that can be pursued in them, as can be heard in works by Rihm and Ferneyhough, or other idioms. For late modernist composers, the inquiry has been a flexible and powerful tool.

So was it for composers earlier in the twentieth century. The inquiry's role in recent music is similar to that played by the inquiry into compositional states. Consistent with the dynamics of continuity and discontinuity in lines of inquiry, the two have run throughout the history of modernism but have shifted course so as to respond to specific needs in the late modernist period. The inquiry into states offered points of structural focus after the decline of serialism, whereas that into the act of expression has come into its own as it has satisfied the interest in forging forceful expressive idioms.

Each of the following chapters offers analyses of works engaged in one or both of the inquiries. Chapter 1 takes up the concept of purity, which has proven to be anything but given the frequent and loose ways in which it has been applied to modernist arts. The most common usage has been to capture the narrow self-reflexivity typical of strands of modernism, particularly the abstract idioms of the 1950s to 1960s. This study picks up on an alternative notion of the pure. Instead of the restriction to a set of intrinsic materials and means, some pieces have evoked purity by embracing a range of materials, means, and associations. The mixture would seem to violate ideals of purity but it has the opposite effect in that the selected elements are all connected to the pure in some way. The works give us a plurality of purity. Two such pieces are Stockhausen's *Gesang der Jünglinge* and Harvey's *Mortuos plango, vivos voco*. The two pair together well in that they not only use a cluster of pure elements but they also feature a particular pure sound, a boy's voice.

Chapter 2 leaps from one end of the twentieth century to the next, starting with Webern in the 1910s and moving to Nono and Sciarrino in the final two decades. All three composers shared an interest in silence. The connection between them is even more specific as they set a similar scene in their works, the borderland between silence and sound. The liminal realm allowed the composers to explore several points, including how close they could bring music to silence and how to suggest the void of silence through musical means. It also provided a space in which to test the act of expression. Each composer re-created the act of expression in that setting, and by doing so each came up with a different formulation of it, particularly with regard to the boundaries of expression (those separating the interiority of the individual and the external social realm) and the outcomes of the act, whether it ends in sound or silence.

In Chapter 3 also, the inquiries into states and expression converge. The ideal of the fragmentary has commanded much attention in late twentieth-century arts, which have turned to it in the attempt to escape entrenched concepts of unity. This chapter begins with a discussion of the writings of Maurice Blanchot, who has left the most far-reaching account of the fragmentary from the latter half of the twentieth century. With Blanchot's theoretical apparatus in hand, we can turn to Nono's *Fragmente-Stille, An Diotima* and Kurtág's *Kafka Fragments* and examine how each work constructs its own version of the fragmentary state. The two pieces emphasize expression, a dimension of the fragmentary untouched by Blanchot. They place the act of expression in both the confined space of the individual fragment and the scattered field of many fragments. Our attention is again drawn to what happens to expression under such intense conditions.

Chapter 4 exposes a rich expressive strand in modernist idioms, the lament. As Whittall has discussed, the lament serves as a recurring topic in twentieth-century music. The fascination stems from tensions within the age-old genre between expression and structural control. Modernist music can turn up the tension by augmenting both sides, employing its forceful dissonances to bolster emotional projection and devising elaborate precompositional schemes to tighten structural designs. The chapter concentrates on the Adagio movement from Ligeti's Horn Trio, the first of the composer's many laments dating from the 1980s and 1990s. Not only is the tension between expression and structure key to Ligeti and other modernist composers' use of the genre but so too is the act of raising a voice central to the lament. The complications of the act and the evocation of traditional lament voices say much about the late modernist use of, and need for, outside voices in creating more directly expressive idioms.

Chapter 5 looks at another coupled inquiry into states and expression. It describes how Saariaho, Lachenmann, and Neuwirth have cultivated aspects of sound to construct a realm that presents sound as a force of unending movement and transformation. They place the act of expression in this volatile space and explore what happens to it, and particularly the voices used in the act of expression, when the surrounding soundworld and the voices themselves constantly change.[64]

---

[64] As the descriptions of the individual chapters make clear, this study focuses on a small number of European composers. No North American composers are discussed in any sort of comparable detail. The focus on Europe was by no means intentional; rather it was the result of looking for pieces related to the topics of the individual chapters. The emphasis on European music should not be interpreted as a statement about the death of modernism in North America. It is true that modernist styles do enjoy more prestige and support (governmental, academic, and performance) there than in North America, but modernist styles of all kinds are still a force in North American music.

The Conclusion sums up where some books open up. A closing gambit employed in many histories that reach an end in the present is to point toward a broad openness, be it an amorphous "post" or an endless pluralism. This study, in contrast, will conclude by attempting to map the contemporary scene and offer a clearer idea of the significant stylistic and aesthetic lines crisscrossing it. The first step is to question, and then to erase, the line drawn between modernism and postmodernism, a line that from the vantage point of a new century seems fainter and fainter. Far from being contained and relegated to the past, modernism still occupies a prominent role in recent music.

By now it should be clear that this study will not entertain a question that has long hung around modern music – whither? The query is one reason that some readers, as mentioned earlier, may suspend a question mark at the end of the title of this book. That it has been put off until now says how much time will be spent addressing it. The question is relevant, and this study, so supportive of modernist styles, has a stake in it. The responses, though, typically call up clichés: an elitist, ugly music taken to intellectual extremes that appeals to deluded cognoscenti or a brave, captivating music that is the one true voice of the time, a music which, if it is dying, is doing so as a martyr. An attempt has been made here to get beyond such hackneyed stances and to offer fresh understandings of modernism, understandings that will increase appreciation of new works. These concepts include the mode of inquiry, compositional states, and the act of expression. The three have all stemmed from the intriguing idea that inspired the book: the modernism of today.

1 Purity

Purity holds many promises. Among them, essence, the absolute, the untainted, and the natural. No wonder advertisers have used it to hawk all sorts of products, such things as water, bread, shampoo, dog food, gas, and even countries. Each, true to the advertising business, brings us closer to a desired, if not impossible, ideal. Creators and theorists of modernist arts have also evoked the concept to describe new works, aesthetic movements, and critical ideas. At worst, they have handled purity like an advertising slogan. It can all too easily become a shibboleth, grand claims oblivious to how demanding the concept can be. The demands, though, have saved purity from being an empty promise. They are part of what has made it a complex, challenging ideal, one rich enough to have provided different ways to create and understand modernist arts.[1]

The concept of purity has long been in the modernist conversation. It typically pops up when the conversation turns to the self-reflexivity that is paradigmatic of many branches of modernism. According to Renato Poggioli, purity aspires "to abolish the discursive and syntactic element, to liberate art from any connection with psychological and empirical reality, to reduce every work to the intimate laws of its own expressive essence or to the given absolutes of its own genre or means."[2] The "mystique of purity," as Poggioli points out, allured artists as far back as Mallarmé, whose works have been considered as part of a tradition of "pure poetry."[3] The "pure work," Mallarmé contends, "implies the disappearance of the poet speaking," in whose absence words create their own play of sound and imagery as "they light each other up through reciprocal reflections like a virtual swooping of fire across precious stones."[4] Jumping ahead to twentieth-century music, critics and composers developed a lexicon to describe the restraint and clarity of neoclassical idioms. "Purity," as in the catchphrase "purely musical," was always near the

---

[1] On the gap between shibboleth and inspiration, see Mark A. Cheetham, *The Rhetoric of Purity: Essentialist Theory and the Advent of Abstract Painting* (Cambridge University Press, 1991).

[2] Renato Poggioli, *The Theory of the Avant-garde*, trans. Gerald Fitzgerald (Cambridge, MA: Harvard University Press, 1968), 201.

[3] Poggioli, *The Theory of the Avant-garde*, 199.

[4] The quotation is taken from the essay "Crise de vers," in Mallarmé, *Divagations*, trans. Barbara Johnson (Cambridge, MA: Harvard University Press, 2007), 208. I would like to thank Geoff Wilson for drawing my attention to this essay.

top of the list, joined by "simple," "objective," "straightforward," and "concise."[5]

The rhetoric of purity flourished during the period after World War Two. The abstract idioms cultivated in the arts at the time encouraged such talk, as they were adamant about shunning outside and familiar elements in the effort to refine intrinsic materials. Perhaps nowhere did this resolve achieve as much attention as in abstract expressionist painting, and nowhere was there a more resolute chronicler of that view than Clement Greenberg. He narrated the history of modernist painting as the push toward "self-definition," or the delving into the medium to reach its essence – "the flat surface, the shape of the support, the properties of the pigment."[6] The historical impulse could be captured in a single word: purity. As Greenberg tersely stated, "purity in art consists in the acceptance, willing acceptance, of the limitations of the medium of the specific art."[7] Or even more succinctly, "'purity' means self-definition."[8] The quotation marks qualifying the word in the latter statement divulge the unease that Greenberg had developed around the concept. In a 1978 postscript to the 1960 article from which the line is drawn, he refers to purity as an "illusion," or, to be more exact, a "useful illusion." Whereas it may be ultimately unattainable, the concept did offer a way "to account in part for how most of the very best art of the last hundred-odd-years came about."[9] Purity also offers a way of accounting for another demanding post–World War Two artistic scene, 1950s electronic and integral serial idioms. Although no single critic affixed the concept to the music like Greenberg did with painting, purity did come close to becoming a byword in the writings devoted to such works. As to be discussed below, the frequent usage conveys how the concept captured many of the ideals envisioned in the music, including essence, perfection, and wholeness.

Contrary to Greenberg, purity is not always useful. It abounds with creative potential as well as hazards. Studies of the concept in both the arts and anthropology often point out the latter. The shared warnings reveal common ground between the two disciplines, more the result of the specific and limited ways in which purity unfolds than of any methodological affinities. Both disciplines track how cultural expressions, be they compositions

---

[5] Scott Messing, *Neoclassicism in Music: From the Genesis of the Concept through the Schoen-berg/Stravinsky Polemic* (Ann Arbor: UMI Research Press, 1987), 108.

[6] Greenberg, "Modernist Painting," in *Clement Greenberg: The Collected Essays and Criticism*, vol. IV *Modernism with a Vengeance (1957–1969)*, ed. John O'Brien (University of Chicago Press, 1993), 85–93.

[7] Greenberg, "Towards a Newer Laocoon," in *Clement Greenberg: The Collected Essays and Criticism*, vol. I *Perceptions and Judgments (1939–1944)*, ed. John O'Brien (University of Chicago Press, 1986), 32.

[8] Greenberg, "Modernist Painting," 86.   [9] Greenberg, "Modernist Painting," 94.

or rituals, approach ideals of the pure and what forms those ideals take. As the two disciplines make clear, purity can breed extremes, which is not surprising for an ideal that itself is extreme, being completely pure or nothing else. In her classic *Purity and Danger*, Mary Douglas describes how arduous rituals can lead to rigid conditions that are "hard and dead as a stone."[10] Integral serial procedures and the sonic experiments carried out in 1950s electronic music studios could be equally painstaking and culminate in "hard" and "dead" pieces.

Purity can also yield contradictions, the consequence of an absolute ideal clashing with the exigencies of the cultural scene in which it emerges. The "logical categories of non-contradiction" mandated by purity, as Douglas explains, cannot hold in the flux of lived experience.[11] In modernist arts, the fixity of the pure especially creates conflicts. According to art historian Donald Kuspit, purity "implies a search for the unchangeable in a field of rapidly changing historical experience."[12] The tension is all the greater when the call for purity coincides with that for innovation, as happened in the 1950s, a decade in which both were highly valued.[13] The ensuing strains, if not futility, sustain what Kuspit calls the "unhappy consciousness" of modernism.

There are ways out of the excesses and contradictions, and possibly even out of unhappiness. Purity can adapt and take on more flexible forms. Douglas presents case studies of adjustment, whereas scholarship in the arts has largely been oblivious to the possibility of change. Kuspit, for example, sees no way out of the void of purity. As Douglas describes and as taken up below, the pure adapts by welcoming materials that it had rejected. The inclusion of once "impure" elements pries apart the narrow categories defining the concept and opens it up to the sprawl of daily life. Through this inclusion, the concept becomes more relevant and the idealism upon which it rests is preserved.[14]

This chapter will document one case study. The subject is the elaborate rites of musical purity practiced in the electronic music studios of 1950s Europe. The focus is on Stockhausen's *Gesang der Jünglinge* (1956), unquestionably the most imaginative electroacoustic work of the time. The

---

[10] Mary Douglas, *Purity and Danger: An Analysis of Concepts of Pollution and Taboo*, 2nd edn (London: Routledge & Kegan Paul, 1969), 161.

[11] Douglas, *Purity and Danger*, 162.

[12] Donald B. Kuspit, "The Unhappy Consciousness of Modernism," in *Zeitgeist in Babel: The Postmodernist Controversy*, ed. Ingeborg Hoesterey (Bloomington and Indianapolis: Indiana University Press, 1991), 52.

[13] Cheetham discusses this pressure in the early modernist period. Cheetham, *The Rhetoric of Purity*, 104.

[14] Douglas, *Purity and Danger*, 159–79.

imagination of the piece has held up well. Whereas most early electro-acoustic works quickly fell into obscurity, Stockhausen's piece pointed to the future and remains as relevant and captivating today.

One way to approach the work is to view it as creating a more adaptable form of purity than that calculated in the two sine-tone-based pieces preceding it. The Stockhausen case study merits attention for several reasons. First, it inspires a rare discussion of how purity can be manifested in a musical work, let alone how it can adapt. New understandings of the aesthetics of 1950s modernism also emerge. Finally, the manifold type of purity forged in *Gesang der Jünglinge* has been taken up in subsequent pieces, furthering a line of inquiry that reinforces the significant role of purity in modernism. Of special interest is Jonathan Harvey's *Mortuos plango, vivos voco* (1980), which in many ways is a companion to Stockhausen's work, the two sharing similar constructions of the pure and one particular pure sound, a boy's voice.

Gesang der Jünglinge, Mortuos plango, vivos voco, and the other works presented here can be viewed as participating in the inquiry into the compositional state of purity. Purity in many ways lends itself to that role, being an ideal to which the musical language of a piece can conform. It also inspires an approach typical of states. Pieces involved with states often keep in play different, and sometimes contradictory, manifestations of the ideal; the Stockhausen and Harvey compositions are no exception. Multiplicity strengthens the presence of an ideal and provides more opportunities to explore its distinct properties. What works for some states, though, would appear to be inimical to purity. Yet another contradiction could riddle the concept. Purity does abrogate diversity and mixture, but the contradiction, if that is how one wants to see it, is more productive than crippling. It is important to keep in mind that works like those by Stockhausen and Harvey do not mix so much pure and impure elements as different facets of the pure. Such mixtures, as in other states, create the crisscrossing dynamics that make states so rich. The combinations also offer an escape from the potential danger of restrictive extremes. In these works, the pure, diverse and adaptable, is anything but restrictive.

The pure elements in these pieces fall into three different categories. The first includes sounds that largely for acoustical reasons are perceived as being pure, such as the boy's voice in *Gesang der Jünglinge* and *Mortuos plango, vivos voco.* The second consists of symbolic associations. The sounds are not just pure but they also evoke cultural topics that have strong links to purity. The Stockhausen and Harvey works, for example, call up both childhood and the sacred. The sounds and symbolic associations reciprocate in the evocation of purity. Identifiably pure sounds may bring out facets of purity in a cultural topic, whereas associations may be introduced that give sounds not necessarily considered to be pure the aura of purity.

The third category requires explanation. Purity is as much an action as it is an inherent quality. It is achieved through some means, which determine how it relates to the impure, the outside world. Or, in the case of the works discussed here, how the pure elements in a piece relate to other pure materials. Anthropological studies, again more so than those in the arts, have considered the means of purity, for example the sequence of events unfolded in a ritual. The specific events, whether it be those in a ceremony or those involved in the creation of an electroacoustic work, can be understood as performing four types of means central to purity. They include reduction, the stripping away of the extraneous to attain some sort of essence; exclusion, the outright rejection of and separation from impure elements; refinement, the clarification of a type of material in and of itself to achieve a specific conception of the pure; and merger, the combination of different materials to create a more flexible form of purity. All four by themselves, it should be stressed, are not signs of purity. Far from it, they are general impulses that play out in a variety of musical settings. One context is that of works inquiring into the state of purity. In that setting, they become the means by which pure sounds and symbolic associations are defined and connected to each other. They also become part of the diverse and dynamic realm of purity.

Stockhausen

The boy's voice in *Gesang der Jünglinge* demands attention. It did so back in the 1950s, when listeners were captivated, some repulsed, by the placement of a voice so fragile and innocent and, because of those qualities, so human in a world of artificial electronic sounds. Even today when the relationship between human voice and synthetic sound has become fluid, listeners still marvel at the ways in which Stockhausen overlays the two sonic worlds, part of the creative longevity enjoyed by the piece. For listeners then and now, the work raises several questions: Why use a voice? Why use a child's voice? What is the relationship between the voice and electronic sounds?

Before turning to these questions, it is necessary to trace Stockhausen's first steps in electroacoustic composition. While studying in Paris, he became interested in *musique concrète* and visited the Club d'Essai studios where Pierre Schaeffer worked. He composed there his one and only *musique concrète* piece, *Étude* (1952), which notably does not build upon the recognizable sounds favored by *musique concrète* composers. It takes the sounds of piano strings being hit by a metal beater and elaborately

Preiset (Jubelt) den(m) Herrn, ihr Werke alle des Herrn –	O all ye works of the Lord –
lobt ihn und über alles erhebt ihn in Ewigkeit.	Praise ye the Lord above all forever.
Preiset den Herrn, ihr Engel des Herrn –	O ye angels of the Lord, praise ye the Lord –
preiset den Herrn, ihr Himmel droben.	O ye heavens, praise ye the Lord.
Preiset den Herrn, ihr Wasser alle, die über den Himmeln sind –	O ye waters that be above the heavens, praise ye the Lord –
preiset den Herrn, ihr Scharen alle des Herrn.	O ye hosts of the Lord, praise ye the Lord.
Preiset den Herrn, Sonne und Mond –	O every sun and moon, praise ye the Lord –
preiset den Herrn, des Himmels Sterne.	O ye stars and heavens, praise ye the Lord.
Preiset den Herrn, aller Regen und Tau –	O every shower and dew, praise ye the Lord –
preiset den Herrn, alle Winde.	O all ye winds, praise ye the Lord.
Preiset den Herrn, Feuer und Sommersglut –	O ye fire and heat, praise ye the Lord –
preiset den Herrn, Kälte und starrer Winter.	O ye cold and hard winter, praise ye the Lord.
Preiset den Herrn, Tau und des Regens Fall –	O ye dew and storms and rain, praise ye the Lord –
preiset den Herrn, Eis und Frost.	O ye ice and frost, praise ye the Lord.
Preiset den Herrn, Reif und Schnee –	O ye hoar frost and snow, praise ye the Lord –
preiset den Herrn, Nächte und Tage.	O ye nights and day, praise ye the Lord.
Preiset den Herrn, Licht und Dunkel –	O ye lights and darkness, praise ye the Lord –
preiset den Herrn, Blitze und Wolken.	O ye lightning and clouds, praise ye the Lord.

Text and translation taken from Stockhausen, *Elektronische Musik, 1952–1960*. Stockhausen Verlag, CD 3, liner notes, pp. 149–51.

Figure 1.1 Text for *Gesang der Jünglinge*

manipulates them so that they come across as blips and bursts of static. Not surprisingly, Stockhausen turned to electronically generated sounds. After his return to Germany, he settled in the studios of the Westdeutscher Rundfunk (WDR) in Cologne. His *Studien I* and *II* (1953, 1954) incorporate sine tones, which are amalgamated to create richer sounds.[15] Tailoring the sounds to his specifications, Stockhausen used them to realize intricate integral serial designs to degrees impossible with human performers. He did, though, want to draw upon human sounds, if not live musicians. The desire to combine the human voice with electronic sonorities inspired *Gesang der Jünglinge.* The work features a boy soprano reciting and singing the text of the Benedicite, the song of praise drawn from the biblical story of the three youths thrown in the fiery furnace (Figure 1.1).[16]

The inclusion of the voice can be understood as an attempt to transcend the two factions that had emerged in the nascent electroacoustic scene, those

[15] The latter work features sounds created by filtering white noise.
[16] The text is drawn from the Apocrypha additions to Daniel, 1:35–68, which can be inserted between Daniel, 3:23 and 3:24. Used frequently in church services, the text would have been familiar to many of the original listeners. Stockhausen chose the twelve-year-old Josef Protschka to sing the vocal parts for the piece.

of *musique concrète* and *elektronische Musik*, that using exclusively synthetic sounds. Stockhausen was not alone in recognizing that the future of the music exceeded such strict categories. Other composers at the time created works blending real-world sounds, including voices, and electronic timbres, notably Varèse's *Poème électronique* (1958) and Boulez's *Poésie pour pouvoir* (1955).[17] The focus of this chapter, however, does not lie upon shifts within a particular compositional scene, as fascinating as they are, but rather upon larger modernist contexts. The three pieces, for instance, can be seen as part of a swerve in 1950s abstraction. With the arts having attained high degrees of abstraction, defined by the divorce from recognizable images or sounds and conventional idioms, some works surprisingly turned to familiar elements. They welcomed back what they had previously rejected.

Art historian T. J. Clark isolates a group of paintings by Jackson Pollock from 1947 to 1950 in which a cluster of recognizable images – the human figure, masks, animal shapes – intrude upon the daedal drips of paint.[18] For Clark, the recourse to such images stemmed from Pollock's contemplation of the signifying power of the figure, a power that he was curious to explore, especially in relation to the abstract space of his imposing canvases. The result is a rumination on "negation." The spontaneous throwing of paint already served as a negation of the figure, pushing it aside and off the canvas, seemingly for good. Now brought back to that space, the figure contravenes those patterns, reasserting a pictorial scheme in which it is primary. As such, the figure functions as "the negation of a negation."[19] Although inspiring intriguing, if not odd, works, Pollock's experiment with the signifying power of the figure was of limited success. It was ultimately abandoned as he returned to his large abstract canvases.

Gesang der Jünglinge presents a parallel case, but one with a far more productive outcome. Familiar elements, the boy's voice and a sacred text, enter a developed abstract idiom, which too emphasized negation. In the *Studien*, Stockhausen had sought to create music "*ex nihilo,*" that is "to compose neither known rhythms nor melodies nor harmonic combinations nor figures; in other words, to avoid everything which is familiar, generally known or reminiscent of music already composed."[20] Similar to Pollock,

---

[17] Boulez later withdrew his piece.
[18] T. J. Clark, *Farewell to an Idea: Episodes from a History of Modernism* (New Haven and London: Yale University Press, 1999), 344–69.
[19] Clark, *Farewell to an Idea*, 344.
[20] Karlheinz Stockhausen, "Hymnen – Nationalhymnen (Zur Elektronischen Musik 1967)," in *Karlheinz Stockhausen*, ed. Rudolf Frisius (Mainz: Schott Musik, 1996), 275. An English translation of this essay can be found in the liner notes to the CD recording of *Hymnen* issued by the Stockhausen Verlag (CD 10, 1995). Stockhausen, liner notes, *Hymnen*, 130. All subsequent references to this essay will be from the English translation.

Stockhausen wanted to explore how the signifying power of the familiar would play out in a sonic realm void of known sounds. In *Gesang der Jünglinge*, the voice does not add to the layers of negation as Pollock's figures do. It instead takes on various meanings and roles. Stockhausen used it to carry a text central to the spiritual import of the work. In regard to the sonic construction of the piece, the voice provides the listener with familiar sounds in an environment that is alien and offputting. Listeners can orient themselves around the voice.[21] Stockhausen found it to be rich material, so much so that in subsequent electroacoustic works he would continue to draw upon real-life sounds. Unlike Pollock who put away the figural shapes, he would not turn his back on the familiar.

The concept of purity provides another modernist context in which to consider the use of the boy's voice. It captured many of the ideals pursued in 1950s integral serial and electroacoustic composition. Stockhausen was drawn to the concept, undoubtedly influenced by his friend Karel Goeyvaerts, who was devoted to the pure. For the latter, musical works could be "absolute purity projected into sound."[22] He reached for an "absolute structural purity" in integral serial designs, self-contained structures that could control every facet of a work and not allow for extraneous elements.[23] Both Goeyvaerts and Stockhausen searched for "pure" sounds and found them in the sine tone.[24] The purity of the sine tone emerged from it being perceived as elemental, a sound of exact pitch with no overtones that exists at the core of all sounds. Herbert Eimert, one of the composers active at the WDR, called it a "pure element," beyond which there was nothing purer or smaller.[25] Eimert and other composers, including Stockhausen, realized that this "purity" was ultimately unattainable, as listeners would always hear additional overtones and colors.[26] Nonetheless, composers worked with these sonic "atoms," seeing them as the building blocks of a new music.[27]

---

[21] Stockhausen referred to the use of "musical orientation phenomena." Stockhausen, liner notes, *Hymnen*, 130.

[22] Jan Christiaens, "'Absolute Purity Projected Into Sound': Goeyvaerts, Heidegger, and Early Serialism," *Perspectives of New Music* 41 (2003), 168.

[23] Karel Goeyvaerts, "Paris: Darmstadt 1947–1956. Excerpt from the Autobiographical Portrait," *Revue belge de musicologie* 48 (1994), 44.

[24] On the fascination with the purity of the sine tone, see Richard Toop, "Stockhausen and the Sine-Wave: The Story of an Ambiguous Relationship," *Musical Quarterly* 65 (1979), 379–80. Goeyvaerts, "Autobiographical Portrait," 47.

[25] Herbert Eimert, "Der Sinus-Ton," *Melos* 21 (1954), 168.

[26] Eimert, "Der Sinus-Ton," 170. Stockhausen, "Zur Situation des Metiers (Klangkomposition)," in *Texte zur elektronischen und instrumentalen Musik*, vol. I of *Texte* (Cologne: M. DuMont Schauberg, 1963), 50–55.

[27] On Karel Goeyvaerts's views of the sine tone, see Herman Sabbe, "Goeyvaerts and the Beginnings of 'Punctual' Serialism and Electronic Music," *Revue belge de musicologie* 48 (1994), 85.

Purity had its champions; it also had its skeptics, none more so than Adorno. In the censorious essay "The Aging of the New Music," he pointed to the "chemical purity" of electronic sounds, a description that holds them up more as laboratory experiments than as vibrant advanced material.[28] The drive to "purification" amounted to a "technocratic attitude," in which "something entirely too binding, violent, and unartistic announces itself."[29] He asks, "what is the raison d'être of this purified music?" The answer is purity itself and the "schematic organization" it supports.[30] The idea takes over, becoming the essence of a work. Pieces like the *Studien* must have only fed Adorno's skepticism. Ideas of purity drive the two works to extremes. They concentrate on a limited group of sounds, "chemical" ones at that, and rigid structural schemes to mold those sounds.[31]

Douglas, as cited above (page 32), describes how purity can be "renewed," a process that captures the ways in which *Gesang der Jünglinge* departed from the earlier pieces. She discusses how systems of purity can be salvaged by welcoming back that which had been rejected, in other words, the impure. The ancient Hebrew Temple, for example, dismissed bodily fluids as grossly unclean only to allow blood to cross the sacred threshold, as long as it was treated in special ways.[32] The use of blood brings together the pure and the impure, "an act of at-one-ment" going beyond the significance of a specific ritual. According to Douglas, such unions nullify the divisiveness upon which the demand for purity thrives and uphold a larger "combination of opposites," which proves a "satisfying" "psychological" and "religious" act.[33] For *Gesang der Jünglinge*, the union of electronic sound and the human voice is no less profound. As realized in the design of a sonic continuum central to the piece, the merger broadens and deepens levels of unity, a "satisfying" state for serial composers, for whom the term "unity" was a mantra. Some composers did indeed prize unity as a religious state. Stockhausen and Goeyvaerts, two ardent Catholics at the time, viewed musical unity, particularly the schemes of integral serialism, as emulating "Divine Perfection."[34]

There is one significant difference between Douglas's model of renewal and the path taken by *Gesang der Jünglinge*. In the former, the pure reaches out to the impure, whereas, in the musical work, pure elements combine with pure elements. The two elements entering the electronic

---

[28] Adorno, "The Aging of the New Music," 194.
[29] Adorno, "The Aging of the New Music," 182.
[30] Adorno, "The Aging of the New Music," 192.
[31] Adorno did see the concept of purity as having positive critical value, as is evident from his comments on Webern discussed in Chapter 2.
[32] Douglas, *Purity and Danger*, 159.   [33] Douglas, *Purity and Danger*, 169.
[34] On this sacred association, see Toop, "Stockhausen and the Sine-Wave," 383.

soundworld – a child's voice and a biblical text – possess acoustic and/or symbolic associations of purity. The boy's voice not only captures the innocence and naturalness by which society defines childhood but it is also a pure sound, a voice with little or no vibrato – a human sine tone, as it were. The biblical text obviously signifies the holy. It is, though, not just pure but also about purity, presenting many different forms of the state. The youths thrown into the furnace embody childhood innocence.[35] They are made even more innocent by the fire, which refines, or purifies, them by bringing them into contact with the divine, the angel encountered in the flames. That presence turns them into fonts of religious faith, pouring out a florid song of praise. Their song calls out the "works of the Lord," which include pure elements, such as water (in its various forms of rain, dew, snow, and ice), air, and fire. Instead of purity, *Gesang der Jünglinge* gives us purities. Why reach out to this plurality? A fear of impurity could be one reason. Any element brought into the electronic sphere would be considered impure. Outside materials, though, were needed. One way to stave off the threat of impurity would be to incorporate elements culturally embedded in the pure. Purity could reinforce purity.

Added to the mix are various means of purity, which are either germane to the materials or offer a way of handling them. Prized as elemental and atom-like, the sine tone appears to possess a natural purity. That sound exists by itself, hidden at the center of all sounds. In other words, it is not made. Or is it? Its purity is achieved by a certain means, that of reduction. Discussing *Studie I*, Stockhausen remarked: "We reduced everything to the element, which is the basis for the variety of sound; the pure soundwave, electrically producible, called 'sine wave.' "[36] To get at these atoms, a sound must be diminished, its thick timbral layers boiled off. Even when these layers have been removed, the sine tone does not exist. It has to be, as Stockhausen mentions, electronically produced, or synthesized. It is nothing more than an acoustic ideal – a wave pattern – given sonic life in the studio, no different from the other electronic timbres in *Gesang der Jünglinge*.

All the electronic sounds, from sine tones to thick masses, result from a related means of achieving purity: exclusion. Sharing an antipathy toward the extraneous, exclusion and reduction overlap. However, there are differences. Whereas reduction gradually removes the contingent, exclusion outright rejects it. Electronic sounds are created in a separate sphere, the studio. From the outset, they have been set apart. At the WDR, Stockhausen

---

[35] In the biblical account it appears that the "youths" are not children but rather adolescents or young adults. At some unknown point, the text became closely associated with childhood.

[36] Quoted in Elena Ungeheuer, "From the Elements to the Continuum: Timbre Composition in Early Electronic Music," *Contemporary Music Review* 10 (1994), 25.

isolated them in the soundworlds of *Studien I* and *II*. In such pieces, and in certain moments of *Gesang der Jünglinge*, electronic sound becomes what Stockhausen calls "pure sound," a realm where sound is no longer tied to, or contaminated by, the known but rather exists in and by itself.[37] Electronic music achieves its essence, becoming sound about sound.

In contrast to electronic sound, childhood – signified by the boy's voice – is a natural form of purity. Children are born pure, a belief reinforced by cultural discourses of childhood since roughly the seventeenth century.[38] Childhood purity, however, is fragile and short-lived. It perishes, succumbing to the defiled adult world around it. Childhood exists more as the threat of impurity than as a means of purity. If childhood purity is shaped by any action, it is that of loss. The danger of violation makes the pure all the more cherished and protected, and thus more frail.

Finally, the biblical text imparts a sacred purity. Unlike other forms of the pure, that state does not arise from a specific means. The sacred, as conveyed in religious traditions, is not created; it has always existed and will never change. It is eternal. *Gesang der Jünglinge*, or any mortal creation, can obviously never commandeer this quality, only evoke it. The text, however, does point to a mode of purity that can be incorporated. The tale of the fiery furnace describes how the flames refine the youths, making them even more pure. Refinement functions as another important means of purity, one by which the impure, or even the pure, can be elevated into a higher form.

The panoply of purity raised in *Gesang der Jünglinge* captures not only the multiplicity characteristic of states but also the way in which such diversity is handled. Works typically emphasize one form of the ideal over the others, especially as a piece nears a conclusion. The closing accentuation brings out the aspect most representative of how a work envisions the governing ideal. With purity, the process of definition is pertinent, as it is a concept expected to reach a high degree of clarification. The process often settles upon one sound and one means. The other elements do not necessarily disappear but rather the elevated sounds and means become the dominant signs of the pure. In *Gesang der Jünglinge*, clarification is particularly needed as it

---

[37] Karlheinz Stockhausen, "Musik und Sprache III," in Stockhausen, *Texte zu eigenen Werken zur Kunst Anderer Aktuelles*, vol. II of *Texte* (Cologne: Verlag M. DuMont Schauberg, 1964), 59–60. This version expands upon an essay that originally appeared in *Die Reihe* 6 (1960). A translation of the latter can be found in the English version of *Die Reihe* 6 (1964), 57–64. A translation of the longer essay can be found in Stockhausen, liner notes, *Elektronische Musik, 1952–1960*, CD 3, Stockhausen Verlag. Unless otherwise noted, the liner notes translation will be cited. "Music and Speech," 160.

[38] For an account of childhood as a cultural discourse, see Philippe Ariès, *Centuries of Childhood: A Social History of Family Life*, trans. Robert Baldick (New York: Knopf, 1962). The centrality of innocence in that discourse is discussed in James R. Kincaid, *Child Loving: The Erotic Child and Victorian Culture* (New York: Routledge, 1992), 72–79.

provides a way of connecting the original "pure" elements, the electronic sounds, with the outside, "impure" materials, the boy's voice and the text. The question becomes which facets of the pure will govern the works. In some ways, the answer depends on how a listener hears the relationship between the two defining materials.

Many of the early reviewers of *Gesang der Jünglinge* held to the purity of childhood. Their interpretations are built around that ideal, revealing how purity, or one particular notion of it, can dominate perceptions of the work. To these critics, electronic sounds could never possess purity, being so far removed from nature and the beautiful. If anything, the sounds corrupted and distorted the pure, as heard in the treatment of the boy's voice. Several reviewers paint vivid scenes in which the voice is polluted, becoming an unnatural, even grotesque, noise, no different than the electronic timbres. Purity, as it takes form in the work, exists as loss, that which is made impure. According to one critic, the voice, "a gift of the divine," was subjected to "the perverse possibilities" of the electronic equipment, which damned it to a "hellish" soundworld.[39] Another reviewer describes how the boy's voice, again a gift from God, was treated in ways going "against nature," mutilated into "howls" and "groans."[40] The homage to divine gifts reveals how some critics also appealed to the purity of the sacred, enshrining both the boy's voice and the biblical text in it. The sacred elevates the voice, thereby allowing reviewers to dramatize its corruption.

The idea of electronic sound purifying the boy's voice would have struck these critics as sacrilege. There is some truth, though, in this blasphemy, as it captures the way in which *Gesang der Jünglinge* approaches the relationship between the two elements. The piece clearly holds to the ideal of purity. Out of all the depicted means of securing that state, it adheres to one: refinement. The biblical story is not lost on the work. *Gesang der Jünglinge*, however, rewrites the tale – yet more blasphemy. Having brought in outside materials, be they pure or impure, the work must make them suitable for the pure realm of electronic sound. *Gesang der Jünglinge* surrounds the child's voice with electronic fire. The blaze, unlike the biblical furnace, does not enhance the voice's own purity; rather, the boy's voice feeds the flames, enhancing the purity of electronic sound. The voice is not so much transformed into divine song as into sounds similar to the electronic timbres.

Douglas's study offers insights into the means of refinement. As she describes, the impure can only be brought into the sphere of the pure

---

[39] A. Neukirchen, *Düsseldorfer Nachrichten*, 2 June 1956. Quoted in Christoph von Blumröder, "Karlheinz Stockhausen – 40 Jahre Elektronische Musik," *Archiv für Musikwissenschaft* 50 (1993), 322.

[40] Ludwig Wismeyer, "Wider die Natur!" *Neue Zeitschrift für Musik* 118 (1957), 136–37.

when handled in specific ways. For instance, the blood used in the Hebrew Temple had to be shed in sacrifice. By following established laws, the outside element can be lifted to the level of the pure.[41] In this elevation, it takes on new qualities, either by assuming different associations (that of sacrifice) or by being directly transformed. *Gesang der Jünglinge* is ruled by a set of laws, by various serial schemes. Stockhausen, to recall, viewed those schemes in general as emblems of "Divine Perfection." Such "perfection" demands purity. Not surprisingly, sine tones were offered to the serial designs of *Studien I* and *II*, pure tones that could complement those laws and be easily molded to accord with them.

A voice, a sound following its own distinct rules, would seem to resist such treatment. Yet it too ultimately follows "the chosen musical order."[42] To unite the volatile electronic sounds with a human voice, Stockhausen held fast to the ideals of integral serialism, expanding them to deal with an unprecedented range of sonorities. The makeup of individual sounds as well as the relationships between them could be serially defined.[43] Those designs involve such parameters as duration, distance between successive sounds, attack, decay, the number of layers comprising a sound, and the spacing between the layers. Even the voice could be pressed into a structural scheme. To that end, Stockhausen established an ordered series of seven degrees of comprehensibility, ranging from clearly understood syllables and words to raucous sonorities comprised of overlapped vocal parts.[44] For Stockhausen, both the voice and electronics were part of a larger sonic continuum.[45] The simple sine tone sat at one end of that continuum and hectic white noise at the other. Different forms of speech fall between those points. Isolated syllables and words stay close to the sine tones, whereas superimposed vocal sonorities push toward the other end. Laid out on the continuum and parsed into units that follow a serial scheme, the voice submits to the overall structural design. As Stockhausen declares,

---

[41] Douglas, *Purity and Danger*, 159.   [42] Stockhausen, "Music and Speech," 152.

[43] The serial schemes of the work are discussed in detail in Pascal Decroupet and Elena Ungeheuer, "Son pur – bruit – médiations: Matières, matériaux et formes dans *Gesang der Jünglinge* de Karlheinz Stockhausen," *Genesis* 4 (1993), 69–85 and Decroupet and Ungeheuer, "Through the Sensory Looking-glass: The Aesthetic and Serial Foundation of *Gesang der Jünglinge*," *Perspectives of New Music* 36 (1998), 97–142.

[44] Stockhausen, "Music and Speech," 156–57.

[45] The idea of a continuum appears in Karlheinz Stockhausen, "Aktuelles," in *Texte*, vol. II, 51–57. The article originally appeared in *Die Reihe* 1 (1955). English translations can be found in "Actualia" in *Die Reihe* 1 (1958), 45–51 and liner notes, *Elektronische Musik*, 137–51. Unless otherwise noted, the English *Die Reihe* translation will be cited. See also Stockhausen, "Music and Speech," *Die Reihe* 6, 58–68. The idea of a continuum was central to early concepts of electronic music. On the importance of that idea, see M. J. Grant, *Serial Music, Serial Aesthetics: Compositional Theory in Post-war Europe* (Cambridge University Press, 2001), 96–102, and Elena Ungeheuer, "From the Elements to the Continuum: Timbre Composition in Early Electronic Music," *Contemporary Music Review* 10 (1994), 25–33.

Section	Timing
A	0:00
B	1:02
C	2:43
D	5:13
E	6:21
F	8:39

The above timings do not include the
ten-second delay used in the Stockhausen
Verlag CD recording of the work.

Figure 1.2 Formal diagram of *Gesang der Jünglinge*

"the sung speech sounds, like all the electronic sounds, follow formal musical laws."[46]

In other words, the voice must become like an electronic sound in order to adhere to the same "laws" that those sounds do. Its purity must be changed, or refined, into electronic sound. The change occurs across the individual sections of *Gesang der Jünglinge*. The work divides into six sections labeled A to F (Figure 1.2).[47] Stockhausen had originally planned and sketched out a seventh concluding (G) section but did not have time to finish it.[48] The junctures between the individual units are demarcated by either thick clusters or silences. Stockhausen contrasts the sections by the treatment of the voice. Each one highlights a specific manipulation of the vocal material. Overall, there are four basic manipulations: clear syllables and words, vocal chords (massed, roughly homophonic groupings of individual lines), vocal polyphony (divergent lines), and choral swarms (very dense and unruly combinations of separate vocal parts).[49] The opening A section introduces the categories of syllables and words, chords, and swarms. Each of the following four units concentrates on a particular category: swarms (B), syllables and words (C), chords (D), and polyphony (E). The final F section serves as a timbral and formal summation (even without the planned G section), bringing together all the vocal categories and a wide range of electronic sounds.

---

[46] Stockhausen, "Actualia," in liner notes, *Elektronische Musik*, 138.
[47] A breakdown of these individual sections can be found in Decroupet and Ungeheuer, "Through the Sensory Looking-glass," 134–39.
[48] Realizing that he would not complete the piece, Stockhausen later approved the six-section version as the final form of the work.
[49] I have adopted the terminology used in Decroupet and Ungeheuer, "Through the Sensory Looking-glass," 134.

The means of purity can be observed by tracking the interaction between what Stockhausen calls "pure speech" and "pure sound." The iterated adjective reveals the composer stirring a mixture of purities and reinforces how much the two defining elements of the work are connected to ideals of purity. As used by Stockhausen, "pure speech" refers to the clear presentation of the text, but it can be broadened to encompass the boy's voice in general, which creates not only lucid words but also other sounds and associations of the pure. Electronic timbres, as mentioned above, claim the status of "pure sound." Stockhausen treats pure speech and pure sound as distant points on the sonic continuum. There are moments when the work ricochets back and forth between them and times when it muddles them in the middle range of the expanse. The overall path, however, is toward the endpoint of "pure sound." It is a path that changes the purity, as well as the sound, of the boy's voice.

The boy's voice does not emerge pure, at least in the sense of consistently clear speech. Throughout the A section, it is broken down into basic parts, including vowels, consonants, and flecks of timbre. The bits can be transformed and combined to create new sounds, like the swarms and polyphony. Along similar lines, the electronic impulse tones – single, percussive sonorities featuring a natural decay – can be presented as either individual blips or in dense swarms. In other words, the voice can be just as elemental and malleable as the synthetic components. Brief moments of melodic imitation tie the voice even closer to the electronic tones. *Gesang der Jünglinge* begins with a rush of impulse tones that dwindle into a series of isolated pitches, approximately e♭''''-g''''-g'''-c♯''''.[50] Out of the sustained e♭ emerges the voice, which sings the word "jubelt" to the pitches e♭''''-b♭'', roughly the outer pitch-classes of the electronic phrase (0:05–0:12).[51] A few seconds later another moment of melodic imitation occurs, as the general contour of a three-pitch electronic figure is taken up by the solo voice on the phrase "lobet ihn" (0:26–0:32). In both cases, the imitation is not exact. Nor would one expect it to be. Ever so modern and multifarious, *Gesang der Jünglinge* has little to do with such a conventional and precisely repetitive gesture as imitation. The aversion to imitation makes these two parallels, no matter

---

[50] As with the bulk of the pitch material in the work, these pitches fall in between the twelve chromatic scale degrees. The score lists the acoustical frequencies as 2533–3067–1600–2267 Hz. These frequencies have been taken from a "realization" score included in a facsimile edition of the materials used in the preparation of the work. Stockhausen, *Gesang der Jünglinge: Elektronische Musik: Facsimile-Edition 2001* (Kürten: Stockhausen Verlag, 2001).

[51] Again these are rough pitches. The frequencies given in the sketches are 1200–933 Hz. Note that these timings do not include the ten-second time delay worked into the track on the Stockhausen Verlag CD.

how loose, all the more surprising and significant. At a moment when the voice claims some degree of purity by enunciating the clearest words in the section, it remains secondary to the electronic tones.

The purity of the voice is further effaced in the B section. The voice behaves more and more like the synthetic sounds. For instance, the choral and impulse swarms both present dense, seemingly chaotic, blends of individual lines and tones. The choral sonorities grow increasingly matted. Once again the clarity of the text suffers, as heard in the gradual disfiguring of the phrase "preiset den Herrn" which reappears throughout the section. Stockhausen regularly interrupts the choral swarms with impulse bursts, using one mass of sound to block and contain another.[52] The section concludes with the choral swarms piling on top of each other into a massive unstable sonority.

Just when there seems to be little left of the voice, it reappears intact in the C section, which opens with the first extended passage for solo speaking voice. Stockhausen fragments and staggers the part, but the text remains clear. The purity of the voice – its sound and the clarity of language – is asserted. So strong is the voice that the electronic sonorities adhere to it. Whereas earlier the voice imitated the textures and even melodies of the synthetic timbres, the latter now behave like the voice. The C section features low individual impulse sonorities. As with the voice, the sounds move melodically from one pitch to the next, as if enunciating lone words or syllables.[53] In their study of the sketches and structural plans of *Gesang der Jünglinge*, Pascal Decroupet and Elena Ungeheuer note that the spoken voice and electronic sounds in this passage have "shared organizational principles," the "melodic contour" of the latter adhering to a structure derived from the inflexions of spoken language.[54]

The conclusion of the C section and the following D section (4:52–5:55) traverse the extremes of "pure sound" and "pure speech." The speech-like impulse tones give way to swarms. The boy's voice similarly grows unintelligible in a host of swarms and chords. At one moment, a vocal phrase from the B section reappears, but now played backwards. The warped, unintelligible voices take us further into the realm of "pure sound." *Gesang der Jünglinge* then unexpectedly swerves back to "pure speech." At the

[52] These bursts articulate the division of the B section into three smaller units, which Decroupet and Ungeheuer label B1 (1:02–1:42), B2 (1:43–2:23), and B3 (2:24–2:42). Decroupet and Ungeheuer, "Through the Sensory Looking-glass," 135–36.

[53] On the development of an "electronic" form of speech during the work and the general relationship between speech and electronic sound, see Metzer, "The Paths from and to Abstraction in Stockhausen's *Gesang der Jünglinge*," *Modernism/modernity* 11 (2004), 707–13.

[54] Decroupet and Ungeheuer, "Son pur – bruit – médiations," 73.

end of the D section, the boy's voice, with little electronic background, clearly recites the phrase "kälte und starrer Winter" (5:56).[55] The phrase is important not only for returning us to speech but also for being the last instance of extended distinct speech in the work. The voice will never sound so pure again; its purity will be refined into another form.

In the E section, the individual impulse tones bounce back and forth. The boy's voice acts like the electronic swarms once did, a blast of noise that interrupts the flow of the other part. The F section is even more dense and harried. Stockhausen structurally realizes the sound continuum, as he breaks it down into twelve fixed segments that are combined to form twenty-three larger sonic groups.[56] The groups are dispersed across the F section in a predetermined order. Quick cuts between the disparate strands create a vacillating timbral surface. The rhythmic conception enhances the timbral vacillation. Much of the section is made up of two passages that Stockhausen calls "rhythmic inserts" (9:53–11:30, 12:07–12:34). In these parentheses, the composer concentrates on the four shortest durations of a larger rhythmic series, durations that last from roughly one twentieth of a second to one second.[57] At such lengths, sounds prick, dissolving as soon as they emerge.

The voice proves just as evanescent. It appears and disappears along with the electronic tones in the sonic commotion. According to the composer, the voice "approaches" "pure sound" and its meaning is "effaced."[58] The treatment of the voice can be understood as a process of refinement. It may seem redundant to refine the pure, but some way is needed to elevate a particular vision of the pure from all the competing ones. As the conclusion makes clear, the purity of electronic sound – or "pure sound" as Stockhausen puts it – is the vision to be upheld. To attain it, the voice cannot remain apart and insist upon its own purity. It must be changed to become like electronic sound.

The change, though, is not complete. The voice adds to that purity but is never completely subsumed into it. No matter how scrambled and disjointed the text becomes, semantic meaning, the chatter of the impure, hovers around the voice, as words and syllables can be heard here and there. Moreover, a child's voice is a very distinct timbre, one not easily dissolved.

---

[55] There is some overlap here, as the prominent **rrr**s in the vocal part match the fizzing sound in the electronics.

[56] On these formal realizations of the continuum, see Stockhausen, "Music and Speech," *Die Reihe* 6, 59–61.

[57] Pascal Decroupet, "Timbre Diversification in Serial Tape Music and its Consequence on Form," *Contemporary Music Review* 10 (1994), 18.

[58] Stockhausen, "Music and Speech," in liner notes, *Elektronische Musik*, 160.

Nor does Stockhausen want to erase the voice, for it, in its more distinctive and intelligible forms, anchors one end of the sonic spectrum. As the piece progresses, though, the voice drifts further and further to the other end, caught in the dense rushes of sound in the final F section.[59]

Gesang der Jünglinge, though, never settles down at that endpoint. It resists the finality of the pure. Refinement – the attainment of purity – is held back by a fear of purity, specifically the hollowness of *Studien I* and *II*, a condition to which Stockhausen had no desire to return. At the same time, a fear of impurity clutches the work. The anxiety perhaps impelled the piece to reach out to the child's voice and biblical text rather than just any foreign elements. It also demands that *Gesang der Jünglinge* attempt to refine those materials, to make them assimilate to the world of electronic sound. Only a piece so obsessed with purity could get caught in such conflicting fears and needs, being pulled in opposite directions by the ideal.

Harvey

The voice of a boy reciting a sacred text reappears in a later major electroacoustic work, Harvey's *Mortuos plango, vivos voco*. As in *Gesang der Jünglinge*, the boy's voice crumbles into consonants and vowels. It too multiplies to form crowds. It too meets sine tones. It too metamorphoses into almost synthetic sounds. That there would be parallels between the two composers' works comes as little surprise.[60] Stockhausen was an influence on Harvey, who authored a major study of his music.[61] *Mortuos plango, vivos voco*, though, is far from a reverential echo. Even with the similarities, it lays claim to a unique soundworld. The foundation of that soundworld is a sound not heard in *Gesang der Jünglinge*, one to which the boy's voice and sine tones defer. It is the first and last sound of the piece – a bell.

---

[59] To recall, Stockhausen had originally planned but never completed a final G section. The facsimile edition of the work provides sketch materials for that section. Although it is difficult to ascertain what exactly this section would have sounded like and what form the relationship between electronic sound and human voice would have taken, it appears that the concluding section would have built upon the fluid soundworld created in the F section. Most of the final events of the work are for electronic sounds; however, the ending includes several prominent choral swarms and chords. It is unclear how intelligible the text would have been in the latter.

[60] In a radio interview, Harvey pointed out two parallels between the pieces: the interest in the boy's voice and the exploration of degrees of intelligibility. He does mention that it was his experiences listening to the cathedral choir, and not Stockhausen's work, that inspired him to use the boy's voice. "Discovering Music," BBC Radio 3, 17 February 2008.

[61] Harvey, *The Music of Stockhausen* (London: Faber & Faber, 1975).

Ex. 1.1 Bell spectrum

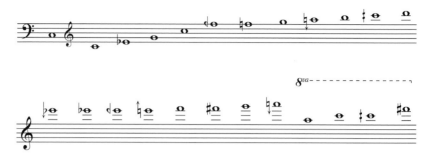

The bell, boy's voice, and electronically generated tones serve as the three source sounds of *Mortuos plango, vivos voco*. The first two originated in a distinct soundworld, Winchester Cathedral. Harvey's son, Dominic, sang in the cathedral choir. The composer recalls the chorus rehearsing amid the tolling of bells.[62] The sounds were transported to another unique sound locale, the studios at IRCAM, where Harvey studied and manipulated them. He recorded the large tenor bell and isolated a sliver in the bell's ring, a half second after the strike. At this moment, the percussive clang has receded and the overtone resonance teems. The spectrum contains the five-point tuning typical of tower and carillon bells, a spectrum different from the natural harmonic series (Ex. 1.1). There is the strike note (c′), the most prominent tone to emerge after the bell has been rung. The hum tone (c) sounds an octave below. It is the lowest partial in the harmonic series, and, given that higher partials decay faster than lower ones, it lingers longest. Above the strike tone are the tierce (minor third), quint, and nominal (an octave higher than the strike tone). After this point, the series ascends by smaller microtonal intervals. Throughout the work, Harvey focuses on the first eight partials. He adds a "secondary strike tone," an unsounded note given a "psycho-acoustical" presence by related pitches in the spectrum.[63] In this case, the pitch is f′, which emerges from partials that suggest a spectrum based on that pitch.

For the part of the boy's voice, Harvey recorded his son singing in different ways the inscription on the bell: "Horas Avolantes Numero, Mortuos Plango, Vivos ad Preces Voco" (I count the fleeting hours. I lament the dead; the living I call to prayer).[64] One recording has him chanting the text on a single

[62] Harvey, "*Mortuos plango, vivos voco*: A Realization at IRCAM," *Computer Music Journal* 5, no. 4 (1981), 24.
[63] Harvey, "The Mirror of Ambiguity," in *The Language of Electroacoustic Music*, ed. Simon Emerson (London: Macmillan, 1986), 181.
[64] Harvey, "Mirror of Ambiguity," 181.

pitch; the individual pitches used include the strike tone, the secondary
strike tone, and some of the first eight partials. Another recording features
Dominic pronouncing individual vowels and consonants. Finally, he sings
a short composed melody drawing upon most of the second through eighth
partials and the secondary strike tone.[65] The bell and boy's voice are joined
by the electronically generated timbres. They are independent sounds in
their own right, but they also double aspects of the other two. Sine-tone-
based sonorities, for instance, are assigned to the frequencies of individual
bell partials to create a synthetic bell. Harvey used the CHANT program
to create synthetic vocal sounds, which often duet with their chorister
counterpart.[66]

Three source sounds appear in *Mortuos plango, vivos voco*; three critical concepts developed by the composer inform it and other works. The
concepts are those of unity, ambiguity, and spirituality. Each bears upon
what was undoubtedly an inspiration for Harvey, the interaction between
disparate sounds. Unity, as described by the composer, is far from a one-
dimensional or settled ideal. It is "dynamic" and "complex," thriving on
the confluence of contrasting materials, such as acoustic and electronic
sounds.[67] The materials exist in "vibrant tension," a condition that, in
turn, has spiritual ramifications.[68] Only in a broad, powerful peace can the
disparate elements be at once themselves and part of a whole. As Harvey
aphorizes: "The greater the conflicts it successfully unifies, the more spiritual
the music."[69] Such fluid conditions foster ambiguity, another condition that
fascinates the composer. A "dialectic between fusion and fission" emerges
as the materials come in and out of profile, one moment being distinct and
the next blurring into each other.[70] In electroacoustic works, Harvey enjoys
making listeners ponder if a sound is either acoustic or synthetic.[71] The flux
of identity too has spiritual significance, as it captures the impermanence
of the material world.[72]

Harvey's three concepts cross lines of thought and compositional practice pursued by Stockhausen. To recall, the latter and Goeyvaerts perceived
a spiritual dimension to unity, one in which the schemes of integral serial
works pointed toward "Divine Perfection." With *Gesang der Jünglinge* and

---

[65] On these materials, see Bruno Bossis, "*Mortuos plango, vivos voco* de Jonathan Harvey ou le
miroir de la spiritualité," *Musurgia* 11 (2004), 124–25.

[66] For Harvey's discussion of the electronic sounds, see "Mirror of Ambiguity," 183.

[67] Harvey, *In Quest of Spirit: Thoughts on Music* (Berkeley: University of California Press, 1999),
26, 28.

[68] Harvey, *In Quest of Spirit*, 28.   [69] Harvey, *In Quest of Spirit*, 52.

[70] Quoted in Arnold Whittall, *Jonathan Harvey* (London: Faber & Faber, 1999), 28.

[71] Harvey, *In Quest of Spirit*, 58, and Whittall, *Jonathan Harvey*, 60. Ambiguities also emerge
between live and recorded sounds.

[72] "Discovering Music," BBC Radio 3, 17 February 2008.

such 1960s pieces as *Hymnen,* Stockhausen saw new possibilities and developed a vision that, like Harvey's, welcomes plurality and ambiguity. Of particular interest is the concept of intermodulation.[73] It involves the coalescing of different elements, such as the folk styles in *Hymnen,* to form new compounds that simultaneously heighten the individuality of the original sounds while creating ambiguous or even unknown sounds. The interaction between the two would create deep levels of unity. Harvey has succinctly summarized the affinity between him and Stockhausen as the "aesthetic urge toward integration without losing individuality." He has also cited the latter's credo: "ultimately I want to integrate everything."[74]

To the three concepts put forward by Harvey, others can be added. In discussing *Mortuos plango, vivos voco,* Whittall points to the "relevance" of the "essential modernist attributes of ambiguity and multiplicity."[75] The former has already been mentioned; the latter captures the numerous individual sounds crowding certain passages and the generation of new distinct sounds from single sonorities, such as the choirs created from Dominic's voice. This chapter of my study places purity on the roster of pertinent critical concepts. It too is an "essential modernist attribute" and plays a compelling role in the work, both as a dynamic within and across sections and as a counterpart to the other leading concepts.

Mortuos plango, vivos voco, like *Gesang der Jünglinge,* commits to materials and means of purity. The materials can be divided between the sonic and the symbolic. Both works trade in similar sounds, a boy's voice and sine tones, similar in that they possess acoustical purity, bearing little or no vibrato, and, in the case of the sine tones, no overtones. In discussing his work, Harvey has referred to "the pure treble voice."[76] The two elements also carry rich associations. The composer has commented that he was drawn to the "connotations" of childhood, particularly that of innocence.[77] The sine tones, as discussed earlier, suggest the elemental.

What about the bell? Bloated with overtones and colors, it is the acoustic antipode to the other two source sounds. Such profligacy detracts from any impression of purity, especially when in comparison to the boy's voice and to the sine tones. Bells, though, abound with symbolic purity. In the case of the Winchester bell, the engraved text points to the sacred. Although not the scriptural words heard in Stockhausen's work, the inscription does proclaim a sacred place and function. The text is a variation on an inlay

---

[73] For a discussion of the technique, see David Metzer, *Quotation and Cultural Meaning in Twentieth-century Music* (Cambridge University Press, 2003), 141.
[74] Harvey, "Mirror of Ambiguity," 186.
[75] Whittall, *Jonathan Harvey,* 57.   [76] Harvey, "A Realization at IRCAM," 24.
[77] "Discovering Music," BBC Radio 3, 17 February 2008.

found on European bells: Vivos voco/Mortuos plango/Fulgura frango (I call
the living/Mourn the dead/Break lightning). Schiller used the inscription
as an epigraph to his "Das Lied von der Glocke," in which the bell serves
as a watchperson and protector in a community. In addition, he gives the
bell a sacred, almost divine, voice. It rings in the heavens and both uplifts
and frightens those who hear it. It is also a pure voice: Dass vom reinlichen
Mettale/Rein und voll die Stimme schalle (That from the pure metal/Pure
and full the voice may sound). Pure metal creates a pure voice; a sacred
place demands such a voice. In its origins and role, Schiller's bell claims a
symbolic purity. Connected to a cathedral and prayer, Harvey's bell similarly
becomes a voice of the pure.

The bell creates a mingled purity, symbolically pure and acoustically
less so. It never comes across as impure, however. Nothing is marked as
impure in the work. The same could be more or less said about *Gesang
der Jünglinge*. It raised the specter of impurity by bringing foreign sounds
into the once pristine realm of electronic composition but sidestepped the
threat by making the interlopers epitomes of purity.[78] Rather than allowing
contrasts between the pure and the impure to persist, both works match
the pure with the pure to create a plurality of purities. As with *Gesang der
Jünglinge*, *Mortuos plango, vivos voco* not only convenes pure sounds but also
exercises means of purity. The operations both emerge from the materials,
such as the process of reduction upon which the sine tones are premised,
and offer a way of shaping the larger mixture of sounds and means. As with
Stockhausen's piece, a single means emerges at the end to clarify one sound
and one vision of the pure.

As is to be expected of such an important work in the electroacoustic
repertoire, *Mortuos plango, vivos voco* has been the subject of several analyses.
Scholars have examined the structural design, the makeup of individual
sounds, and the technological processes involved in the creation of the
piece.[79] Michael Clarke's analysis is exemplary in many respects, particularly
his scrutiny of sonic events in specific passages.[80] My discussion profits from
the observations made in those studies, and, with much of the analytical
dissection of the work already accomplished, it takes an interpretative turn,

---

[78] Nor is there the threat of impurity with the child's voice as some felt in *Gesang*.

[79] Bossis, "*Mortuos plango, vivos voco*," 119–44; Michael Clarke, "Jonathan Harvey's *Mortuos plango, vivos voco*," in *Analytical Methods of Electroacoustic Music*, ed. Mary Simoni (New York and London: Routledge, 2006), 111–43; Patricia Lynn Dirks, "An Analysis of Jonathan Harvey's *Mortuos plango, vivos voco*," cec. Concordia.ca/econtact/9_2/dirks.html; Paul Griffiths, "Three Works of Jonathan Harvey: The Electronic Mirror," *Contemporary Music Review* 1 (1984), 87–109; Pamela Smith, "Towards the Spiritual – The Electroacoustic Music of Jonathan Harvey," *Contact* 34 (Fall 1989), 11–16.

[80] Clarke, "*Mortuos plango, vivos voco*." This study is especially indebted to Clarke for his detailed analyses of specific passages.

Ex. 1.2 Formal diagram of *Mortuos plango, vivos voco*

a direction that some of the studies begin to make but do not fully pursue. The subject of the critical reading offered here is, of course, purity, a topic that has been neglected in previous analyses.

Harvey divides *Mortuos plango, vivos voco* into eight sections. Each is based upon either one of the first seven partials or the secondary strike tone (Ex. 1.2).[81] The individual parts begin with a statement of the central pitch by the bell. Across the eight sections, the structural tones do not sound in the sequential order of the spectrum, although, true to a bell ring, the strike tone appears first and the hum tone last. The durations of the parts are related to the frequencies of the central pitches. Consistent with the quicker decay of upper partials, the higher the central pitch lies, the shorter the section. The structure coaxes us into what Harvey calls "abnormal" listening. He "de-composes" the spectrum so that instead of the expected simultaneous throng we hear separated, "de-fused" partials.[82] 'Normal' listening, though, is still encouraged. There are moments in which the partials appear more or less together or, at least, in close quarters. Moreover, we become so familiar with the spectrum during the course of the piece that we can 're-compose' it in our heads, even across the eight sections. True to the emphasis on ambiguity, we can hear the bell one way or another or sometimes both at once.

Another perspective on the work, one befitting its cathedral origins, is that of a series of panels elaborating upon a theme, be it the sounds of a spiritual place or purity. In considering the eight sections, or panels, attention will be paid to which sounds are featured in each part, how they are presented, and the connections made between them. All of the sections present the pure sounds of the boy's voice and/or sine tones, but they differ when it comes to the means of purity. Some carry out specific means, whereas others reject the push to purity and concentrate instead on diversity and mixture. The restrictive demands of the means and the expanding heterogeneity of the sonic compounds form opposing dynamics in the eight-part structure.

---

[81] Each section also concentrates on a particular phonetic element of the sung words.
[82] Harvey, "Mirror of Ambiguity," 181.

The work negotiates them by twice progressing from the mixtures to the points of focus characteristic of purity.

The first section presents a scene of acoustic diversity. It introduces the three source sounds one after another. The pealing of bells opens the work and serves, according to the composer, as "a call to the faithful to approach the holy place."[83] Or, more accurately, there is the pealing of a lone bell. Harvey creates the impression of a rack of bells by transposing the bell to the pitches of the first eleven partials. The bell choir gives way to a choir of boys, which, similar to the bell passage, is derived from the voice of one boy chanting the textual inscription on the pitches of five partials (0:15). Both parts emphasize c', the central pitch of the section. The sine tone sonorities follow the real-world timbres. Like them, they too are pegged to the partials, here seven of the eight pitches used as centers for the structural sections (0:51). By stating the three sounds in sequence, Harvey draws attention to the uniqueness of each one. At the same time, he begins to connect them. The three move within the same spectrum, sharing five pitches between them. Moreover, they all suggest the outpouring of single pitches characteristic of pealing, although the pealing gets slower with the boy's choir and very slow with the electronic tones. The ties create not only affinities between the separate sound realms but also the ambiguities valued by the composer. Even at this early point in the work, and in a moment when the three sounds are especially distinct, the lines between them blur. The play between what Harvey calls "bellness" and "boyness" begins here, as the boy's voice takes on aspects of the bell.[84] The links and ambiguities continue without the lead of the bell. The rest of the section consists of an exchange between the sine tones and the boy's voice, both of which carry on stating the opening partials of the spectrum. During the back and forth, the electronic tones assume qualities of the voice. Instead of the rapid decay typical of the bell, they feature an acoustic envelope suggestive of the voice, in which a tone is sustained before fading away. Boys sound like bells, and synthetic tones sound like boys.

The second section thickens the mix of the first. Rather than stating the three source materials successively in exchanges, Harvey overlaps them in sustained sonorities. The opening bell strike on the central pitch g'' is drawn out (no longer a bell envelope) and suspended with held sine tones and some vocal tones (1:41). The pitches are largely that of an Eb major triad, but, even with that harmonic glue, the mix barely holds together.[85] The sine tones dominate the blend, which is interrupted by the voice with bursts

---

[83] Quoted in Bossis, "*Mortuos plango, vivos voco*," 131.
[84] Harvey, "A Realization at IRCAM," 24.   [85] Clarke, "*Mortuos plango, vivos voco*," 124.

of consonant sounds, a complement to the vowel sounds in the sustained pitches. The boy's voice has been broken down into its own kind of partials, the flecks of speech.[86]

Although variegated and unsettled, the sonority, which is held throughout most of the section, offers the first indication of a means of purity. The potential for merger is raised, something never hinted at in the first part. The three sources could come together in a cohesive sonority, similar to the acts of "at-one-ment" described by Douglas. The possibility is not taken up, but the general idea of merger is not lost. In the closing gesture of the section, a pitch in the boy's voice smoothly progresses to the opening bell strike of the third section via a sine tone glissando (2:05). If not a single sound, all three at least form a continuous one. "Boyness" and "bellness" have been joined together. Even more important, the glissando emerges as a sound in its own right.

The figure becomes the focus of the third section, which consists of twelve glissandi divided into three groups demarcated by bell strikes. It is the most sonically circumscribed section of the work. Whereas the single glissando at the end of the previous part contains all of the source sounds, the twelve presented here are made out of synthetic sonorities. The bell is reduced to a periodic punctuation, and the voice is absent. There is one material, or close to one material. The means of purity are at work. The third section draws upon a means almost as old as electroacoustic music itself – exclusion. In Stockhausen's *Studien*, purity was achieved by concentrating on wholly synthetic materials. The third section of *Mortuos plango, vivos voco* does not go that far, but it does take the surprising step of banishing the voice and relegating the bell to a minor role.

The means of exclusion shape the passage, and so too do those of reduction. The line between the two, as mentioned above, can be a fine one. In 1950s *elektronische Musik*, for example, sine tone sonorities not only arose to the exclusion of all other sounds but they also represented the act of boiling sounds down to an elemental core. So bare are the sine-tone sonorities in *Mortuos plango, vivos voco* that they too appear to have reached such an essence. The work emphasizes the means of reduction through both the sounds in the glissando and the figure of the glissando itself. The latter emerges from another type of reduction. As I will discuss in Chapter 5, the glissando is a sonic archetype, a figure that encapsulates fundamental qualities of sound and is experienced along the lines of sound rather than conventional conceptions of music. Two key qualities inhere within the glissando, the tendencies of sound to be in constant motion and in the process of

---

[86] Clarke, "*Mortuos plango, vivos voco*," 124.

Ex. 1.3 Saariaho, *Vers le blanc*

continual transformation. Evading traditional notions of melody, let alone the fixity of pitch, the figure is always moving somewhere and changing in register and sometimes color along the way. With the glissando and other archetypal figures, we hear sound as sound, following its own dynamics in its own world.

The glissando archetype comes into its own in Saariaho's *Vers le blanc* (1982). Composed two years after *Mortuos plango, vivos voco* at IRCAM, the piece consists of, or is reduced to, a single glissando, which slides between two three-note chords and lasts for around fifteen minutes (Ex. 1.3). Both the chords and the glissando are made from synthetic vocal sonorities, created by the CHANT program employed by Harvey. At such a speed, the changes in pitch become imperceptible, but transformations in "harmonic structure" and timbre come through.[87] Saariaho has called *Vers le blanc* an "extreme" work.[88] Extremes, as has often been the case in modernist arts, serve visions of purity. The title conjures such a vision, as we move to (and from?) a color traditionally associated with the pure. Saariaho even implicates herself in the purity of the piece. She has remarked that she used the piece to "purify" herself of past "influences," a reference to her shift to spectralist idioms after beginning work at IRCAM.[89] It is one thing to strip sounds of superfluities; it is another to have a piece purify a composer of her own past.

The "extremes" of *Vers le blanc* put into relief how far the fourth and fifth sections of *Mortuos plango, vivos voco* take the glissando. Like Saariaho's work, the fourth part builds upon a single glissando, or, to be more specific, the focus of the section (30 out of 38 seconds) is on a long glissando, which is flanked by two brief ones. It makes for a striking change from the twelve small glissandi heard in the previous section. As in *Vers le blanc*, the figure moves slowly and the changes in pitch are nearly imperceptible, not because of the glissando's duration, as in Saariaho's piece, but rather because of a small melodic and harmonic range. The glissando operates

[87] Kaija Saariaho, "Timbre and Harmony: Interpolations of Timbral Structures," *Contemporary Music Review* 2 (1987), 94.
[88] Pierre Michel, "Entretien avec Kaija Saariaho," *Kaija Saariaho* (Paris: Éditions IRCAM, 1994), 16.
[89] Michel, "Entretien," 16.

within the boundaries of a B♭ minor chord (created by transposing bell partials), moving slightly higher and then back down again.[90] The effect is that of nudged stasis.

Despite the perceived immobility, two means of purity busily play out. Harvey reduces an already reduced figure, presenting a single and circumscribed version of the archetype. Unlike those in the previous section, the glissando in the fourth part involves more than one type of sound, blending synthetic sine tones and the boy's voice. Through the combination, the possibility of a merger arises. The beginning of the second section pointed to such means, but the overlap of the three source sounds proved unstable. The mix in the protracted glissando is peaceful, but the union is not complete, as the two sounds remain ultimately distinct. Nonetheless, the figure brings us closer than before to the synthesis of opposites.

The fifth section consists of four glissandi. As in the third part, the figures are made out of one type of material (here synthetic vocal tones rather than sine tones), and just as the three groups of glissandi in that section were interrupted by bells, the four individual ones here are separated by appearances of the boy's voice. The voice catches our attention as it offers the first clear speech, "ad Preces" (to prayer), that we have heard in a while, and, it should be mentioned, the last discernable words that we will hear (4:31).[91] The extended appearance of the boy's voice, lengthier than the bell interruptions in the third section, twists the means of exclusion used in the previous part. On the one hand, the fifth section is restricted to one type of material, the vocal, be it synthetic or real. On the other hand, it keeps the two distinct, there being no attempt at a merger. Indeed, when the boy's voice drops in, it appears to be coming from a different realm and breaking into a sequestered sonic world.

The third, fourth, and fifth sections stand out as a group. A tranquil quality distinguishes them from the other parts. Moreover, the bell is largely absent. The three sections also establish purity as a state. The appearance of the boy's voice and sine tones in the beginning of the piece gave purity a presence, but the plural and dynamic state does not emerge until the sounds are combined with various means. The three sections act as a set of variations on the sounds and means of purity. Each highlights particular sounds: sine tones in the third, a sine tone/boy's voice mixture in the fourth, and the separation of synthetic and real vocal tones in the fifth. The means also change per section: the third utilizes reduction and exclusion; the fourth

---

[90] Clarke, *Mortuos plango, vivos voco*, 131.
[91] As Bossis points out, the call to prayer is given weight by placing it at the center point of the work. Bossis, "*Mortuos plango, vivos voco*," 139.

draws upon reduction and merger; and the fifth relies on reduction but resists merger. The constant between the sections is the means of reduction, as realized in the archetype of the glissando. If purity is the theme, the glissando is the motive.

The sixth and seventh sections break the chain of variations by returning to the sonic diversity of the opening. Not only does a thick heterogeneity reappear but so too do some of the sounds from the first two sections. They include the eight-chord sequence presented in the first section, which is reconfigured in the sixth.[92] The pulsating mixture of sustained vocal and synthetic sonorities in the sixth recalls the uneasy overlap at the beginning of the second section (5:01). As in the latter, the compound gives way to a spray of isolated consonants and vowels, what Harvey refers to as in the sketches "coloratura" (5:26).[93] The synthetic tones respond with an even more virtuosic splurge, a reply that evokes the imitation between boy's voice and synthetic tones in the first section (5:32). Moreover, the flurry of individual pitches in both parts recaptures the rapid pealing of bells, a sound that the two evoked at the beginning of the work.

The seventh section continues the recollections by presenting further alterations of the eight-chord sequence.[94] It also introduces a new sound, one that both enriches the diversity and reasserts the means of purity. A pulsating ostinato made up of interlocking sonic swells runs throughout the entire section. Little more than a second in length, it contains four different sounds. The figure begins with a real bell strike, moves to a synthetic bell tone, links that sound with a synthetic vocal tone, and concludes with a real vocal pitch.[95] All of this is done with the slight lift and fall of a glissando. The ostinato looks back to another figure heard from the beginning of the work, the one from the close of the second section that moved from the boy's voice to the bell via a sine tone glissando. Despite the similarities, there are notable differences between the two glissando figures. In the figure from the second section, the endpoints are distinct and the overall effect is that of a bridge erected between remote sounds. The brevity of the ostinato in the seventh part compresses the sounds so that no one element stands out. The ostinato appears as a single gesture rather than as two distant, yet connected, sounds. With the ostinato, the three source sounds merge together into a new sound. It is as near to "at-one-ment" as the work will ever get.

With the eighth, and final, section, the bell returns to prominence, having largely disappeared since the third section. The hum tone rings throughout the section, which reconstructs the acoustical realm surrounding the bell.

[92] Clarke, "*Mortuos plango, vivos voco*," 134.   [93] Clarke, "*Mortuos plango, vivos voco*," 134.
[94] Clarke, "*Mortuos plango, vivos voco*," 136–37.   [95] Clarke, "*Mortuos plango, vivos voco*," 135.

In a closing exchange of "bellness" and "boyness," the voice forms chords based on the fifth through eleven partials.[96] The chords adhere to a bell, rather than vocal, envelope, as the lower pitches resonate longer than the higher ones. Finally, the vocal sonorities toll, sounding at first with every five strikes of the bell and later less regularly. Add to this the pulsating ostinato from the previous section, which carries on for the first thirty seconds of the eighth section, and the effect is that of off-kilter tolling. Near the end of the work, sine tones, the third source sound, reappear (8:00). They present high partials in the spectrum with an inverse envelope, in which the upper tones outlast lower ones. The high synthetic tones linger after the last strikes of the boy's vocal chords, creating, as Clarke aptly describes, an "aura" for the hum tone.[97] In the concluding passage, just the bell sounds. It is, though, a strange bell, as with a closing touch of ambiguity, Harvey alters the tone so that there is no clear initial strike and gives it a smooth, almost vocal, decay.

That only the hum tone remains at the end of the work should come as no surprise. *Mortuos plango, vivos voco* has schooled us well in the acoustic behavior of bells. It has also instructed us in the sounds and means of purity. Acoustics may seem to offer a more convincing explanation of what happens in the eighth section. Indeed, Barry Truax's *Basilica* (1992), another electroacoustic work based upon bell sonorities, arrives at a similar ending. The closing passage focuses on the resonances of one of the three bells that the piece samples. *Basilica*, however, makes no appeal to purity, be it the sounds, symbols, or means of the state. *Mortuos plango, vivos voco* does, and the commitment allows us to hear the eighth section as a culminating moment of purity. The means of reduction are exercised in an exposed and exacting manner. One by one the boy's voice and the synthetic tones drop out until just the hum tone is heard. Previously, the means attained a basic figure of sound in the glissando; now they secure the most basic sound of the work. The hum tone lies at the heart both of the bell ring and of *Mortuos plango, vivos voco*, where it is much more than an acoustical fact, taking on the symbolic values of essence and core.

In *Bhakti* (1982), Harvey again makes much, both symbolically and sonically, out of a single pitch. The work begins with the pitch g′ stated by several instruments and tape. The pitch gradually changes octaves before other pitches appear, notably a cascading rush of the harmonic series based on g′. The opening movement suggests a sonic awakening, an image further evoked by the textual postlude drawn from the *Rig-Veda* that describes the creation of the world. In the ninth movement, the single g returns, now

---

[96] Clarke, "*Mortuos plango, vivos voco*," 137.   [97] Clarke, "*Mortuos plango, vivos voco*," 138.

stated in eight octaves at once.[98] For Harvey, the idea in both movements "is to explore the inner life of a static sound, a spiritual turning-inwards."[99] *Mortuos plango, vivos voco* also turns inwards. Elaborating upon the textural contrast between the opening and closing passages, Harvey describes:

> the central image of the piece, the progression from outwardness to inwardness. (The Eastern meditation mantra "OM" is designed to express the same movement.) The spectacular brilliance of the attack gradually transforms to the prolonged calm of the deep hum note, the last to decay. Doubtless that is why bells are "sacred" in many cultures.[100]

Bhakti journeys into the interior of a single pitch; *Mortuos plango, vivos voco* pushes into a bell ring to reach a single pitch. According to the composer, both works arrive at a similar place, that of spiritual reflection and the sacred. Spirituality is one way to interpret the closing hum tone of *Mortuos plango, vivos voco*. Purity is another. It is not so much a question of one or the other as that the two are so close that they commune. The sacred is often considered as being pure, and, if not that, it invites associations of purity. Such is the case with the texts used in Stockhausen and Harvey's pieces. Pure elements have traditionally hallowed holy places and rites. At the end of *Mortuos plango, vivos voco*, they enrich the sacredness of a single tolling bell.

Having discussed the eight sections individually, it is now time to step back and consider the structure as a whole. An important question is whether or not there is a larger progression unfolding throughout the work. Inspired by Harvey's notion of ambiguity, Clarke describes a structure that is both static and teleological.[101] On the one hand, the piece is "an articulation within stasis," as "everything is enveloped within the bell timbre from beginning to end."[102] On the other hand, the piece moves through the bell partials used as central pitches in the separate sections until it reaches the inevitable conclusion on the hum tone. The formal reading proposed here agrees with Clarke on the ambiguity between stasis and progression, but it offers a different way of understanding the latter. Whereas Clarke sees melodic and timbral elements driving the progression, this study focuses on changes in texture. It should be acknowledged, though, that it is difficult to separate the three areas, so fused are they in this and other spectralist works. The overall textural movement is that from the crowding of sonic

---

[98] For a discussion of the two movements, see Palmer, *Jonathan Harvey's "Bhakti,"* 93–97 and 118–21. The Winchester Cathedral bell appears in the seventh movement of the work.

[99] Harvey, "Mirror of Ambiguity," 184.   [100] Harvey, "Mirror of Ambiguity," 181.

[101] Clarke, "*Mortuos plango, vivos voco*," 139–40.

[102] Clarke, "*Mortuos plango, vivos voco*," 139.

diversity to a point of concentration on one or two elements. Harvey, to recall, discussed the piece in similar terms, describing how it replicates the "transformation" in a bell from the "spectacular brilliance of the attack" to "the prolonged calm of the deep hum note."[103] Whereas he presents one larger "transformation," the above analysis has pointed out two such developments, or processes of reduction as they have been depicted here. The eight sections of *Mortuos plango, vivos voco* can be divided into two groups, each moving from timbral and textural heterogeneity to a more reduced texture. The first group consists of the initial five sections. The opening two introduce the three source sounds in various forms and combinations, a multiplicity diminished in the following three sections, which employ a restricted timbral palette and focus on the glissando figure. In the second group, the restored sonic diversity of sections six and seven is gradually thinned out until there is only the concluding hum tone in the final section.

The textural progression can also be seen in terms of purity. As the sonic mix winnows so too does the plurality of the state. In *Gesang der Jünglinge*, the multiple purities give way to an emphasis on one type of sound, electronic timbres, and one means of purity, that of refinement. *Mortuos plango, vivos voco* settles the plurality along different lines. It narrows in on an acoustic sound, the bell, instead of electronic sounds. The bell inspires the means of reduction emphasized in the work. Bells slowly quiet to a single pitch then silence. *Mortuos plango, vivos voco* calms clangor to reach first a basic type of sound, the glissando, and then, in the closing moments, a more fundamental and spiritual sound, the dying note of a bell.

On the evidence of *Gesang der Jünglinge* and *Mortuos plango, vivos voco*, the modernist devotion to purity could appear to be a small sect, the articles of faith limited to electroacoustic media, a boy's voice, sine tones, and, for one of the two pieces, a bell. Other works, though, reveal that devotion to be an ecumenical faith. A brief description of two more pieces shows how diverse the state of purity has proven to be. Both hold to the mix of associations, sounds, and means typical of the state, but they offer different combinations than those found in the Stockhausen and Harvey compositions.

In *Xi* (1999), Unsuk Chin blends electronics with a live ensemble. The title is the Korean word for "the origins or smallest unity of things."[104] Organicist approaches prize this microscopic level, and not surprisingly the work adopts such an outlook.[105] It expands upon and integrates "cell"

---

[103] Harvey, "Mirror of Ambiguity," 181.

[104] "Programme Note," www.boosey.com/pages/cr/catalogue/cat_detail.asp?site-lang=de&musi-cid=15297&langid=2.

[105] Whittall discusses the organicist and classicist bearings of the work. Whittall, "Meditations and Mechanics," *Musical Times* 141 (2000), 25–26.

sounds. Purity also holds at that level. *Xi* opens with sounds that have an elemental quality to them, like the raw, agitated timbres produced through granular synthesis and the breathing noises created by the instruments. The piece has a clear arch structure. It begins with fleeting sounds, builds to packed sonorities, and closes with references to the opening sounds. Consistent with the organicist development of the materials, the "cell" sounds are given new but related shapes and then restored to more or less their original forms. The design also accommodates the state of purity. Indeed, organicism and purity are akin; they both concentrate on the elemental and shun the extraneous. The two approaches home in on the same elements in *Xi* but offer contrasting perspectives. Purity, for instance, accentuates how much reduction rules the conclusion of the work. The initial sounds are taken down to an even more basic, pure level. The use of granular synthesis characteristic of the opening timbres is now pushed to an excessive point. The closing sounds vibrate so much that it is unclear if they are sound or rhythmic pulsation. They come across as the origins of sound.

Claude Vivier's *Lonely Child* (1980), like *Gesang der Jünglinge* and *Mortuos plango, vivos voco*, finds purity in childhood, but it makes a connection unknown to those two works: childhood and death. It is an old connection, one that reached mournful kitschy heights in the Victorian images of peaceful and well-dressed dead boys and girls. The image embalms the child in innocence and forever protects him or her from the corruption of age.[106] *Lonely Child* for soprano and orchestra is a lullaby, in which to sleep is to enter an afterlife of eternal fairytale wonder. An opening instrumental melody, punctuated by a Japanese temple bell, evokes the ritualistic, particularly the funereal.[107] The body of the piece conveys the magic of the fairytale realm through a soprano line surrounded by lucent spectral harmonies. The conclusion contemplates the figure of the dead child through means of purity. The piece winds down with a series of reductions, first to a group of chords (mm. 183–84), then to an interval (a descending half step, nonetheless; mm. 185–86), and finally to the opening melody (mm. 195–212). The melody is prefaced by a statement of the harmonic series on E played by a solo double bass (mm. 192–93). The passage reduces the rich spectral harmonies to their source, after which the ritual melody comes across as particularly stark. Vivier overlays it with glissandi played in harmonics by the strings, lines heard previously in the childhood wonder sections (mm. 113–40). The combination of the glissandi and the ritual

---

[106] Kincaid, *Child Loving*, 80–82.
[107] The bell is another parallel with Harvey's work, yet not a strong parallel. In Vivier's piece, it does not generate harmonic, melodic, and sonic material as it does in the electroacoustic work. Vivier, though, does have the bell appear between major sections, in a way similar to Harvey's strikes at the beginning of each of the eight formal units.

melody brings the piece down to two basic sounds, the archetypal glissando and a solemn chant. Both consecrate aspects of the dead child. The string glissandi are the glow of the empyrean of eternal childhood; the chant is the melody leading there.

In closing, it should be mentioned that intricate states are not the only method by which late modernist works have evoked purity. For some, the blunt contrast between purity and impurity is sufficient. These pieces do not court the rich associations that the compositions of Stockhausen and Harvey do. Instead of childhood and the sacred, they suggest general acoustic qualities of purity. In such works, sounds are set apart as pure and either juxtaposed with or defiled by unstable, motley timbres. In the conclusion of Lachenmann's *NUN* (1999), a sequence of clear, vibratoless E♭s are either blotted out by crashes or disappear into the sputtering, blowing, and scraping typical of the composer's music (mm. 590–612).[108] The to and fro between purity and impurity is one way to hear the works of Giacinto Scelsi, particularly his *Quattro pezzi per orchestra* (1959). Each piece is based on a single tone. The pitches are not only played in a pure manner similar to that in *NUN* but they also connote the pure by being the one and only element. The purity of the pitch, though, succumbs to disruptions, tremolos and extended techniques, and contamination, brief neighbor tones and microtones. In both pieces, purity proves to be a fragile sonic ideal, an ideal set upon by pollution and loss.

The darting off to discuss a different view of purity and the rush through four new pieces admittedly brings this chapter to a hectic close. This is not the points of refinement and reduction reached at the ends of *Gesang der Jünglinge* and *Mortuos plango, vivos voco*, respectively. Such an outcome may seem more fitting, but it would not be practical. Whereas the Stockhausen and Harvey pieces conclude by closing in on single visions of purity, this study opens up the concept. To look at purity in new ways it is important to look at many pieces, even if it means quickly throwing in several compositions at the end of the discussion. These works by Stockhausen and Harvey along with those by Chin, Vivier, Lachenmann, and Scelsi provide fresh angles, all of them revealing purity not to be restrictive and static but rather manifold and dynamic.

---

[108] The sounds are appropriate to the purity of thought, time, and place described in the works of philosopher Kitaro Nishida upon which the piece draws.

2 Modern silence

Theirs is a closed relationship – always two, never three. When brought together, words and music keep to themselves. There may be others but they are merely observers, standing on the outside listening in. They are the ones who discuss the ups and downs of the relationship: how well the two get along with each other, which one has more to say, and who does so more clearly. Some of the observers have even written dramatic works about the two. Think of Salieri's *Prima la musica, poi le parole* and Strauss's *Capriccio*.

Think of Beckett's *Words and Music*. Turning to the radio play, we can hear a very different presentation of the starring pair. With Beckett, Words and Music are actual characters instead of being represented by the stand-in poets and composers of the earlier two operas.[1] More than that, they speak their own languages – Words utters words and Music utters only music. There is no Countess to choose between them, as in Strauss; rather, a tyrant named Croak bullies the two and commands them to elaborate upon a series of words and images, including love, age, and "the face." Imploring them to "be friends," he grows tired of them talking past each other and departs. Words and Music are left in tantrums and despair.

Pettiness, ennui, and quarrels are not ways in which the relationship between words and music is usually depicted. Amid all the squabbling, an even more shocking departure from convention can go unnoticed. Beckett breaks up the closed relationship by adding a third character. The character does not say a word or play a note. How can it, when the part belongs to silence. Throughout the play, as in many of Beckett's works, extended moments of silence set in, marked either as such or as "pauses." As the play goes on, the moments grow more prominent, reaching an unsettling climax for the title characters when the sounds of the departing Croak trail off into nothingness. What disturbs them is a new and persistent "sound," one that is neither speech nor tone. Silence interrupts their private dialogue, demanding their attention and ours.[2]

It is hardly surprising that quiet broods in Beckett's drama and does not play even the smallest part in the works by Salieri and Strauss. Modernist

---

[1] The characters are also called Joe and Bob, respectively.
[2] Morton Feldman wrote incidental music for the radio drama. Surprisingly, his score does not engage silence, or near silence, as much as some of his other works do.

arts have engaged silence to an unprecedented degree. Silence, of course, has been a long-standing site of artistic, philosophical, and spiritual rumination, but it was not until the twentieth century that it assumed such an extensive presence in artistic creation.[3] As for music, silence forms a large part of the soundworlds explored by modernist composers. To be sure, silence appears prominently in works from previous periods, as in the engulfing pauses in Beethoven's works, but it was never mined so deeply or used to such diverse effects prior to the twentieth century. As Sciarrino, a master calligrapher of quiet, has remarked: "Sound has an intimate relationship with silence; the consciousness of that connection is new."[4]

The "intimate relationship" between modernism and silence has been interpreted in different ways. In what has become a critical trope, silence stands as the larger artistic and social oblivion awaiting modernist arts. Adorno, for example, calls attention to the irreversible slide of new music into silence. So removed has this music grown from audiences and so absorbed has it become in its own practices that it recedes further and further away until it becomes unheard, or silent.[5] Susan Sontag situates silence as a "termination" for contemporary art. According to her, art, as material or even ideal, torments the modern artist, who views it as an impediment to a desired "transcendence." The block can only be removed by silencing – no longer creating – the work of art, a step taken by Rimbaud, Wittgenstein, and Duchamp.[6] Umberto Eco describes a less severe form of renunciation. Restlessly stripping away the superfluous, be it the familiar or the past, modernism reaches a point of nullity, attained in the white canvas, the blank page, or four minutes and some of silence.[7]

These writers show little interest in silence as artistic material. It remains first and foremost a broad cultural and aesthetic fate. Sontag mentions the

[3] For a discussion of the contemplations of the relationship between music and silence across the centuries, see *Silence, Music, Silent Music*, ed. Nicky Losseff and Jenny Doctor (London: Ashgate, 2007).

[4] Salvatore Sciarrino, "Entretien," *Entretemps* 9 (1991), 139. Some studies deal exclusively with the role of silence in twentieth-century music. Two notable ones are Martin Zenck, "Dal niente – Vom Verlöschen der Musik," *MusikTexte* 55 (1994), 15–21, and Gerhard Stäbler, "About Silence or What Happens When Nothing Happens?" *EONTA* 1 (1991/92), 68–81. A modified version of the latter appears as "Stille Schrei Stille," *Positionen* 10 (1992), 24–26. This volume of *Positionen* deals exclusively with the topic of silence.

[5] This view is reinforced in the sections dealing with Schoenberg in Adorno's *Philosophy of New Music*. Elaborating upon Adorno's "negative teleology," Edward Said remarked that "the reversed course toward silence becomes [modern music's] raison d'être, its final cadence." Said, "From Silence to Sound and Back Again: Music, Literature, and History," *Raritan* 17, no. 2 (1997), 10.

[6] Susan Sontag, "The Aesthetics of Silence" in her *Styles of Radical Will* (New York: Farrar, Straus and Giroux, 1969), 3–7. Sontag, like Adorno, sees the alienation of new styles as leading into a larger cultural silence.

[7] Umberto Eco, "Postmodernism, Irony, the Enjoyable" in *Postscript to "The Name of the Rose,"* trans. William Weaver (New York: Harcourt Brace Jovanovich, 1984), 67.

"self-conscious" and "traditional" use of silence but sees it as "unrelated," even "antithetical," to the larger "termination," an insignificance making it unworthy of critical elaboration.[8] Adorno may discuss the role of silence in the music of Webern and others but he subsumes that role into the cultural *morendo* of modernism.

This study, in contrast, explores how silence has been used as artistic material in ways that speak to the creative vigor and longevity of modernism. It approaches silence in two ways: as a compositional state and as an expressive scene. As a state, silence proves more elusive than such conditions as the fragmentary or complexity. After all, absolute silence, as Cage reminded us, does not exist. Pure silence may not exist, but silence does. It takes various forms, including an ideal (that of absence), a symbol (of mystery and death, for instance), a sensation (unease, tranquility), or even a sound (stillness). This chapter will discuss how three composers have used these different forms in creating the state of silence: Webern, the first modernist composer to scrutinize silence, and two Italian successors of his in the latter half of the twentieth century, Nono and Sciarrino, each equally captivated by quiet.

All three composers have had to evoke silence in some way. Musicians, unlike artists in some other fields, have access to the real thing, the patches of quiet gapped in rests and pauses. Surprisingly, many composers, notably Webern, do not exploit this resource. They instead rely on musical means of evoking quiet, a paradox of having something convey nothing. The means include chromatic clusters played very softly; extended stretches of low dynamics; short, murmured phrases that quickly yield to nothingness; and transitory tones that no sooner emerge from quiet than they return to it. Gestures of this kind do not give us silence but rather qualities of silence, such things as stillness, hush, and fragility. It is through these traits that silence, the ideal of nothingness, can be evoked; but of course these traits can also convey sensations and settings distinct from silence. For instance, clusters have been used to suggest expectancy (Sciarrino), nature (Webern), and night (Ives and Bartók). The varied uses serve as a reminder of how vague and multivalent silence can be, as it easily melds with different ideas and feelings.

The same gestures have been employed for centuries by composers to evoke quiet. Softly played chords, fragmentary phrases, and muffled tones are hardly modernist discoveries. Modernism, though, has rendered them

---

[8] Sontag, "The Aesthetics of Silence," 6. In a 1964 article on Michel Leiris's *Manhood*, Sontag briefly mentions that silence has become "a positive, structural element in contemporary music" since Webern. Sontag, *Against Interpretation* (New York: Farrar, Straus, and Giroux, 1967), 68.

in new ways by having them partake in its harmonic and sonic liberties. The chords become clusters, the phrases grow more sparse and perishable, the tones, now typically produced by extended techniques, sit awkwardly on top of a bubble of sound. The transformations in turn heighten evocations of silence. Clusters weave a thicker, eerier quiet; multiphonics barely whisper.

These means are crucial to the second conception of silence proposed here. Webern, Nono, and Sciarrino employ them to set an expressive scene that situates silence in a specific role and place. The scene occurs at the border between sound/music and silence. All three composers locate their works in that ephemeral realm. For his part, Cage sought to erase once and for all the line between sound and silence (and, along with it, that between music and sound). It would seem easy to do. The line is very thin, for at this point music is close to disappearing. The borderland is a realm of traces, where sounds – the clusters, the faint tones – waver before an expanse that appears to be empty of sound.

Modernist artists have frequently settled this space, drawn there by the insubstantiality of sound and the proximity to the nothingness prized and feared in silence. For insights about the terrain, we should once again turn to Beckett. In *The Unnamable*, the title character exists in a liminal realm, caught between the fracas and refuse of the everyday world – trash cans, a back alley, and a slaughterhouse – and an ultimate silence. Like many of Beckett's characters, he cannot stop talking. One of the things he chatters about is silence, two different kinds. On one hand, there are the spells of quiet that visit him, "grey" silence as he calls it, since it is besmirched by "murmurs." Beyond the "door" and "walls," a more imposing quiet awaits. "Black" or "real" silence perplexes him – does it even exist? Doubts aside, he feels that it is out there, in some removed space. Obsessed by it, he at once dreads it and yearns for it, as this form of quiet would bring an end to his unceasing words and life.

The works discussed in this chapter create spaces similar to Beckett's limbo. "Murmurs," faint tones and fragments, and "grey" silence, defiled rests and pauses, fill the pieces. They make up the state of silence, materials with which composers work. The sounds are as close as we can get to silence, the "black" or "real" kind. As in Beckett, that realm exists outside of a piece. It is a void into which we will never cross. Although Beckett's language lends itself to the works of Webern, Nono, and Sciarrino, each sets the scene of a borderland in a unique manner. One of the appeals of the scene is its flexibility, allowing artists to establish all sorts of relationships between fragile sounds and the unknown realm of silence. With each work, we look to see where the line has been placed and what type of mystery lies on the other side. Webern locates the boundary in the tranquility of nature, having reflections on loss point to a deeper silence. Nono and Sciarrino inscribe a line between the emotional interior of the individual and the external social world.[9] The former is a space of silence, holding either deep feelings (Nono) or the obscurity of madness and spiritual communion (Sciarrino).

The different settings reveal the borderland to be an expressive place. Indeed, expression has driven many composers to the realm. As with such other states as the fragmentary, the pursuit of silence not only provides a compositional focus but also rich means of expression. Many of the states have unique potential for expression. Silence offers composers two rich means – one age-old one, the other relatively new. The former, the expressive quiet experienced in tense pauses and serene stillness, is not the main concern of this chapter. The works discussed here do indulge in many such gestures, but they also bring out a different expressive side of silence, one exploited by late modernist composers. They place the act of expression within the austere conditions of the compositional state. Silence has contributed to the inquiry into the act by offering a way of isolating the expressive utterance. Just as silence, a supposed non-sound, can serve as a backdrop against which sound can be presented and dissected, so too can it – the supposed absence of expressive utterances – throw into relief the act of expression. Once it has been exposed, we can study the act and ask pertinent questions: where does it come from, how is it done, and what happens to it?

Raising these and other questions, modernist music has used silence as a way of commenting on the act of expression. Webern's pieces hint at this commentary. His works make us wonder what happens to the voicing of loss when the musical utterances so quickly evanesce. Indeed, what happens to the need or desire to voice loss under such conditions? Late modernist pieces, such as those of Nono and Sciarrino, have grown more pointed and analytical. They depict the act in detail and pose specific questions about how it proceeds. The commentary adds to the inquiry into the act of expression and has steered modernist idioms further away from Romantic expressive stances. As witnessed in Webern's music, quiet refutes the munificence of Romanticism. In the works of Nono and Sciarrino, it also reveals expression not to be the natural and effortless impulse that Romanticism had presumed it to be. When set against silence, expression can emerge as forced, violent, or withdrawn. Its outcomes can be ambiguous and scattered. However, as

---

[9] In the case of Webern, the line can shift, as the inner reflections on loss often take place in nature. As Anne Shreffler remarks on the texts chosen by the composer in his early songs, "these poems are concerned primarily with nature images as metaphors for the subject's inner state." Shreffler, review of *Webern and the Transformation of Nature* by Julian Johnson, in *Music Theory Spectrum* 24 (2002), 295.

realized in late modernist styles, the depictions of expression are not merely analytical; rather, they can transcend commentary and become expressive.

Webern

People rarely boast about silence. But Schoenberg did. In a preface to Webern's Six Bagatelles for String Quartet (op. 9, 1913), he divided the "heathen" from the "believers," that is, the foes and friends of new music. For the latter, he held up a prize, proclaiming "may this silence [Stille] sound for them."[10] The heathen, their ears blocked by ignorance, could never appreciate the cultivation of quiet in Webern's work. Silence would forever remain silent to them. On the other hand, the believers, their ears quickened to the modern, could appreciate the quiet folds of what amounted to a new kind of sound. To Schoenberg, silence was another modernist innovation, one more new direction taken, one more new element uncovered.

In many ways, he was right. Modernism focused on sonic aspects of music to a degree unequaled in earlier music. With the idea of *Klangfarbenmelodie*, Schoenberg isolated the color of sound, using it as a primary – even structural – element rather than as mere gloss. It was perhaps inevitable that modernist composers would eventually turn to silence, the non-color of sound. It was perhaps also inevitable that the composer to do so would be Webern, the disciple who often pursued Schoenberg's ideas to understated extremes. No other early modernist who explored timbre – Debussy, Schoenberg, Varèse – took to silence with comparable intensity. Only in Webern's works does silence have a strong presence, which is remarkable given that true silence – rests and pauses – appears only here and there. What does "sound" are the brief phrases, very soft dynamics, and fleeting timbres, all of which place the listener at the border realm between music and silence.

The pursuit of silence provides one narrative to describe the direction taken by Webern in what Adorno refers to as his "second period," which produced such works as the Bagatelles for String Quartet and the Five Pieces for Orchestra (op. 10), both from 1913. Compositions from this time are characterized by concise forms, extremely fragmentary thematic writing, and thinner textures.[11] Adorno offered another narrative, one built around

---

[10] Webern, *Sechs Bagatellen für Streichquartett* (Vienna: Universal, 1952), 2. The German word "Stille" enfolds more meanings than the English word "silence," as it evokes silence, stillness, and peace, among other things. Such breadth is appropriate for Webern's works, which offer various forms of quiet.

[11] Theodor Adorno, "Anton Webern," in his *Sound Figures*, trans. Rodney Livingstone (Stanford University Press, 1999), 96.

expression and silence. He depicts a music not headed toward silence but
rather toward "pure expression" and "pure lyricism."[12] Purity, as described
in Chapter 1, is just as much an action, a way of attaining a state, as it is
an actual state. It is achieved through some means – reduction, refinement,
or exclusion – that in turn becomes a force that shapes a piece. Adorno
focuses on reduction. The Bagatelles and other second-period works shed
anything extraneous, ranging from "pre-existing forms" to melodic connective tissue.[13] Through this purging, the music attains such a concentrated
lyricism that a four-note melodic phrase can hold a wealth of emotions,
a quality that Schoenberg captured in his memorable line "a novel in a
single gesture."[14] The individual subject, the site of expression in Adorno's
criticism, is also purified. Raising an expressive voice in those few germane
pitches, the subject attains a "pure sonority."[15]

Silence is apparently not part of this purity, which is not to say that it
is impure. It exists outside Adorno's purity/impurity opposition. Indeed,
it exists outside the work altogether. Adorno does acknowledge the silence
at the end of a piece, but he points to a greater end and a greater silence,
that of death. The incessant casting-off eventually leads music to a "point of
silence." Once there, a work takes on new expressive meaning, as it becomes
a "simile" for "the moment of death," specifically the moment when the
soul takes flight and departs the body. The expressivity in Webern's music
arises in part from the faint musical sounds suggesting the "disembodied"
"beating of wings" in that flight.[16]

The idea of a piece tarrying at the border between music and silence plays
no role in Adorno's account of Webern. How could it? Such a realm would
amount to a purgatory, not the afterlife of silence. For Adorno, silence points
to an end and beyond. The pockets of quiet emerging here and there during
a piece are barely mentioned, only the impending moment of death. Even
the faint sounds exist in some sort of quiet welkin beyond the piece they

---

[12] This chapter will focus on Adorno's 1959 essay on Webern. It first appeared in the journal
Merkur (13/1959) and was included in the collection of essays *Klangfiguren* published the same
year. An English translation can be found in *Sound Figures*, 91–105. Over the course of his
career, Adorno's conceptions of composers would change, as he emphasized different qualities
at different times. Webern's music is a case in point, as can be seen in comparing a 1926 review
of Webern's Five Pieces for Orchestra, op. 10 and the above essay. The concept of purity does not
appear in any extended fashion in the earlier review (there is a mention of "absolute lyricism").
Purity, however, becomes a key word in the 1959 piece. The emphasis is surprising, for Adorno
expressed skepticism about the notion of purity around this time, particularly the types of
purity sought by integral serial and electroacoustic composers. He found the pursuit of purity
by these artists to be a "technocratic attitude" leading to sterility. See Adorno, "The Aging of
the New Music," 182. For the earlier review, see "Anton Webern. Zur Aufführung der fünf
Orchesterstücke, op. 10, in Zürich," in *Gesammelte Schriften*, ed. Rolf Tiedemann (Frankfurt
am Main: Suhrkamp Verlag, 1984), vol. 18, 513–16.

[13] Adorno, "Anton Webern," 93.   [14] Webern, *Sechs Bagatellen*, 2.
[15] Adorno, "Anton Webern," 93.   [16] Adorno, "Anton Webern," 104–5.

inhabit. Yet to insist on purgatory – the timbral variety – offers insights, as it presents a different type of relationship between silence and expression than the one described by Adorno.

Webern situates us at the border by evoking different forms of silence. Like purity and the fragmentary, silence is a state that often exists in multiplicity, made up of distinct, individual forms of the state. The borderland scene set by Webern and other composers depends on this plurality. Various types of silence are required to sustain the realm, even if for only ephemeral stretches. In Webern's music, four types appear prominently: stillness, extremely soft dynamics, brevity, and fragmentation. Stillness, the blank background against which other sounds emerge, comes across through repeated or sustained figures, which are performed *ppp*. For many composers, the marking amounts to an endpoint, as it either approximates silence or acts as the last stage before it. In Webern's music, though, it can be a starting point. His works, as has often been pointed out, scale gradations of *piano*. The movement from *ppp* to *pp*, infinitesimal to some, can be dramatic in his compositions. So too can movement in the opposite direction. Webern explores ranges below *ppp*, a realm that is "barely audible" (kaum hörbar) as he notes in his scores. Beyond this level, he can only point, telling the performer to play a tone "verklingend" – the gradual fade into nothingness. The dynamic markings and score indications function as signposts in the borderland between music and silence, showing it to be so vast that directions are needed in moving from here to there.

The severe brevity of individual pieces and movements also serves to heighten the presence of silence. In so little time, the work arises from and retreats into quiet, making us more aware of the pool of silence around it. Jankélévitch claimed brief pieces tie music closer to silence not so much because they exist as mere bubbles on its surface but rather because they respect quiet, desiring to trouble it as little as possible.[17] Briefer yet are Webern's melodic phrases. Like fragments (as to be discussed with Nono's work), the phrases are surrounded by silence, which they barely break before disappearing. They are sometimes fragmented, in the more conventional sense of being broken down into smaller parts, so that the presence of silence is intensified. Adorno does not point out this disintegration, preferring to have the phrases be expressive essences.

We can now turn to one of the first pieces to settle the borderland, the Five Pieces for Orchestra, particularly movements three and four. These two

---

[17] Vladimir Jankélévitch, *Music and the Ineffable*, trans. Carolyn Abbate (Princeton University Press, 2003), 141.

movements bring together ideas of silence, nature, and loss, all of which
have played a role in the criticism of Adorno and in a recent book by Julian
Johnson. The following discussion relates the three elements in ways different from those two authors, in particular showing how the mediation of loss
through silence deepens both the sense of loss and the level of silence. The
third movement is one of many evocations of nature to appear in Webern's
oeuvre; this one and others, as described by Adorno and Johnson, offer a
mountain vista, evoked in particular by the use of cowbells (Ex. 2.1).[18] In
the opening A section of the overall ternary form (mm. 1–4), the cowbells
help create a spell of stillness, which is enhanced by the shimmering sound
of plucked strings (mandolin, guitar, and harp), bells, and celesta.[19] The
sound inheres in a chromatic cluster, made up of pitch classes grouped
together in an augmented fifth (ab-a-bb-c♯-d-e) with the actual sounding
pitches stretched out over the range of 29 semitones (Ex. 2.2a). The individual tones are either struck repeatedly or rolled, to create a sustained yet
vibrating sonority – and a very quiet one, the dynamic markings hugging
ppp. The sonority calls to mind the stillness of nature, particularly the quiet
residing in the mountains. It also calls to mind works by other early modernist composers who similarly used chromatic collections in softly played
sustained or repeated patterns to evoke stillness. In the third movement
of his Five Pieces for Orchestra (op. 16), Schoenberg depicted a summer
morning by a lake through a sustained collection that constantly changes
tone color. In *Wozzeck* (Act III, scene iii), Berg turned to like means to create
a very different lake scene, the nighttime quiet that emerges after the title
character drowns. Night has especially attracted the use of such patterns and
sonorities, as heard in Ives's *Central Park in the Dark* and Bartók's "Night
Music" (*Out of Doors Suite*, mvt. 3).

In the last two works, sounds, particularly man-made ones, jostle evening
tranquility. Webern's mountain serenity is similarly interrupted. One of his
"pure" melodies emerges, a four-note phrase played by a solo violin that
breaks the stillness by entering at a relatively loud *pianissimo*. The phrase

[18] For a discussion of the importance of nature in Webern's musical thought, see Julian Johnson,
      Webern and the Transformation of Nature (Cambridge University Press, 1999). The cowbell
      connection has been mentioned by several commentators. Adorno heard cowbells as referring
      to mountain scenes, commenting on the cowbell-like sound of harps in the Symphony, op. 21.
      For Adorno's remarks and Webern's appreciative response, see Johnson, *Webern*, 7.
[19] A fair copy of the movement provides a written list (no music) of the instrumentation: trombone,
      harmonium, mandolin, celesta, harp, bass drum, snare drum, and double bass. The instrumen-
      tation in the final published version expands upon this early conception, but we can already see
      that the instruments involved in the stillness sonority were central to Webern's conception of
      the movement. Fair Copy, Third Movement, Five Pieces for Orchestra, op. 10, Sammlung Anton
      Webern, Paul Sacher Stiftung, Basel.

Ex. 2.1 Webern, Five Pieces for Orchestra, op. 10, no. 3

suggests a voice calling out into the dell, an impression reinforced by an echo-like response in the muted horn. As with Echo's replies, this phrase repeats only the end of the call. The four-note figure becomes a three-note phrase, the melodic intervals of which restate the last two of the call

Ex. 2.1 (*cont.*)

(perfect fifth and tritone, now descending instead of ascending).[20] The echo characteristically fades away. Silence uncharacteristically does so as well. Even before the echo, the stillness sonority dwindles, as, following the

---

[20] Moreover, the three-note phrase contains the 3–5 pitch-class set (0,1,6) part of the larger four-note set. The pitch-class system developed by Allen Forte is used here. Allen Forte, *The Structure of Atonal Music* (New Haven: Yale University Press, 1973).

Ex. 2.1 (*cont.*)

favorite Webern exit cue "verklingend," it goes from *ppp* to nothing. Only the bells and rolled bass drum are left to absorb the faded echo.

The extremely brief central section of the ternary design (mm. 5–6) contains little of the stillness sonority (except for bells and cowbells) and instead concentrates on overlapped melodic statements. With the concluding A section (mm. 7–11), the stillness sonority settles back in, now rescored

Ex. 2.2 Stillness sonorities in Webern, Five Pieces for Orchestra, op. 10, nos. 3
and 4

(harmonium, mandolin, celesta, harp, bells, cowbells, and cello playing harmonics) and placed in a higher register, all of which make it sound more
ethereal and faint (Ex. 2.2b).[21] Webern also reconfigures the harmonic
makeup of the sonority. The pitch classes create a smaller collection of a
diminished fourth (c♯-f), which is now concentrated in an actual cluster
rather than being dispersed over more than two octaves as in the opening
collection. As before, the sonority fades away into nothingness, but, unlike
the first statement, it breaks apart during the withdrawal. Small rests disrupt
the repeated pitches and sustained sonorities, leaving us with flecks of stillness. This crumbling away hints at another means of silence, fragmentation,
but we only get a hint, for pieces of the sonority are quickly claimed in the
final "verklingend." The calling phrase also returns in the last A section,
thereby adding to the impression of a deeper silence. The trombone plays
a four-note phrase (which begins with the same tritone pair, pitch classes
c-f♯/g♭, that closed the opening violin line).[22] It receives no answer. Echo has
been struck mute. The call meets silence, which, as heard in the treatment
of the stillness sonority, is not only growing fainter but also breaking apart.

The unrequited call and fractured quiet both point to a silence beyond
stillness. The fourth movement takes us into such a silence, inching closer
to the border. It does so through connections with the previous movement.
Given that the two movements were written at different times and originally
intended for different works, the possibility of connections between them
needs to be clarified. As argued here, there are no direct motivic ties but
rather similarities in pitch and instrumentation which serve to link the
two in general ways.[23] The first link is an echo. The forlorn trombone call

[21] In a discussion of the piece, Shreffler describes this sonority as capturing a "moment of stasis."
She mentions other works by the composer featuring such moments. Shreffler, review, 296.
[22] It refers to the earlier melodic phrases in the opening A section, as it too is built around the set
consisting of a half step and tritone.
[23] Movement IV was the first to be composed (dated 19 July 1911 by Webern) and was to be part
of a never-completed set of seven pieces for orchestra. Movement III was written two years
later (8 September 1913, Webern's date) for a group of four orchestral pieces that also went
unrealized. Webern most likely assembled the collection making up op. 10 for a performance

may yet stir a response. In mm. 2–3 of the fourth movement, the clarinet plays an a′, the same pitch sounded at the end of the trombone phrase. It may seem fanciful to hear the clarinet pitch as an echo, especially across the divide of separate movements, but manuscript materials for the work invite such an interpretation. In earlier versions of the movement, Webern marks the repeated a′ in the clarinet (mm. 2–3) "Echoton."[24] The Echoton technique creates an extremely soft, muted tone. Contemporary Viennese composers, notably Mahler and Berg, used the sound to evoke echoes and other effects.[25] Whereas the manuscript evidence adds to the suggestion of an echo, the composition history of the work complicates such an idea. The fourth movement was written two years before the third, thus making for the rather unlikely case of an echo of a piece yet to be composed. Moreover, Webern deleted the marking in the final published version. This study, though, deals with connections that emerge between the movements as heard in a performance of op. 10. One such bond is the a′ left hanging by the trombone at the end of the third movement and sounded by the clarinet at the beginning of the fourth. The connection raises the possibility of hearing the latter as an echo, especially given the prominent role of echoes at the beginning of the third movement. The direction "Echoton" is an archival detail that encourages us to hear it that way. It is also raises the

of an arranged version of the work by the Society for Private Musical Performance in 1919. As Meyer and Shreffler point out, the composition history of the work "should be kept in mind in any attempts to describe op. 10 as a cycle, and should also caution us against finding specific motivic connections between movements." This study does not claim the work to be a cycle nor does it point out specific motivic relationships. As described below, it focuses on similarities between the two movements, one in terms of pitch (a shared prominent a′) and the evocation of stillness in each through similar means. That the movements were conceived of independently does not rule out such similarities. Webern may have been aware of affinities between the two. In assembling op. 10, he could draw upon eighteen short pieces, including the eleven written for the two abandoned sets. That he put these two pieces side by side suggests that he perceived some affinity between them, perhaps one dealing with the evocation of silence. What Webern planned is, of course, unknowable and ultimately beside the point. As this study argues, there are similarities between the two movements and it is the job of an analysis to call attention to those connections and to interpret them. The topics of silence and loss provide one way to understand the connections. Felix Meyer and Anne C. Shreffler, "Webern's Revisions: Some Analytical Implications," *Music Analysis* 12 (1993), 357. On a compositional history of op. 10, see Hans Moldenhauer and Rosaleen Moldenhauer, *Anton von Webern: A Chronicle of His Life and Work* (New York: Alfred A. Knopf, 1979), 194–99.

[24] The marking can be found in two different manuscripts. The first is a copy of the original 1911 version of the movement. The manuscript was discovered in the Stadtbibliothek in Winterthur. It is reproduced in Meyer and Shreffler, "Webern's Revisions," 358. The second is a fair copy of the fourth movement found in the Sammlung Anton Webern, Paul Sacher Stiftung.

[25] See Mahler's Second Symphony (mvt. 1, m. 126) and the second of Berg's *Four Pieces for Clarinet and Piano* (mm. 3 and 7). The Mahler symphony offers a good example of how the technique is not limited to imitation of echoes. A few measures after the example cited above, Mahler uses the tone to set off a new theme as being distant (mvt. 1, m. 135). Berlioz praised the clarinet for "its precious capacity to produce distant effects or echoes, or echoes of echoes, or half-shades of sound." He does not describe the specific "Echoton" technique, but he does mention muting the instrument by placing it in a leather bag. *Berlioz's Orchestration Treatise: A Translation and Commentary*, ed. Hugh Macdonald (Cambridge University Press, 2002), 125–27.

possibility of another type of echo. Taking the fourth movement by itself, we could be listening to the echo of a call that was made but lost to us, a fitting role given the prevailing emphasis in the movement on loss and disintegration.

Besides an echo, the fourth movement also evokes stillness, doing so in ways similar to those heard in the third movement. The instrumentation and part writing in the fourth movement have strong similarities with those used to create the stillness sonority at the end of the previous movement. Stated in the order in which they appear, the orchestration elements include sustained viola harmonics (evoking the previous cello harmonics), snare drum (not part of the stillness sonority yet present at the end of the third movement), harp harmonics, half steps in the celesta (now played simultaneously instead of in alternation), and repeated pitches in the mandolin (although with longer rhythmic values) (Ex. 2.3).[26] The instrumentation of the two sonorities may be similar but the registration is very different. The collection at the end of the third movement is packed into a tight cluster set in a high range (Ex. 2.2b), whereas the sonority in the fourth movement, like that in the opening of the third, is spread out over a broader range (18 semitones compared to 29 in the beginning of the third, Ex. 2.2c). The harmonic makeup of the fourth movement sonority and that of the initial sonority in the third are similar. The pitch classes in the former create a cluster a perfect fifth in range (e-f-f♯-b♭-b), one semitone smaller than the augmented-fifth group in the latter (a♭-a-b♭-c♯-d-e). Moreover, both contain a prominent 4–5 set (0,1,2,6) sequence.

Despite these parallels, we never hear stretches of stillness, as in the third movement. The flecks are too diffuse for it to inhere. To buttress quiet, other types of silence appear, including quiet dynamics and fragments. The movement offers an intriguing case of how Webern handles the plurality of silence. Different kinds of silence are needed to sustain the faint borderland. One is not enough. One, though, is required to give quiet a particular cast. As in states such as purity and the fragmentary, a selected type assumes prominence over the other kinds. In the third movement, stillness sets the scene of tranquil quiet. With the fourth movement, fragmentation ascends. Only it can take us into a more removed and engulfing silence.

Fragmentation pervades the movement, to the point that we get fragments of fragments. Disintegration can be heard in the opening and closing phrases.[27] The opening six-note line in the mandolin stands out by virtue of

---

[26] Discussing the earlier manuscript version of the work, Meyer and Shreffler point to some "noisy" elements in the original orchestration, specifically a glissando in the trombone part and the concluding clarinet trill being played by the horn. "Webern's Revisions," 360.

[27] Meyer and Shreffler discuss the role of disintegration in the movement. They, however, hear the final violin phrase as "re-establishing order." "Webern's Revisions," 360.

Ex. 2.3 Webern, Five Pieces for Orchestra, op. 10, no. 4

IV.

being the loudest (*piano*) and longest phrase in both this movement and the preceding one. The closing line in the violin amounts to a reduced form of the mandolin line (another echo?), consisting of only five notes that share key intervallic correspondences to the earlier phrase.[28] Now played very softly, it is, as Webern indicates, barely more than a "breath."[29] Adding to the fragmentation is the brevity of the movement (a mere six measures), which sounds like a fragment itself. What is most remarkable is the fragmentation of silence, the stillness sonority. Webern breaks it into pieces so as to give us a more heightened form of the state. How different from the evocation of stillness in the works by Schoenberg, Berg, Ives, and Bartók cited above. They maintain the sustained sonorities or repeated patterns throughout the movements in question. If anything breaks apart and disperses it is the sounds of man, not quiet. These works cannot imagine a silence beyond stillness; Webern's pieces, though, can, and they create it by fracturing the peacefulness of quiet.

For a performance of the Five Pieces for Orchestra in 1919, Webern gave titles to the individual movements: "Urbild" (original form), "Verwandlung" (transformation), "Rückkehr" (return), "Erinnerung" (remembrance), and "Seele" (soul).[30] He urged listeners not to interpret them programmatically.[31] Needless to say, many have done so. Johnson, for instance, sees the work as responding to the death of Webern's mother. In particular, he believes, the third movement restages a scene in which the mother assumes an angelic presence in the splendor of nature.[32] To Johnson, the sonorities of bells, plucked strings, and celesta in the composer's works do not so much evoke stillness as "brightness and the sparkling of sunlight on reflective surfaces," all of which are emblematic of the mountains, even heaven.[33] To hear silence (especially an expanding silence) forces us to experience loss in a very different way. Instead of being mollified by nature, it is intensified through silence. Webern's works testify to a search for new means of expressing loss, means different from the thick and protracted

---

[28] There are clear parallels between the opening and closing phrases. They share some pitch classes (d, e♭, e, a♭), feature a prominent tritone (a♭-d), begin with an opening whole-step movement (displaced by an octave in the last phrase) followed by a tritone, and end with half-step movement around the pitch class e. More elaborate analytical observations on this connection can be found in Forte, *The Structure of Atonal Music*, 89–90 and David Lewin, *Musical Form and Transformation: Four Analytical Essays* (New Haven: Yale University Press, 1993), 68–96.

[29] The last line is marked "wie ein Hauch," a marking used by Schoenberg in the quiet aphoristic closing movement of the Six Little Piano Pieces (op. 19).

[30] Moldenhauer and Moldenhauer, *Anton von Webern*, 198.

[31] Moldenhauer and Moldenhauer, *Anton von Webern*, 198.

[32] Johnson, *Webern*, 38–127.   [33] Johnson, *Webern*, 120.

emotionality of Romanticism. A refracted natural serenity may be one such way. Silence is another.

It proves an efficacious way. In the approach to silence, so much is lost – melodic loquacity, accompaniment, answering phrases. For Adorno, the approach is to a purified space and, beyond that, death. As mentioned in this study, it is to a borderland between music and silence, where many elements exist in a lost state, either having disappeared or being poised to do so. Such a space is of course enigmatic and can be open to different types of interpretation (Adorno's purity, Johnson's Alpine radiance), but loss exerts a strong presence (as it does for both Adorno and Johnson).[34] It emerges especially in the third and fourth movements of the Five Pieces for Orchestra, where musical depletion offers a way to interpret Webern's sparse titles. The person or object "returned" – perhaps Webern's mother – now exists as a "remembrance." Yet memory falters. Everything falters, the musical fragments and even silence. The object or person can never be restored. The piece underscores a larger modernist statement about the fragility of memory.[35] Many of Ives's works unfold nostalgic dramas in which the object of memory (often a tune associated with the composer's childhood and father) is evoked, takes form, and breaks apart, once again consigned to the irrecoverable past.[36] Webern's work takes a characteristically more oblique and reticent approach. There is no musical entity standing in for the object of memory, as with Ives's quotations; there is indeed little suggestion of such an object. Instead we encounter an atmosphere hospitable to recollection, be it the natural tranquility described by Johnson or what Adorno calls "a mysterious dimension of an endlessly questioning contemplativeness."[37] Rather than effacing the object of memory, Webern's work takes the unique step of dissipating the contemplative atmosphere, thereby diminishing the space for reminiscence. Silence, particularly stillness, can be conducive to

---

[34] Shreffler offers a contrasting interpretation of the third movement, one that departs from Johnson's reading. Accepting that the ostinati may suggest a celestial, radiant music, she describes how the solo melodic lines of the violin, horn, and trombone stand apart from that music. The three parts do not share many pitch classes with the two ostinati. Moreover, there are pronounced timbral differences. The violin plays on the g string, creating a dark tone. The horn and trombone play softly with mutes in very high registers, which produces narrow, pressed tones lacking the fullness typical of the two instruments. According to Shreffler, the three parts suggest human voices of loss. With this in mind, she writes of the end of the movement: "Maybe these anguished earthly voices cannot hear the sublime 'heavenly' music. The way I hear it, both the grief of bereavement and the radiant vision of the mother are represented in the piece simultaneously. The utopia articulated here is unreachable: the human subject, straining to the utmost, can at best hear only brief echoes of it before it fades away into noise." Shreffler, review, 298.

[35] For a discussion of modernist perspectives on memory, see Richard Terdiman, *Present Past: Modernity and the Memory Crisis* (Ithaca and London: Cornell University Press, 1993).

[36] For a discussion of such scenarios, see Metzer, *Quotation and Cultural Meaning in Twentieth-century Music*, 19–42.

[37] Adorno, "Anton Webern," 93.

recollection but now that particular type of quiet is fragmented. The disintegration takes us closer to the border between music and silence, where memories of a loved one and pieces of silence crumble. At this point, the feeling of loss deepens as does the presence of silence.

Like memory, the act of expression wavers in this space. The closer one gets to the border, the more the musical materials – the means used to communicate – fall apart, as do certain types of silence, themselves expressive. There are fewer and fewer materials to enlist, a diminishment that has repercussions for the individual subject. The drive toward pure expression and lyricism in Webern's music crystallizes around what Adorno calls the "pure sonority of the subject."[38] It is a curious phrase, for purity implies wholeness, some sort of essence being achieved with nothing missing or broken off. Adorno built his theoretical elaborations on modernism around the fragmented subject, a state inevitable given the stresses and strains of historical influence, the alienation of the new, and the regimentation of capitalist society. Webern's music, it appears, offers the possibility of wholeness, albeit fleetingly. If one hears a growing silence in lieu of purity, the expressive subject takes on a different guise. It is once again fragmented. The more the subject nears the border realm, the more it falls apart. Drawn there by the promise of new expressive means, the subject forfeits the means it once possessed and must now rely on comparatively thin and evanescent gestures. The voice of loss may even fall silent. Sonic fascination also lures the subject into the liminal realm; however, the sounds claimed there, those making up its "sonority," barely stay intact, existing as shards.[39]

The liminal state presents dangers as well as rewards, particularly new expressive and sonic resources. Brittleness and fragmentation not only undermine the expressive actions of the subject but also heighten them. In other words, the growing fleetingness of the subject becomes expressive, similar to the expressive effects created by the fragmentation of the subject described by Adorno. The sonic shards, the pieces of the subject's "sonority," also have sonic value, as music had never explored such timbral ephemera before. Fragility and loss are central to the borderland opened up in Webern's works. In pursuing silence, the musical language and the subject experience those qualities to the point of breaking apart and possibly disappearing. It is through that process, though, that the expression of fragility and loss becomes so much richer.

[38] Adorno, "Anton Webern," 93.
[39] This idea of fragmentation (of music and implicitly the subject) appears in Adorno's 1926 review of Webern's Five Pieces for Orchestra, which describes a general disintegration of melody, harmony, and form. Adorno, "Fünf Orchesterstücke," 515–16.

Nono

Since the premiere in 1980, Nono's string quartet *Fragmente-Stille, An Diotima* has attracted much critical attention, including two book-length analytical studies.[40] The rich scholarly discussion covers issues to be taken up here: the titular fragments and silence as well as expression, contemplated now at the borderland between sound and music. As with Webern's work, we will consider how Nono sets the scene, particularly what types of silence he draws upon and how they relate to each other. Instead of Webern's one- or two-minute forays into the borderland, Nono's work lasts around forty minutes, quite a long period of time to sustain such an ephemeral realm. The String Quartet situates the border in a different location than Webern's Five Pieces for Orchestra. It now separates the silent emotional interior of the self from the surrounding outside world of sound. The equation between silence and interiority has significant implications for the act of expression. It shapes the forms assumed by the expressive utterance and sways where it will ultimately head, either to silence or to sound.

The String Quartet not only approaches the borderland but also enters the state of the fragmentary, which, as will be discussed in detail in Chapter 3, is built upon a series of brief sections, many less than a minute in length, that contrast with each other to create the impression of sharp discontinuities and juxtapositions. The units bear headings drawn from poems by Friedrich Hölderlin, some of which revolve around the character Diotima, who appears prominently in the writer's oeuvre.[41] The headings too are fragments, comprising individual lines, groups of words, or just single words shorn from a larger whole. Surrounded by ellipses, they remain incomplete and cryptic: "... geheimere Welt ..." (world of deep secrets), "... ich sollte ruhn? ..." (should I rest?), and "... Staunend ..." (wondering). In discussing the work, Nono offers a paradoxical conception of the fragment, the

[40] The two book-length studies are Werner Linden, *Luigi Nonos Weg zum Streichquartett* (Kassel: Bärenreiter, 1989) and Herman Spree, *"Fragmente-Stille, An Diotima": Ein analytischer Versuch zu Luigi Nonos Streichquartett* (Saarbrücken: Pfau, 1992). Other noteworthy studies include Doris Döpke, "*Fragmente-Stille, An Diotima*: Réflexions fragmentaires sur la poétique musicale du quatuor à cordes de Luigi Nono," in *Luigi Nono* (Paris: Festival d'Automne/Geneva: Contrechamps, 1987), 98–114 (originally in German, "*Fragmente-Stille: An Diotima*: Fragmentarische Gedanken zur musikalischen Poetik von Luigi Nonos Streichquartett," *Zeitschrift für Musikpädagogik* 36, no. 9 (1986)); Nicola Gess, "Dichtung und Musik: Luigi Nono *Fragmente-Stille, An Diotima*," *MusikTexte* 65 (1996), 18–30; Wolf Frobenius, "Luigi Nonos Streichquartett *Fragmente-Stille: An Diotima*," *Archiv für Musikwissenschaft* 54 (1997), 177–93; and Carola Nielinger-Vakil, "Quiet Revolutions: Hölderlin Fragments by Luigi Nono and Wolfgang Rihm," *Music and Letters* 81 (2000), 245–74.

[41] Many writers have expanded on the significance of Hölderlin in the work's aesthetics and political import. See Linden, *Luigi Nonos Weg zum Streichquartett*, 4–81; Spree, "*Fragmente-Stille: An Diotima*," 79–87; Gess, "Dichtung und Musik," 21–24; and Nielinger-Vakil, "Quiet Revolutions," 245–58.

quality of being simultaneously momentary and endless.[42] Isolated from the original text, fragments come across as transitory, thoughts that evanesce and can never cohere into a larger whole. At the same time, freed from the specific meaning of the original, they, in their incompleteness, can take on a vast range of meanings, as if following a perpetual trail of ellipsis dots.[43]

For Nono, silence too can be paradoxical.[44] *Tristan und Isolde* harbors what he calls an "infinite" silence.[45] His own string quartet, on the other hand, collects terse, self-contained units of quiet, fragments of nothingness. Silence is also dynamic. As depicted by Nono, it does things – "anticipates, derives, and dreams."[46] Immersed in this activity, we become aware, alert to all the things it can do and to all the places it can lead.[47] Lachenmann has aptly described silence in Nono's work as "a fortissimo of agitated perception."[48] Silence can do so many things because it takes so many different forms.[49] Many of these forms appear in Webern's works, including fragmentation, stillness, soft dynamics, and the gradual fade to nothingness, whereas others significantly extend elements in those pieces or are altogether new. The Nono String Quartet features numerous long and prominent rests, large stretches of quiet as opposed to the fissures in Webern's music. Nono also highlights fragile sonorities, ones that barely emerge – or can barely emerge – before subsiding. Many of the sonorities are produced through extended techniques. In his Bagatelles for String Quartet, Webern also used such gestures, notably pizzicato and tremolo. Nono, however, assembles a lexicon of these techniques, around forty altogether. Some of the more percussive ones, like gettato and spiccato, produce fleeting, brittle sounds. At the opposite end of the spectrum are the sustained pitches and chords. Out of all the extended-technique sonorities, these are the ones that bring us closest to silence. Nono selects sounds that are difficult to produce in the first place, such as harmonics and awkward chords, and asks the players

---

[42] This conception of the fragment is discussed in Chapter 3.

[43] Frobenius, "Luigi Nonos Streichquartett," 182, n. 9.

[44] For a dialectical view of silence, see Stäbler, "About Silence," 74.

[45] Enzo Restagno, ed., *Luigi Nono* (Turin: Edizioni di Torino, 1987), 256. It should be mentioned that Nono does not see a strict opposition between silence and sound. He mentions that "silence is also sound" and that silence can be filled with sounds, even if they are the listener's memories of other sounds. Restagno, ed., *Nono*, 16–17.

[46] Restagno, ed., *Nono*, 61.

[47] Klaus Kropfinger, ". . . kein Anfang – kein Ende . . . Aus Gesprächen mit Luigi Nono," *Musica* 42 (1988), 167.

[48] Helmut Lachenmann, "Touched by Nono," *Contemporary Music Review* 18 (1999), 27.

[49] In his discussion of silence in the String Quartet, Guy Gosselin also distinguishes between different types of silences, not so much the compositional means discussed here but more conceptual varieties. Gosselin too places the work at the "frontiers of silence." Gosselin, "Le silence comme matériau premier de la composition du quatuor à cordes de Luigi Nono," *CIREM*, nos. 32–34 (1994), 81. Another extended account of silence in the work can be found in Linden, *Luigi Nonos Weg zum Streichquartett*, 82–91.

to hold them at very quiet dynamic levels and usually with special bowing techniques (for instance, flautato and playing close to the bridge). Making matters more difficult, they are to be sustained for twenty or so seconds or, in some cases, "as long as possible" – a paradox for a fragment. The sounds are fragile to begin with but now they become perilous, as we hear them struggle to keep above silence and then finally relent to it. As silence becomes sonic destiny, its presence becomes all the stronger.[50]

Underneath the various forms of quiet lies another type of silence, one we don't hear, or don't hear directly. This silence gathers around the Hölderlin texts. Nono directs that the headings are not to be recited or even interpreted programmatically. As he wrote to members of the LaSalle Quartet (the ensemble that premiered the piece), to render them in such a way would debase them to the level of "vulgar excerpts."[51] If the fragments are mute, why have they been included in the first place? In fact, they turn out to possess a voice. The performers are to "'sing' them inwardly," within their "hearts." The "silent chants" will resonate within the individual players and perhaps by doing so inflect the music that they produce. According to Nono, the songs are "of other spaces, other skies."[52] Consistent with the imagery developed in this study, they do belong to another realm, the far side of the border between music and silence. Whether or not the songs exert a sonic presence, they command our attention, for they represent an attempt to cross over the border and create from the other side. The border now emerges as a two-sided space instead of a one-sided realm in which we can only imagine or sense the sphere of true (or Beckettian "black") silence. The latter is still ultimately mysterious and unclaimable, but Nono has found a way to send messages from there, no matter how faint or vague.

With silent songs and imperiled sonorities, the String Quartet offers a compendium of ways to approach quiet, including two particular strands of silence that merit attention here: stillness and fragmentation. Appearing beside each other, the two offer insights into how Nono handles the plurality of silence through means very different from those employed by Webern. Three sections (figs. 18, 20, 22) in the String Quartet bear the heading "wenn in reicher Stille" (if in richer stillness/silence). The proscription not to link textual and musical fragments in any sort of illustrative way seems rather forced here, as the music strongly suggests stillness. It does so through a

---

[50] Martin Zenck sees silence in the work playing a larger role of destiny. He sees the work as nearing the end of a paradigm shift in twentieth-century music, one from sound to silence. Nono's String Quartet, the last piece he discusses, represents the "fading away" (Verlöschen) of music. Zenck, "Dal niente," 20–21.

[51] Archivio Luigi Nono, folio 44.32/08rsx.

[52] Nono, *Fragmente-Stille, An Diotima* (Milan: Ricordi, 1980), Introduction. Letter to the LaSalle Quartet, Archivio Luigi Nono, folio 44.32/08rsx.

Ex. 2.4 Nono, *Fragmente-Stille, An Diotima*, fig. 18
© Copyright G. Ricordi. Reproduced by permission

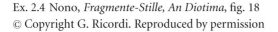
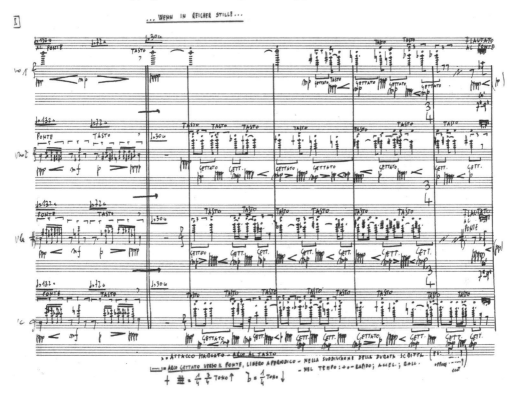

conventional gesture, a high sustained g played softly and often in harmonics
and/or flautato (Ex. 2.4).[53] The gesture appears earlier but it, and the quiet
it imparts, comes to the fore in these sections. Nono ensconces the pitch
within a microtonal cluster, thereby expanding upon the chromatic clusters
used by Webern and other earlier modernist composers to convey stillness.
He also subjects the cluster to different bowing techniques, which ripple the
sustained sonority.[54] Some of the gestures (like the gettato in fig. 18) agitate
the sonority whereas others (the flautato in fig. 20) enhance its ethereality.

This "rich" stillness is interrupted by a particularly fragmentary phrase.
In a piece in which everything is a fragment (including the high G stillness),

[53] In the letter to the LaSalle Quartet, Nono equates the sonority with a Mirage airplane, a
comparison which underscores not only the high range of the sonority but its sense of being
removed and quiet. Archivio Luigi Nono, folio 44.32/04v. I would like to thank Erika Schaller
at the Archivio Luigi Nono for making this aeronautical suggestion.
[54] Adding to the shifting effect are the constant and overlapping small crescendo and decrescendo
patterns, most of which move in between different degrees of *piano*.

Ex. 2.5 Nono, *Fragmente-Stille, An Diotima*, fig. 17
© Copyright G. Ricordi. Reproduced by permission

it would be hard to isolate any one gesture for being distinctly so. This one stands out nonetheless, as it amounts to little more than sonic scrawl. The gesture first appears in fig. 5 and consists of a rapid series of sixteenth notes (often grouped as a quintuplet) performed with very soft dynamics and either on the bridge or moving near it so as to create a splintery sound (Ex. 2.5). Like the wispy pencil scratches in a Cy Twombly canvas, the figures prove insubstantial, a mere trace on the surface of silence – so ephemeral are they that, like Twombly's scratches, they have to be grouped together in order to give them and the silence they signify a marked presence.

Two means of silence appear, but neither ascends here as in the end of the fourth movement in Webern's work. The stillness and scrawl figures keep side by side for most of the first half of the composition.[55] Rather than one lording over the other, each pursues its own ideal. The stillness sonority returns in a fourth section (fig. 24, "ruht" [sleep]), by which time it is no longer nettled by percussive bowing. It now soars in an aerial flautato, with

[55] The work is not clearly demarcated into halves, but one can hear the piece more or less breaking into two sections (figs. 1–25, 26–52), each of which concentrates on specific material. For instance the first half deals more extensively with the high stillness and scrawl gestures. Many of these gestures do return in the second part of the work, although not as prominently.

Ex. 2.6 Nono, *Fragmente-Stille, An Diotima*, fig. 48
© Copyright G. Ricordi. Reproduced by permission

each part dropping out (sleeping?) until only the cello sounds. Hovering in a lone line played *ppp* in harmonics, stillness almost becomes silence.[56] In the following section (fig. 25), the scrawl figure becomes even more shadowy, the culmination of gradual disintegration. Now it is a mere wisp within a crowd of more solid fragments, so near to being a rest, a moment of silence, amid the other lines. In these sections, both gestures have come closer to attaining a particular type of quiet, and by doing so they take us closer to the borderline.

Near the end of the work, we cross over that line, or the String Quartet suggests that we do. One of the final sections (fig. 48) features a quotation from the Renaissance chanson "Malheur me bat," which is attributed to Ockeghem in some sources (Ex. 2.6).[57] The inclusion of a quotation enhances the fragmentary scheme, as the phrase is excised from a larger whole. Quotations are also outside elements, snippets that breach the borders of a work, settle in the piece, and force the new musical surroundings to respond to

[56] Nicola Gess offers a similar account of this group of fragments, seeing them reaching a more quiet point in the last unit, among other changes. Gess, "Dichtung und Musik," 27–28.

[57] Doris Döpke proposes that the quotation may be a memorial to Nono's teacher Bruno Maderna, who made an arrangement of the chanson for three violas. Döpke, "Réflexions fragmentaires," 106–8.

them in some way. Nono's "silent songs" emerge from the other side of the border between music and silence, cross the line, and inflect the music that we hear to some unknown degree. Given the parallels, we can imagine the quotation as the voicing of a "silent song." Songlike it is, as the stepwise motion and small melodic range make it the most conventionally lyrical moment in the String Quartet. Moreover, the somber text ("misfortune strikes me") and Phrygian mode are suitable to the type of song that could be inspired by the accompanying Hölderlin fragment: "...wenn ich trauernd versank,...das zweifelnde Haupt ..." (if I sank into sadness...the head consumed by doubt).

The viola alone takes up the chanson, thereby making the quotation seem more like a melody sung by an individual. A mere fragment, the opening phrase from the tenor line, it becomes more fragmentary in its new surroundings, as it is shattered into smaller phrases, each separated by either rests or long-held pitches. It also becomes gradually softer, entering *piano* and concluding *ppp*. If the melody has broken into the world of sound, it can barely sustain itself there, for it crumbles and fades away – all the time returning to silence.

The other parts adhere to the quotation in a strict homophonic fashion, creating chords or sounds that move with each pitch of the melody. They spin out figures, harmonies, and timbres heard elsewhere in the piece, including high-pitched stillness, the major structural intervals of the tritone and augmented octave, the low g string in the violin, the g-d open fifth, sharply ascending and descending melodic phrases (reminiscent of the opening and fig. 26), and flautato, gettato, and battuto bowings. The appearance of so many of these elements in the passage inspires a new way of appreciating them and other similar gestures. The ephemeral materials seem to be sitting on the surface of silence, and now we can hear them as hovering over a specific strand of quiet, the "silent song," as materialized in the quotation.[58] They hover so closely that they react to every move in the borrowed melody. The sensitivity suggests that the twitching and shadowy phrases throughout the work are responding to "silent songs," the voices from beyond the border. Silence, be it Nono's "chants" or merely the idea of another realm, acts as a force beneath the music, a force felt on an ever-shifting surface.

The String Quartet features another borrowing, not a melody but rather a score direction.[59] Midway through the work, there appears a fragment

[58] Gosselin hears these effects as another type of silence, one that "silences" the normal bowed, more conventionally lyric sound of the viola (discussed below). Gosselin, "Le silence," 81.
[59] Nono also draws upon the "scala enigmatica" used by Verdi in the Ave Maria of his *Quattro pezzi sacri*. As discussed in Chapter 3, the scale serves as a larger pitch collection upon which many of the chords and melodic lines draw.

Ex. 2.7 Nono, *Fragmente-Stille, An Diotima*, fig. 26
© Copyright G. Ricordi. Reproduced by permission

(fig. 26) marked "mit innigster Empfindung," a line used by Beethoven in the third movement of his String Quartet no. 15 ("A Convalescent's Holy Song of Thanksgiving to the Deity") and the third movement of the Piano Sonata no. 30 (Ex. 2.7).[60] The call for deep feelings befits this particular passage. The fragment offers some of the more lyrical phrases of the work, lines more suited to imparting those feelings than scrawls or still clusters. The lyricism, though, is short-lived, as it, like all the passages in the work, is abruptly cut off. Even briefer are five following sections (figs. 34, 36, 38, 43, and 45), which draw upon chords from fig. 26 and also bear the Beethoven direction.[61] They are left with only the upper and lower chords in the arching phrases, nothing in between – a gap that makes them sound all the more fragmentary and non-lyrical. The intense emotion called upon by the Beethoven direction is to be thrown across a melodic chasm, the wide gap in range between the chords in some of the phrases. It is also to be winnowed down to nothing. All of the five sections begin *pianissimo* and decrescendo "al niente," sliding to emptiness. Moreover, they use normal

---

[60] The direction also appears in the Adagietto of Mahler's Fifth Symphony.
[61] They also share the Hölderlin fragment "das weisst aber du nicht" (however, this you do not know).

bowing as opposed to the array of extended techniques heard throughout the String Quartet. In fact, these sections and the chanson quotation are among the few passages to employ normal bowing, making it clear that Nono reserves such production for lyrical and expressive moments, in particular, moments that suggest some sort of voice singing to us.[62]

The idea of a voice is reinforced by another score direction: "sotto voce." The pairing of this inscription with "mit innigster Empfindung" may come across as a contradiction. Deepest feelings, it would seem, are never to be so muted. In fact, Beethoven accompanies the phrase in the sonata with the word "gesangvoll." Even the end of the convalescent's song, the moment at which the direction appears, suggests robust health and voice.[63] According to Nono, there is no contradiction – quite the opposite, as the combination of the two takes expression to a "new level."[64] Nono places intense, heartfelt emotion on the cusp of silence, the quiet fragment quickly giving way to nothingness. At this point, the scope of expression – very soft dynamics, the shortest of durations, and understated delivery – has been constrained, but the constraints make the music all the more intense. Nono's work seems to suggest that after the emotional extravagances of Romanticism, the borderline may be the last place left to voice feelings "mit innigster Empfindung."

Or it may be the next to last. What happens to the utterances of passionate feelings? Do they, as dictated by the "al niente" marking, fade into nothingness? Is their intensity so quickly dissipated? Another score marking – Beethoven's, not Nono's – may hold answers to these questions. The direction should be interpreted literally – with the most inner feelings. With this in mind, we can hear the utterances as heading toward an interior realm: a silent realm, a space where the subject shelters emotions, and keeps them from the outside, sounding world. Nono has already evoked this realm through the "silent songs," which are to be sung "inwardly," a delivery that may or may not leave some resonance in the sounding world. If the Hölderlin lines are any indication, this interiority is a vast and rich expressive space, in which a range of emotions can be conveyed with a vigorous, yet silent, voice. The *innigste Empfindungen* we do hear in the String Quartet appear to be heading back to the inner realm. Shorn into fragments

---

[62] Döpke refers to this type of production as "le beau son," which becomes a quotation in itself, recalling a more conventional type of lyricism. Döpke, "Réflexions fragmentaires," 108.

[63] The song (the opening statement of the double-variation form) begins with the direction "sotto voce." Nono could be seen as telescoping the dynamic, emotional endpoints of the convalescent's song by combining the directions. In the sketch materials for the work, he does write out all the markings from the Beethoven movement in the order in which they appear. Archivio Luigi Nono, folio 44.04.03/02v.

[64] Quoted in Kropfinger, ". . . keine Anfang – kein Ende . . . ," 167–68.

and thinned to sotto voce, the deep emotions come across as having grown weary of the sounding world and the travails of expression. The rich, inner song offers refuge as well as fulfillment. All these emotions have to do is follow the final decrescendo and cross over the borderline. Silence is the ideal space for them.

Nono's appeal to music "mit innigster Empfindung" revises an ideal of nineteenth-century Romanticism. As Hegel emphasized, the "true principle" of "Romantic art" is inwardness (Innerlichkeit), or the emotions gathered in the "shrine of the soul."[65] Beethoven's score direction also upholds interiority as the locus of expression. For the composer, deep-seated feelings were to be released and given external form, an outpouring as spontaneous and direct as a "song of thanksgiving." Hegel describes how musical works could "absorb" or provide a "home" for such feelings.[66] Although it adopts the rhetoric of inwardness, Nono's String Quartet complicates the ideal of interior emotion released in external artistic form. What distinguishes Nono's expressive path from the Romantic one is the association between interiority and silence, a connection made by neither Hegel nor Beethoven. With the two closely linked, the projection of the expressive utterance is either occluded or reversed. The "silent songs" do not transport feelings all the way beyond the threshold of interiority, whereas the sounded *innigste Empfindungen* fade away and head back across the line. In either case, the expressive utterance knows the other side of the borderland, the side we cannot know. By placing the interior at such a remove, Nono significantly changes Romantic conceptions of the realm. It is no longer a wellspring set to release expressive ideas; rather, it and the emotions sheltered there remain mysterious and inscrutable.[67]

---

[65]   G. W. F. Hegel, *The Philosophy of Fine Art*, trans. F. P. B. Osmaston (London: G. Bell and Sons, 1916), vol. II, 283 and vol. III, 358.

[66]   Hegel, *The Philosophy of Fine Art*, vol. III, 358 and vol. II, 295.

[67]   In his discussion of interiority and silence in the String Quartet, Danuser describes how the subject emerges from an absolute silence and how the work draws attention to realms of interiority in both the performers and listeners. Danuser, "Innerlichkeit und Äußerlichkeit in der Musikästhetik der Gegenwart," 25–27. For another discussion of interiority, see Luigi Pestalozza, "Ausgangspunkt Nono (nach dem 'Quartett')," in *Luigi Nono*, vol. 20 of *Musik-Konzepte* (Munich: Text + Kritik, 1981), 3–4. One aspect of expression not discussed here is the political significance of the work. The absence of the direct political engagement heard in the composer's previous pieces struck many critics, who accused him of retreating into the bourgeois realm of chamber music or a secluded individuality. See Gerhard Müller, "*Fragmente-Stille, An Diotima* per quartetto d'archi von Luigi Nono," *Musik und Gesellschaft*, 40 (1990), 352–60, and Herbert Stuppner, "Luigi Nono, oder: die Manifestation des Absoluten als Reaktion eines gesellschaftlich betroffenen Ichs," *Musik-Konzepte* 20 (1981), 83–92. Holding on to political ideals, some writers have placed the String Quartet in the context of an ongoing leftist interest (in particular, of Adorno and Bertaux) in Hölderlin. See Linden, "*Luigi Nonos Weg zum Streichquartett*," 13–24, and Nielinger-Vakil, "Quiet Revolutions," 245–49. For a discussion of the political import of silence in the work, see Matteo Nanni, "Luigi Nono: Le silence de l'écoute," *Atopia* 7 (April 2005). www.atopia.tk.

Sciarrino

Salvatore Sciarrino may be the only composer to have invoked a god of silence. His *Un'immagine di Arpocrate* (1979) offers a "picture in sound" of the Egyptian deity Harpocrates. The surviving pictures of Harpocrates show a cherub pressing his index finger against pursed lips so as to issue a cosmic *ssshh*. His hush extends throughout *Un'immagine di Arpocrate* and other of the composer's mature pieces that stretch tissues of slight, ephemeral tones.[68] With these works, Sciarrino emerges as arguably the contemporary composer most devoted to silence, a living follower of Harpocrates. Not all of his pieces, though, would please the god. There are no hushing cherubs in some compositions; rather, passionate characters fracture silence with cries and outbursts. Far from belonging to an ancient sect of quiet, the characters participate in a modernist fascination with silence. In particular, they point to different ways of shaping the relationship between silence and expression, ones in which the figures achieve expression not so much through embracing silence as by reacting against it.

The silent worlds occupied, and disturbed, by these characters have many things in common with those cultivated by Webern and Nono. Sciarrino too relies on fragmentary phrases and the stillness of sustained high-pitched sonorities in creating quiet. He, however, skims a sonic layer untouched by the other two composers. The residues of performance – breaths, the patter of keys, tongue noises, knocks, the raw scrape of bow against string – are no longer covered up but appear in the open.[69] Whole passages can be exclusively built upon these sounds, as in sections consisting of nothing more than tongue stops and key clicks. With them, a realm that is supposed to be made as quiet as possible in instrumental performance now represents the possibilities of quiet. The noises capture, in the composer's words, the "infinite rumbling of microscopic sonorities" that taint the silence around us.[70]

Sciarrino's silent worlds harbor another noise unheard in most works that explore the border realm – the voice. It is not surprising that the voice has been unwelcome there, for it can easily overwhelm an ensemble of muffled instruments and the quiet they depict. Sciarrino, though, is a composer who thinks dramatically, often operatically, and such thinking

---

[68] The literature on Sciarrino is quickly growing. Some notable studies include Martin Kaltenecker, "L'exploration du blanc," *Entretemps* 9 (1991), 107–16; Gavin Thomas, "The Poetics of Extremity," *Musical Times* 89 (April 1993), 193–96; Nicolas Hodges, "'A Volcano Viewed from Afar': The Music of Salvatore Sciarrino," *Tempo* 194 (1995), 22–24.

[69] These gestures have been used by other composers to a wide variety of effects. As mentioned below, Sciarrino's works are set apart by the almost exclusive use of these gestures and the association with quiet.

[70] Sciarrino, "Entretien," 139.

Ex. 2.8 Sciarrino, *Infinito nero*, mm. 90–91

has led him to perceive the expressive potential of placing the voice in these still arenas. The potential arises from the contrast between the voice and the quiet "rumblings" of the instruments, one facet of the broader contrast between the act of expression and silence.

The voice used by Sciarrino is not the standard operatic instrument, the volume and tone of which would obliterate his delicate realms. He has instead cultivated a style of vocal writing more suited to those spaces. The singer spits out short, almost spasmodic, phrases. The lines possess a dynamic quality, as they forcefully emerge, push to a certain point, and then instantly wither or just stop. Sciarrino often has them arise from "nothing" (indicated by the notational device of an altered crescendo sign) and then swerve back and forth between *ppp* and *piano*. The most extreme phrase is a two-note sigh figure consisting of a microtonal glissando over the range of a whole or half step (Ex. 2.8). While sliding downward, the voice rushes through syllables and words. Unlike a typical sigh, the gesture does not tragically faint away. It instead begins with intensity and becomes more intense as it drives through the glissando and text. Several sigh figures and smaller phrases built around narrow melodic orbits typically join together to form longer phrases. The flow between the short phrases escalates the textual and melodic momentum. The energy quickly dissipates into silence as the phrases, short or long, come to abrupt ends. The overall effect is that of breaking quiet, not sinking into it. The voice leaps into the realm of sound and by doing so momentarily dispels the surrounding silence.

Sciarrino's voices may not sound traditionally operatic but the emotions and psychological states conveyed by them surely are. Rage, jealousy, madness, and desire, the furies swirling in opera houses, do not loom in the quiet worlds of Webern and Nono. Emotions can be experienced there, but they are either understated, as with loss in Webern's music, or diffuse, like Nono's "mit innigster Empfindung" passages. The feelings and sensations in Sciarrino's works, on the other hand, not only ring out but are declared. Characters wear their hearts on their sleeves, telling us passionately and pointedly about the envy that overwhelms them, the entanglements of lust, or the delirium in which they wander.

They do all these things by singing against silence. Sciarrino's works configure the bond between expression and silence in ways strikingly different from those pursued by Webern and Nono. In pieces by the latter two composers, expression can be fulfilled in silence. It approaches quiet, is drawn to it. Each soft step to the border in Webern's music underscores the evocation of loss, until music itself is lost. Nono's String Quartet secures the cusp of silence as the place to release intense personal feeling and points beyond to the harbor of a silent interior realm. Sciarrino's compositions, on the other hand, poise expression against silence. Put differently, pieces by Webern and Nono turn to silence for expression, whereas Sciarrino's pieces encounter silence in seeking to express.

The encounter is one way of presenting the relationship between speech and silence. The pair has long demanded attention, as it brings together the most human of sounds, one central to the act of expression, and its supposed opposite, the blankness of quiet. Philosophers, scholars, and artists have configured the relationship in various ways. It is worth taking the time to present three different vantage points in order to show both the contrasting forms the relationship can assume and where Sciarrino's music fits into a larger discourse. Depictions of the pair typically differ in two key respects: how much the two overlap, if at all, and how the one side acts with or against the other. For Heidegger, "language speaks as the peal of stillness." It mingles with silence (stillness), like the resonance of a bell hanging in the air. Language gives silence a sound, as both the emergence from quiet and the eventual return to it point to stillness, a remote state that exists beyond mere soundlessness. Heidegger's formulation stands out in the degree to which the two exist simultaneously and give form to each other, speech as a sound of silence and silence offering material to speech.[71] The philosopher and theologian Max Picard approaches silence as an "autonomous" realm. It may stand apart from speech, but at the same time it is necessary for the creation of speech. Silence is the "pregnant mother" giving birth to language, as each word is preceded by silence and comes from it.[72] Whereas Picard claims that speech arises "unobtrusively" from quiet, others portray the emergence of speech as a violent rending of silence. The Romantic writer the Comte de Lautréamont presents a character trapped in the silence sustained by deafness and muteness. The torment experienced by him finally wells up into a cry, which, with the force of a volcanic eruption, blasts the surrounding silence and releases him into the world of sound.[73] In his work *Infinito nero* (1998), Sciarrino espouses a similar view of speech and silence, placing a moment of violence at the center of the relationship.

Infinito nero, "An Ecstasy in One Act" for mezzo-soprano and chamber ensemble, takes us into the cell of Sister Maria Maddalena de'Pazzi. For around twenty years at the end of the sixteenth and beginning of the seventeenth centuries, Maria Maddalena experienced religious visions in which she would commune with Christ.[74] Captured by the ecstatic dialogue, her fellow sisters at a Florentine convent circled around her and listened in. During a period of seven months in 1584–85, they wrote down Maria Maddalena's speeches. Transcription posed challenges as there was only her side of the dialogue to be heard and her lines were spat out at a rapid pace as they careened between seemingly unrelated images. Making matters even more difficult was what she did not say. Maria Maddalena reposed in long periods of silence, unpredictably breaking them with her twitching interjections. Desirous to capture everything, eight sisters took to the task. Four would immediately repeat Maria Maddalena's phrases and four would write them

---

[71] Martin Heidegger, *Poetry, Language, Thought*, trans. Albert Hofstadter (New York: Harper & Row, 1971), 207–9. Hofstadter translates the word "Stille" as stillness, a practice used by many Heidegger scholars. Aware of the breadth of the word "Stille," I have used "silence" so as to be consistent with the terminology adopted in the essay. For a discussion of the give and take between speech and silence in Heidegger's thoughts, see Ute Guzzoni, "Thoughts on the Sound of Silence," *Atopia* 7 (April 2005). www.atopia.tk.

[72] In a Big Bang type of scenario, Picard does mention that the arrival of the "Divine Word" did "tear open" silence. Max Picard, *The World of Silence* (Chicago: Henry Regnery, 1964), 1, 8, 15.

[73] Comte de Lautréamont, *Les chants de Maldoror*, trans. Guy Wernham (New York: New Directions, 1965), 77–78.

[74] For a discussion of Maria Maddalena's visions, see Armando Maggi, *Uttering the Word: The Mystical Performances of Maria Maddalena de'Pazzi, a Renaissance Visionary* (Albany: State University of New York Press, 1998).

down. They even recorded the silences, viewing them as essential to the mystery.

The sisters used one specific symbol to notate the spiritual pauses. In his musical elaboration of their textual transcriptions, Sciarrino draws upon various ways of evoking quiet. Once again, a plurality of silence unfolds. No single type dominates. The composer often employs one or two types to define individual sections of the work. For instance, the concluding section (mm. 190–210) sustains an ethereal stillness of high-pitched harmonics performed sul tasto by violin and cello (d''''/e''''). Against and within the floating and suggestively sempiternal sound, Maria Maddalena (represented by the mezzo-soprano soloist singing her lines) closes her dialogue by telling Christ that he is without end, only to add, in one of her strange reversals, how she would like to "see" "that end."

Used by Webern and other early modernist composers, floating clusters were by 1998 a traditional means of evoking silence. Sciarrino opens his work with yet another means. The first ten minutes consist of a series of inhalations and exhalations made into the flute headpiece, tongue stops by the oboe and clarinet, and very soft bass drum strokes. These are not indistinct "infinite rumblings." They are the sounds of breathing and heartbeats. Ours? The expectant sisters? Maria Maddalena's? It is not clear. One way to hear them is as a sound pointing to silence. Drawing upon his experience in an anechoic chamber, Cage used such sounds to make the point that silence, the absolute kind, does not exist.[75] Sciarrino, in contrast, uses them to evoke silence, the kind we sense. Presenting the sounds by themselves, his works suggest the mysterious realm behind them. The noises are the last thing between us and nothingness.

Infinito nero focuses just as much on disrupting silence as on creating it. To express in this work is to break through quiet, and to do so violently. Each statement by Maria Maddalena has to make that passage. With each one, we experience the transitory moment when the expressive utterance comes into contact with silence. We hear an event that typically does not capture our attention and are made to hear it again and again. Sciarrino's vocal phrases heighten the moment. They are fragments, kernels of melody (often the two-note sigh figure) combined with Maria Maddalena's terse, incomplete thoughts. The fragments, though, do not behave as fragments usually do in the realm of silence. Instead of lapsing into quiet, they cut it. The phrases emerge with frenetic urgency, as the plosion of the opening syllable and harried vocal sounds quickly slice through quiet. The cut is made all the deeper as Sciarrino often has the vocal entrances fortified by

---

[75] John Cage, *A Year from Monday* (Middletown: Wesleyan University Press, 1967), 134.

Ex. 2.9 Sciarrino, *Infinito nero*, m. 109

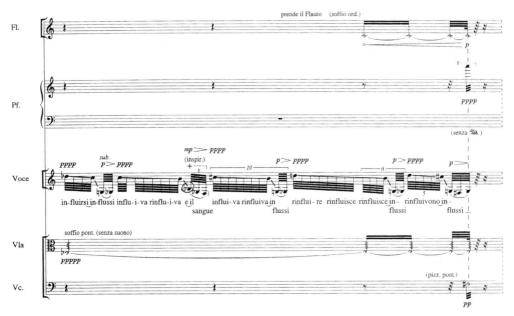

attacks on the piano and other instruments. Even the ends of phrases, the spot where fragments supposedly acquiesce to silence, are often accented by piano pitches and drum strokes. These fragments dispel into noise rather than into quiet.

Once aired, the expressive utterance attempts to stave off silence and thereby escape having to relive the torturous moment of rending quiet, at least for a while. To that end, Maria Maddalena extends her ideas, often by linking together broken thoughts. In her discourse on the influence (*influssi*) and reinfluence (*rinfluisce*) of blood (mm. 108–20), a flow (*flussi*) of repeated melodic phrases and different forms of the former two words creates her longest, if not necessarily clearest, thought (apparently, however, visionaries can be clear enough to enjoy wordplay).[76] The effort seems to work, for silence, when and where it is evoked in this passage, is worn down to its thinnest level in the composition, a single string harmonic to be produced "senza suono" (Ex. 2.9). Silence is vulnerable as well, for Maria Maddalena has not only ruptured quiet but also filled it. In one of her short pauses, the flute, playing tones only with the hushed sound of breath, imitates her melodies. Elsewhere, the solo violin repeats a childlike

---

[76] Sciarrino draws attention to this wordplay. Sciarrino, liner notes, *Infinito nero; Le voci sottovetro*, Kairos CD 1202, 23.

tune bounced around by Maria Maddalena (mm. 194, 200), and the viola states in harmonics a phrase reminiscent of her sigh figures (mm. 191–210, first heard in m. 106).[77] Instruments that usually mimic silence now mimic Maria Maddalena. The repetitions suggest utterances so forceful that they have been inscribed into quiet. The etchings, however, soon fade, and quiet returns, unmarred and resilient. The voice once again has to break silence and we once again have to wait and listen to the inevitable, yet always strained, rupture.

In waiting we, like the attendant sisters, have been drawn into Maria Maddalena's visions. The sisters took from them tales of a romance with Christ. We can extract from them something more analytical than romantic, a commentary on the act of expression. Of course, Sciarrino is the one making the commentary, and it is telling that he chooses to do so through an extreme figure, a mystic nun who was most likely mad. As the composer points out, lines between religious visions and mental illness have been entangled for centuries.[78] Partaking in the ambiguity, *Infinito nero* has no interest in freeing the lines. Whether mystic or hysteric, Maria Maddalena serves to place expression in stark terms. In her visions, expression comes across as a mysterious and brutal act, the mystery and brutality of which have much to do with silence. The expressive utterance emerges from an unfathomable and silent inner state, be it the sanctuary of religious ecstasy or the recesses of madness. Raw and unmediated, it takes shape and is projected from the internal locus with driving force. The utterance collides with the screen of silence separating the inner state and our sounding world, an impact that, as heard in Maria Maddalena's spasmodic vocal phrases, proves violent. How different from Nono's "silent songs," which float away from a silent interior realm and leave only suggestions in the sounding world, never having to rupture the screen of silence. Although severe, the impact in Sciarrino's work does not completely obliterate the screen. Maria Maddalena gives the sisters and us only strewn and partial thoughts. The fragments suggest that not everything makes it through quiet. Silence resists here and there, blocking the fullness of expression and leaving the utterance to be always incomplete and sundered.

Sciarrino's opera *Luci mie traditrici* (1998) sets up the interaction between the act of expression and silence along different lines. *Infinito nero* rests upon the notion that the act ruptures silence. The break is never complete in the

---

[77] The viola figure does not exactly imitate a phrase sung by the vocalist. In fact, when the violist first introduces the phrase, the vocalist has yet to sing the pitch class a. The similarities to, yet independence from, the vocal line suggest resonances of Maria's lines taking on distinct shapes in the realm of silence.

[78] Sciarrino, liner notes, 23–25.

work, but *Infinito nero* nonetheless takes to the notion by dramatically dilat-
ing the moment when the utterance rends quiet. *Luci mie traditrici*, on the
other hand, imparts the idea that silence, the true, deep kind, sooner or later
stills the act of expression. The opera builds suspense around the moment
when quiet will settle upon the yearning exclamations of the characters,
who are haunted by an ultimate silence.

To haunt his characters and us, Sciarrino has conceived of another means
of presenting silence. He surrounds the voices with rings of quiet. These
rings pack together Sciarrino's trademark particles, the "rumbling" sonorities, stillness clusters, and breathing noises. They function as an aureole of
nothingness, a floating realm existing outside of the vocal music. The voices
have little impact on the rings of quiet. The characters may momentarily
break them with outbursts or inscribe a phrase into them, but the aureole
remains intact. Intact, and indifferent. Silence continues in its own realm.
By virtue of sounding, the voices have already broken through silence, but
there are apparently many layers of quiet. Just as one is dispelled another
emerges. Some layers, like those in the corona, are ultimately out of reach
and can never be vanquished. Nor do the characters want to disturb them.
What sets these figures apart is that they keep a distance from silence, afraid
of what it means and what it can do.

Like *Infinito nero*, *Luci mie traditrici* takes us back to late sixteenth-century
Italy. For his libretto, Sciarrino adapted the play *Il tradimento per l'onore*
by Giacinto Andrea Cicognini, which recounts Gesualdo's murder of his
wife and her lover in 1590. Sciarrino offers a "very narrow" perspective on
Cicognini's text, stripping away the names of the main characters (leaving us
with an anonymous Duke, Duchess, Guest and Servant), all the secondary
characters, and any historical references. The result is an opera that exists
outside of a specific time or place. Gesualdo's story is now part of the broad
"explosion of a love tragedy, marked by violence and death."[79]

For the characters caught in it, the explosion remains quiet, menacingly
so. They become increasingly aware of the silence surrounding them, even
acknowledging it at times. The most direct response occurs in scene iii, the
moment when the Duchess and Guest admit their love for each other. Sciarrino may remove the characters from the Baroque, but he keeps the period
affectation of the dialogue. The two speak in the coupled phrases so common to declarations of passion in madrigals and Baroque dramatic works.
One character finishes the other's thoughts, elaborates upon the other's

---

[79] Salvatore Sciarrino, "*Luci mie traditrici* par Salvatore Sciarrino; Propos recueillis
par Gianfranco Vinay." Program notes available at www.festival-automne.com/public/
ressourc/publicat/2000scia/23.htm.

images. Each word and idea is embraced, consummated. In the Baroque period, the music for such dialogues effuses. Individual vocal phrases join together to form flowing lines. Sciarrino's vocal writing follows suit. The typically terse, jabbing entries commingle to form longer, propulsive phrases. Some of the bare sigh figures become arabesques, albeit convulsive ones. In Baroque opera, the enraptured dialogue excites the orchestral accompaniment, which can dress beguiling words in rich chords or fuel the ecstatic momentum with a passacaglia. Here is where Sciarrino parts company with earlier styles. In *Luci mie traditrici*, the lovers' entwined phrases confront rings of indifferent silence floating in the orchestra.

In scene iii, the Duchess and Guest get near those rings of silence. The lovers begin the scene bewildered by their senses and emotions: "What do I see?" "What do I feel?" They never ask "What do I hear?" To do so would force them to confront the surrounding silence, an aureole made up of whistle tones in the flutes and a dissonant dyad (c♯''''''-d'''''') in the violins played in harmonics with a rapid tremolo (mm. 1–5).[80] Of the two separate rings of quiet, the former is the most distant, a "freely unstable" glissando unfurling in its own realm. The string layer hovers between the remote whirring and the lovers' voices, the ethereal quiet above and the mortal din below. It eventually mingles with the latter. At first, though, it keeps away from the lovers, or, more accurately, they try to keep away from it. With the exception of one pitch class (c♯) sung by the Guest, the pitch classes in the vocal lines do not overlap with the pitch classes of the dyad. Emphasizing g′, the Countess's line stays furthest away.[81] The melodic separation suggests that the lovers are attempting to hide from silence or that they are not yet aware of its presence and power.

They experience that power soon enough. Near the end of the scene, the Duchess exclaims "I sink into silence" (mm. 131–37). At this moment, the aureole from the opening measures returns. True to her words, she does sink into silence, as does the Guest who breaks off the incessant vocal coupling and falls mute for the longest period of time in the scene. Although still singing, the Duchess gets closer to silence. Unlike earlier in the scene, the pitches making up the second of two phrases in her vocal line (phrase 1: g♯-a-b, phrase 2: b-c′-d♯″) now near the pitch classes of the dyad (c♯-d). Besides the proximity to the dyad, the pitch classes in the second phrase

---

[80] The aureole sonority returns a few times during the scene. It is also transformed into another recurring sonority, this one made up of the d'''''' and c♯'''''' along with an f♯'''' in the viola which is repeated in a more regular rhythmic fashion (m. 85).

[81] The pitch g′ is the focal point for her phrases, which do include some pitches nearer to the pitch classes of the dyad. The Guest's pitches (prominent e′ and f′) do bridge the gap between the pitches associated with the Duchess and those in the dyad.

also combine with those in the dyad to create a larger cluster, a traditional stratum of stillness. No longer removed from silence, the Duchess merges with it and recognizes its power.

The effect is immediate. Silence imposes itself. The Duchess and Guest exhort each other to "listen," as if to find any sound other than silence. The attempt is futile, as they concede that they can only hear "nothing." Closer to silence than ever before, the two experience "shock" and "confusion." For a moment, silence stills expression, leaving the lovers dazed and mute. Its powers extend well beyond that moment. As Sciarrino says, *Luci mie traditrici* is a tragedy. In traditional forms of the genre, moments of foreshadowing set up the final blows. This brief "shocking" spell of silence too presages. It points to the silence, or silences, awaiting the lovers. One such silence is rather untraditional, the aura of nothingness that eventually overtakes the act of expression. The other is an age-old conception of quiet. This one awaits the lovers at the end of the opera. It is a type of silence that they may have sensed in the rings of quiet – the silence of death.

Fredric Jameson begins his study of postmodernism by sweeping away foundations of modernism and earlier periods. Dismissed immediately are a series of "depth models." One of them is familiar to us: the model of expression premised upon separation between the interiority of the subject, a deep space where the expressive utterance is formed, and the external social world into which the utterance is launched. According to Jameson, this model and along with it the "very aesthetic of expression itself" have "vanished away" in the ascendant postmodern culture. Their disappearance stems from several developments that have formed the cornerstone of Jameson's and other theorists' concepts of postmodernism: the death of the subject (the monad who harbors this interiority), the erosion of grounding oppositions like inside/outside, and a fascination with the surface and hollowness of simulacra, which possess no expressive depths.[82]

What are we to make of Nono's and Sciarrino's works? They hold on to this "depth model" well after its supposed demise. The pieces caution us once again not to accept the large-scale and totalizing aesthetic shift described by Jameson, a shift in which such a fundamental concept of expression disappears. The concept endures. So too does the "aesthetic of expression," or, we should say, aesthetics. Plurality, be it of different aesthetic positions or styles, offers a more encompassing and detailed view of late twentieth-century culture than Jameson's sea change. The idea of an unprecedented artistic pluralism has served as one of two leading ways to view the period,

---

[82] Jameson, *Postmodernism*, 11–16.

the other being the rise of a new postmodern culture, itself characterized by plurality.[83] The former, though, is not without its shortcomings. Many critics have used the notion of pluralism as a curtain that can be stretched out to hide an unruly multiplicity behind it. The suggestion of pluralism is much easier to deal with than its reality. The critical challenge is to find the similarities and antinomies within the array, particularly those between what can be called modernist and postmodernist works. The focus on a compositional state or expressive position can offer a way of drawing such connections. This point is made by two very different women: Maria Maddalena, whose eruptive cries have been revived by Sciarrino, and Marilyn Monroe, whose image was endlessly reproduced and hollowed out by Warhol. They reveal two contrasting aesthetics of expression active at the end of the twentieth century, the former emblematic of modernist anguished depths, the latter, postmodern depthlessness.[84] Both speak to the time.

Maria Maddalena, of course, speaks very loudly, especially to the continuing vitality of modernism within an allegedly pervasive postmodern culture. In particular, the works of Sciarrino and Nono enrich one endeavor of modernism, the inquiry into the act of expression. They contribute to the inquiry by taking apart and complicating what appears to be a natural, effortless model of expression, one that served Romantic composers well. The String Quartet has the expressive utterance withdraw into silence. Sciarrino's work depicts it as aggressive and blocked. The pieces of both composers comment not only on Romantic expression but also on early modernist dissections of the model. The inquiry builds upon itself. Nono's work, for instance, can be heard as responding to the enigmas in the third and fourth movements of Webern's Five Orchestral Pieces. The latter sets a typical nineteenth-century scene of a figure expressing loss, or other intense emotions, within the stillness of nature; however, it dissipates both the stillness and the utterance of loss. In doing so, the two movements suggest another realm, a silence deeper than stillness, where utterances are so fragmentary that they are close to being silent. The rich interiority of music "mit innigster Empfindung" and silent songs lays claim to the deeper silence spied by Webern's pieces and also achieves expressive utterances in silence.

Sciarrino's work focuses on the Expressionist side of the Second Viennese School. With its small ensemble (flute, oboe, clarinet, piano, percussion,

---

[83] Jameson conceives of the two different approaches along these lines: "I cannot stress too greatly the radical distinction between a view for which the postmodern is one (optional) style among many others available and one which seeks to grasp it as the cultural dominant of the logic of late capitalism." *Postmodernism*, 45–46.

[84] Jameson draws a similar comparison between Van Gogh's painting of a pair of boots and Warhol's *Diamond Dust Shoes*. *Postmodernism*, 6–11.

violin, viola, and cello), frenzied cross of speech and song, and mad character, *Infinito nero* is one of many descendents of *Pierrot lunaire*. Schoenberg's piece and Expressionist arts in general challenged Romantic ideals by removing some of the last-standing barriers, social or artistic, placed on expression, so as to have utterances spring unfettered from dark psychic regions. Sciarrino's piece descends into the same areas but erects a barrier between them and us. With a screen in place, the emotional blasts of Expressionism take on a new guise as well as a new kind of intensity. They now come across as obstructed and strained.

Sciarrino's screen is made of silence. Nono's interiority exists in silence. Capturing quiet, both composers extend another exploration undertaken during the early modernist period, namely the joining of the act of expression and silence heard in Webern's works. As observed in the music of all three composers, the union opens up a range of new expressive and sonic possibilities. In particular, one element offers a means of examining the other. Silence can be used to scrutinize the act of expression, showing that it can assume a range of dynamics, at times violent or fleeting. The state of silence, as Beckett has told us, appears to be always beyond reach, a mysterious realm. All we can ever experience are qualities of it. Yet aspects of expression, as realized in the still echo, the thinnest of *innigste Empfindungen,* and the cries of a visionary nun, can bring us close to this mystery.

3 The fragmentary

Fragment. It is a common title in 20th- and 21st-century music – a title largely unknown in previous periods. Among the composers writing such pieces are Birtwistle, Carter, Ligeti, Henze, Nono, and Kurtág. With his . . . *agm* . . . , Birtwistle has gone so far as to fragment the title, giving us just the central letters. In addition, there are compositions that, although not bearing the title, have nonetheless been described as fragments by critics and listeners. John Zorn's "filing card" pieces come immediately to mind. At the beginning of the 20th century, Adorno heard works by the Second Viennese School composers as existing in shards.

Fragment. It is an object, or concept, crucial to modernism. In T. S. Eliot's poem *The Waste Land*, the protagonist "shores" up "fragments," all part of the "heap of broken images" compiling early 20th-century Western culture. Adorno attended to the fragmented subject, the individual broken by the strains of modern life. Ironically, one of the continuities between modernism and postmodernism is the shattered fragment. Paul Virilio links the latter with "the art of the fragment."[1] Many theories of postmodernism, notably those of Jameson, deal in stylistic and historical pieces.[2] The inherent ambiguity and incompleteness of the fragment and the resulting resistance to unity have also elevated it in branches of deconstruction and poststructuralist criticism.[3]

The prominence of the fragment suggests that there would be a rich critical conversation around its role in modernist composition. Surprisingly only a few words have been said here and there, mostly in regard to individual composers and works.[4] No broader account of the fragment across twentieth-century pieces or styles exists. In fact, the most

---

[1] Paul Virilio and Sylvère Lotringer, *Pure War/Twenty-Five Years Later*, trans. Mark Polizzotti (Los Angeles: Semiotext(e), 2008), 49.

[2] The idea of the fragment appears prominently in Jameson's conception of postmodernism, although he uses it carefully since the term has connotations of "privation." Jameson, *Postmodernism*, 25.

[3] The fragment, for instance, plays an important role in the writings of Barthes, DeMan, and Derrida.

[4] Studies of the fragment in the works of Kurtág are discussed below. For studies of two other composers who have fostered the fragment, Debussy and Birtwistle, see Linda Cummins, *Debussy and the Fragment* (Amsterdam: Rodopi, 2006); Rachel Iwaasa, "Fragmentation and Eros in Debussy's *Chansons de Bilitis* and *Six épigraphes antiques*" (DMA thesis, University of British Columbia, 2006); Robert Adlington, *The Music of Harrison Birtwistle* (Cambridge University Press, 2000).

extended discussion of the fragment in music deals with nineteenth-century repertoires, specifically the connections drawn between compositions by Schumann and the writings of the Schlegel brothers and the early Romantic Jena School.[5] Although studies of this earlier musical-philosophical bond offer general ideas for a consideration of the modernist fragment, they understandably fall short in coping with the various forms assumed by the fragment over a hundred years later.

This chapter looks at different conceptions of the fragment in late modernist music. It begins by asking basic questions. What exactly is a musical fragment? What does it sound like? How does it act? To address these questions, we need to start with the individual fragment and then move on to collections of such bits. The move is prompted by the musical works themselves, which typically assemble crowds of fragments. Together the shards form a compositional state called the fragmentary. Like other states examined here, it involves an ideal that a work emulates by shaping the musical language in ways consistent with the dynamics and associations of the ideal. As is to be expected of a kaleidoscopic condition, the fragmentary abounds with different structural dynamics, such as incompletion, interruption, and separation, and associations, including loss and ambiguity.

Amid that diversity, there are two basic types of fragments: the remnant and the invented.[6] The former consists of surviving scraps of a once-intact work or object, like the stray words or letters of a Sappho poem or the decapitated torso of a Roman sculpture. Surrounded by a lost past, remnants proved especially captivating in the Renaissance and in the eighteenth century.[7] Artists in both periods eulogized ancient ruins in paintings and poems. They even created ruins, be it a new marble torso without a head or a new crumbling Greek temple in a country garden. The new fragment, though, does not always have to mimic the old. Fragments can be invented that neither survive nor resemble a previous complete work. They are fragments of nothing. Their origins lie in the idea of the fragment, particularly the notions of incompletion, loss, and vagueness. One way

---

[5] See Charles Rosen, *The Romantic Generation* (Cambridge, MA: Harvard University Press, 1995), 41–115; John Daverio, *Nineteenth-century Music and the German Romantic Ideology* (New York: Schirmer, 1993); Beate Julia Perrey, *Schumann's "Dichterliebe" and Early Romantic Poetics: Fragmentation of Desire* (Cambridge University Press, 2002); and Richard Kramer, *Unfinished Music* (New York: Oxford University Press, 2008), 311–45.

[6] Other taxonomies of the fragment are discussed in Elizabeth Wanning Harries, *The Unfinished Manner: Essays on the Fragment in the Later Eighteenth Century* (Charlottesville: University of Virginia Press, 1994), 3–8.

[7] For a discussion of the appeal of the fragment in the two periods, see Harries, *The Unfinished Manner*, and David Rosand, "Composition/Decomposition/Recomposition: Notes on the Fragmentary and the Artistic Process," in *Fragments: Incompletion and Discontinuity*, ed. Lawrence Kritzman (New York Literary Forum, 1981), 17–30.

to partake in those qualities is to produce brief and enigmatic works. In other words, one can create a fragment to get at all the effects created by fragments.

Both remnants and invented fragments share a similar rhetoric, one that holds across centuries and across the different arts. It builds upon a defining property of the fragment, incompleteness. In some way, a fragment appears incomplete, be it a sliver cut off from a larger whole, an unfinished work, or a work that seems insubstantial. Incompleteness yields two other key characteristics, ambiguity and loss. The fugitive boundaries of a fragment – the random tear from an original source or the amorphous start and stop of a slight work – invite obscurity. We ponder what once joined the ripped line or the inscrutability of what lies across the border. The space surrounding a fragment is just as important as what is inside the terse form. The outside is a world of vast possibilities. It is also a realm of vast rumination, as we must constantly try to make sense of the space and to grasp the impressions and possibilities abounding there. One such impression is that of loss, be it of the original material from which the piece came or the broader absence of wholeness and substance.

The central relationship for a fragment is that between part and whole. The fragment obviously plays the role of part, but part of what? The whole can take on a range of forms; which, befitting the reciprocal relationship between the two, depends on the type of fragment. It can be the object or work from which a fragment splinters off and to which it harkens back. The fragment can point to a larger context or figure that acts as a whole, as Kurtág's work discussed below does with musical types such as the circle of fifths and the canon. The whole can also be the larger form, or the possibility of a larger form, in or around which a fragment sits. Moreover, it can be the ideal of such values as unity, coherence, and system.

If the fragment and the whole can assume different forms, so too can the relationship between them. With the remnant, the bond is one of loss, the forsaken piece and the irrevocably broken source. An oppositional relationship often develops. In its independence, a fragment torments ideals of unity and completion. Here is an object that, whether by design or fate, resists those ideals. Finally, the roles can be reversed. Anytime we interpret a fragment, we run the risk of approaching it as a self-contained work, implicitly ascribing to it degrees of totality and coherence.[8] Under such a lens, it can appear as a whole. To avoid such a misinterpretation, we must concentrate

---

[8] Hans-Jost Frey elaborates upon the misperceptions that can arise when interpreting a fragment. To him the risks are so great and unavoidable that he removes the fragment from the part/whole relationship, claiming that the fragment "is neither a whole nor a part." Frey, *Interruptions*, trans. Georgia Albert (Albany: State University of New York Press, 1996), 25–26.

on the defining features of fracture, incompletion, and ambiguity. On the other hand, as long as a fragment exists, the whole can never be complete. The latter could be an object with a piece missing, or it could be an ideal that has been cracked. In either case, the whole is not intact; it comes close to being a fragment. Such a fate is avoided by our habit to conceive of the whole as a something that was once complete or as a larger, encompassing ideal. We could appeal to what Hans-Jost Frey calls the "infinite whole," that "which includes everything and outside of which there is nothing," but such a construct, even if it was fully comprehensible or let alone possible, would preclude the possibility of a fragment and the productive relationship between part and whole.[9]

The rhetoric of the fragment also sustains layers of paradox. For instance, fragments lie impoverished. Bereft of context, they possess little or no specific meaning. At the same time, both the vague material within the fragment and the vast space around it hold an excess of possible meanings. A fragment is both closed and open.[10] Not connected to anything, it can shut itself off and become a secluded speck. In an oft-quoted line, Friedrich Schlegel compared the fragment to a rolled-up hedgehog, complete in itself and separated from its surroundings.[11] Schlegel's conception, as discussed below, applies more to a particular type of miniature, the aphorism, than to the fragment.[12] Ambiguous and porous, the fragment can never withdraw completely. With its transient boundaries, it bleeds into the outside realm. Fragments require a double focus. We always look into them, scrutinizing the incomplete traces that they hold. The traces also force us to look out, as we try to connect them to something larger, be it an original whole or a familiar idea that they resemble. Finally, fragments prove both fleeting and prolonged. Incomplete and/or insubstantial, they evanesce. Unable to sustain an idea, image, or sound, they may seem briefer than they actually are. Or broader than they appear. Ambiguity once again adds dimensions to a fragment, giving it a range of possible meanings that encourage extended reflection.

---

[9] Frey, *Interruptions*, 27.
[10] For an elaborate discussion of this paradox, see Françoise Susini-Anastopoulos, *L'écriture fragmentaire: définitions et enjeux* (Paris: Universitaires de France, 1997), 31–33.
[11] "A fragment, like a miniature work of art, has to be entirely isolated from the surrounding world and be complete in itself like a porcupine [hedgehog]." Friedrich Schlegel, *Friedrich Schlegel's "Lucinde" and the "Fragments"* (Minneapolis: University of Minnesota Press, 1971), 189.
[12] The distinction between the aphorism and the fragment is difficult to demarcate clearly, especially in the Jena School, which drew upon the use of the aphorism in eighteenth-century writings and transformed the form to something more befitting its conception of the fragment. On the relationship between aphorism and fragment at this time, see Susini-Anastopoulos, *L'écriture fragmentaire*, 12–30 and Matthew Bell, "The Idea of Fragmentariness in German Literature and Philosophy, 1760–1800," *Modern Language Review* 89 (1994), 372–92.

This chapter examines what happens to the rhetoric of the fragment during the late twentieth and early twenty-first centuries. It looks at how a group of artists have conceived the fragmentary, including the writer Maurice Blanchot and several late modernist composers. In both criticism and fiction, the former produced one of the most far-reaching theoretical accounts of the fragment. His writings have much to say about the potential of the fragment and its place in late twentieth-century arts, and they prove a rich resource upon which to draw for a discussion of late modernist music. With his writings in mind, we can move on to analyses of two of the most important fragmentary works of the twentieth century, Nono's *Fragmente-Stille, An Diotima* and Kurtág's *Kafka Fragments*.

Beginning in the 1960s, Blanchot pursued what he called fragmentary writing. The style of the prose and its theoretical bearings offered a reconception of the fragment. Two of the most distinctive ideas put forward in Blanchot's works are the emphasis on collectivity and the relationship between the fragment and the whole. Blanchot's collections of fragments establish a new aesthetic experience, one that moves beyond (a crucial word for Blanchot) both traditional notions of the fragment and values of unity, system, and totality.

Blanchot has specific views as to what a fragment is. First, it is not an aphorism, a terse, self-contained expression of thought. He rejected the equation between fragment and aphorism made by Schlegel.[13] For Blanchot, the fragment is perpetually incomplete. As such, it gapes open to an endless range of meanings and contexts. Blanchot extols this expanse, holding it up as one of the most rewarding elements of the fragmentary. No wonder then that he vilifies the aphorism as a "violent" "force that limits and encloses."[14] Moreover, the fragment is not a remnant. It may appear broken and splintered, but it has not been chipped off from any existing original, at least none that we will ever find. He describes it as "a piece of meteor detached from an unknown sky and impossible to connect with anything that can be known."[15]

Blanchot may isolate the single fragment but he always places it in a collective. A fragment is never, or should never be, alone. It is characteristically part of a larger field. Blanchot refers to the field in several ways, the two most frequent being "the fragmentary" or "fragmentary writing." He

[13] Blanchot, *The Infinite Conversation*, trans. Susan Hanson (Minneapolis: University of Minnesota Press, 1993), 351–59. For a discussion of changing conceptions of the fragment from the nineteenth century to the twentieth, see Timothy Clark, "Modern Transformations of German Romanticism: Blanchot and Derrida on the Fragment, the Aphorism, and the Architectural," *Paragraph* 15 (1992), 232–47.
[14] Blanchot, *The Infinite Conversation*, 152.   [15] Blanchot, *The Infinite Conversation*, 308.

also uses the phrase "fragmentary exigency." The demands of the field are broad. There are the creative forces that drive the curious writer to the new possibilities of the fragmentary, or, as Blanchot puts it, "thought seeking to escape the power of unity."[16] Once there, both writers and readers face the challenges posed by this unpredictable space. Blanchot never uses the word "state," but his conception of the fragmentary accords in many ways with the notion of compositional states developed here. Blanchot's fragmentary writing surges with energy and is ruled by specific structural dynamics. The forces originate in the inherent incompleteness of the fragment. The bits precipitously stop and trail off. One fragment doing so after another creates a relentless "energy of disappearing."[17] Incompletion also creates an overall "experience" of "discontinuity" and "separation."[18] Each ragged ending obstructs a sense of flow, what amounts to "the interruption of the incessant."[19] Or should we say incessant interruption, as all we ever experience are continuous breaks? With these incisive cuts, gaps emerge between the fragments, leaving them separated from one another. At the same time, the individual bits are not completely alone. The porous endings open up the fragments to an array of meanings, including those found in surrounding pieces. In this sense, fragments are "unfinished separations."[20]

The fragmentary is a realm ruled by dynamics of incompletion, separation, and discontinuity. As such, it stands apart from the whole, which, as used by Blanchot, is a philosophical concept for a totality premised upon esteemed epistemological ideals of unity and completion. For Blanchot, fragmentary writing is an assault on the whole. The fragment has long played that role for many philosophers and critics. Nietzsche, as cited approvingly by Blanchot, enlisted the fragment to "get rid of the whole – to shatter the universe."[21] For Nietzsche and others, the fragment represents the antithesis of the whole. Adorno succinctly described the fragment as "that part of the totality of the work that opposes totality."[22] Blanchot rejected an oppositional approach. He places the fragmentary "beyond" the possibility of a whole.[23] He sets it apart from the valued terms of completion and cohesion comprising the whole as well as the opposing-yet-related concepts of incompletion and separation. The fragment is not merely incomplete. How

---

[16] Blanchot, *The Infinite Conversation*, 350.
[17] Blanchot, *The Writing of the Disaster*, trans. Ann Smock (Lincoln: University of Nebraska Press, 1986), 61.
[18] Blanchot, *The Infinite Conversation*, 308.
[19] Blanchot, *The Writing of the Disaster*, 21.   [20] Blanchot, *The Writing of the Disaster*, 58.
[21] "It seems to me important that we should get rid of the Whole, of Unity; . . . we must shatter the universe." Quoted in Blanchot, *The Infinite Conversation*, 152.
[22] Adorno, *Aesthetic Theory*, 45.
[23] Hans-Jost Frey also resists oppositional thinking. As mentioned in note 8, he claims that "the fragment is neither a whole nor a part." Frey, *Interruptions*, 26.

can it be when there is no sense of completion with which to compare it in this realm? At the same time, it is not separated, as it is not detached from any known thing and furthermore cannot be connected to anything. Instead of incompletion and separation, there are "effects" of those qualities.[24] A world of effects, one lying beyond engrained concepts, is hard to imagine, let alone to attain. Blanchot realized as much. As he pointed out, we can never fully escape the whole as we, like Nietzsche, are forever conditioned by its ideals. Even within the deepest disarray of the fragmentary, we "turn toward a still absent unity."[25]

Blanchot's explorations of the dynamics of fragmentary writing offer much to draw upon in discussing the inquiry into the compositional state of the fragmentary. His writings, though, have little to contribute to a study of the inquiry into the act of expression, which intersects with that into the compositional state. Throughout his critical writings, Blanchot reveals a space untouched by expressive forces, or, to be more exact, a space untouched by the subject, the figure who makes expressive utterances. So scattered is the fragmentary that no "I" can form there. The space demands the "complete diffusion of the subject position."[26] Amid this dispersion, Blanchot introduces the neuter. As described by Lycette Nelson, "the essential feature of the neuter in Blanchot's overall critique of the idea of presences as all is its displacement of the subject as the locus of self-presence. Beginning from the neuter, Blanchot displaces first the subject, then identity in general, and finally the present itself."[27]

Contrary to Blanchot's theoretical visions, compositions occupying the musical fragmentary insist upon both the locus of the subject and the act of expression. The works are absorbed in the act, drawing upon the state as a way of intensifying it. That the urge to express has taken root here should come as no surprise. As with the border between sound and silence, expression has been pushed to, or found refuge in, an extreme space. Late modernist music once again declares that these spaces are the only ones left in which to make expressive utterances, so corrupted and hollowed out have more traditional forms and genres become.

To explore the role of expression in the fragmentary, we need to call upon a figure that has often been invoked in both modernist and postmodernist criticism: the fragmentary subject. As depicted in modernist criticism, the

---

[24] Blanchot, *The Step Not Beyond*, trans. Lycette Nelson (Albany: State University of New York Press, 1992), 49.

[25] Blanchot, *The Infinite Conversation*, 153.

[26] Stephen Barker, "Nietzsche/Derrida, Blanchot/Beckett: Fragmentary Progressions of the Unnamable," *Postmodern Culture* 6, no. 1 (1995) (electronic journal).

[27] Blanchot, *The Step Not Beyond*, ix.

figure by itself is expressive, the embodiment of the crushing strains of modern life. Moreover, the expressive utterances of the figure emerge as isolated, incomplete shards, which can no longer form a whole.[28] Different lines of postmodern criticism, on the other hand, consider the figure to be neither expressive nor capable of expression. The subject has become the byproduct of an irrevocably shattered cultural environment, existing in pieces with little expressive depth.[29]

This chapter not surprisingly sides with those interpretations upholding the expressive dimensions of the fragmented subject. Yet it once again takes a contrasting approach. Most accounts focus on the subject, describing the forces that fracture it and how the broken figure relates to the surrounding world. This study begins with the fragments, and asks what happens to the subject and its expressive utterances within the space of the lone fragment and across the broad realm of the fragmentary. Fragments, as used by many late modernist composers, hold intense bursts of emotions. How these emotions play out in such cramped spaces is a question that has been barely raised. Of particular interest are the enigmatic endings, at once a sudden closure and an open sprawl. What happens to the expressive utterance at that point? Is it instantly terminated or does it waft into other spaces? Moreover, fragments come in bunches, which stirs another question: how do the utterances in the individual fragments relate or not relate to one another. As with the border between sound and silence, the fragmentary offers us a chance to see how the act of expression fares in a particular space, one that threatens it but which can also enhance it.

Nono

In a talk given before the 1980 premiere of *Fragmente-Stille, An Diotima* by the LaSalle Quartet in Bonn, Nono spent a considerable amount of time explaining what fragments are and what they do.[30] It was an explanation he had made several times before, to the performers and to himself. The need for the commentary emphasizes how challenging the fragmentary realm created by Nono was at the time, and continues to be. As described in Chapter 2, the work consists of a rush of both musical and textual fragments,

---

[28] In particular see Adorno's *Philosophy of New Music*. The fragmented subject also plays a role in the early criticism of Lukács. He presents the surrounding social world as fragmented. As it breaks down so too does the subject occupying it. Georg Lukács, *The Theory of the Novel*, trans. Anna Bostock (Cambridge, MA: MIT Press, 1971), 53.

[29] Jameson, *Postmodernism*, 1–54.

[30] "Luigi Nono: Streichquartett *Fragmente-Stille, An Diotima*," in *Luigi Nono: Dokumente, Materialien*, ed. Andreas Wagner (Saarbrücken: Pfau, 2003), 156–67.

the latter taken from poems by Hölderlin.[31] To explore this realm, we will begin with Nono's various explanations, as found in the opening-night address, letters, and notes from his sketches.

At some point during the long gestation of the quartet, Nono felt the need to write down what he considered to be defining characteristics of fragments. His jottings take the form of a list.[32] At the top of the slate is the exclamation "Fragments Not Aphoristic!!!" He immediately clarifies the point with the observation "always open." Like Blanchot, the composer rails against the idea of the self-contained fragment, impounded within its minuscule dimensions – a fate suffered by the aphorism. The idea of openness was elaborated upon in the later comments he made about the completed piece. Nono told the premiere audience that fragments "do not reach an end."[33] In a letter to Hans-Jürgen Nagel, leader of the Beethoven Festival in Bonn, the composer, focusing on the Hölderlin excerpts, added that once freed from the original succession of words from which they come, fragments can take on qualities of the "infinite," as they welcome a host of possible meanings. In the same letter, fragments are described as "moments."[34] The latter conception is not present in the sketch list, but it comes to the fore in subsequent commentary. Writing to the LaSalle Quartet, Nono refers to fragments as "flashes" (Blitze).[35] For the Bonn audience, they are "moments" of "potential" and "possibilities."[36] The last formulation brings out the contradictory essence of the fragment. The bits are at once "moments" and "flashes" and a threshold to "infinite" meanings and limitless "potential" and "possibilities."[37]

---

[31] In an earlier conception of the piece, Nono had decided to use fragments taken from the diaries of Franz Kafka. As described in one sketch, the work was to consist of two large sections, each of which would divide into three subsections. For the first section, Nono labels the subsections A–C, which in order are linked with the following fragments: "Oggi ho sognato," "Oltre a ciò sognai," and "Poi sogna" (all three lines are taken from the diary entry of October 28, 1911). The second large section is entitled "Malor me bat," the title of the Renaissance chanson discussed in Chapter 2. It has three Kafka fragments associated with it: "Sogno sul mattino" (November 24, 1913), "Sogno" (November 21, 1913), and "Soltanto sogni, niente sonno" (July 21, 1913). It is unclear from the sketches how these lines would fit into the overall form. The first two are crossed out. The marking of the third suggests that it could be either a separate large unit or a smaller section of the second large unit. The sketch reveals that the earlier conception of the work was not as fragmentary as the final version. It has longer, more extended sections (fitting into an estimated twenty minutes of music according to the annotations) and only a few textual headings compared to the forty some headings resting above over fifty smaller sections (as demarcated in the score). Archivio Luigi Nono, Venice, Folio 44.04.01/01vDx.
[32] This page is from the sketch materials for the work at the Archivio Luigi Nono, 44.04.03/12.
[33] "Nono: Streichquartett *Fragmente-Stille, An Diotima*," 159.
[34] Nono, *Scritti e colloqui*, ed. Angela Ida De Benedictis and Veniero Rizzardi, vol. I (Lucca: Ricordi, 2001), 485.
[35] Archivio Luigi Nono, 44.32/08rDx.
[36] "Nono: Streichquartett *Fragmente-Stille, An Diotima*," 159.
[37] "Nono: Streichquartett *Fragmente-Stille, An Diotima*," 159.

Ex. 3.1 *Scala enigmatica*

Turning to *Fragmente-Stille, An Diotima*, the paradox plays out in various ways. Moments of a particular sound, style, or effect are all we ever hear before a fragment is severed. The jarring endings of many fragments escalate a sense of interruption and discontinuity. At the same time, the fragment, as described by both Nono and Blanchot, pours open. Even the briefest piece lingers in the ear and mind, sustained by an intriguing timbral or harmonic ambiguity. Some fragments merge with a closing extended silence, creating the impression of having entered a vast, unknown realm. To recall, silence, so intimately coupled with fragments in the work, similarly partakes in paradox. It too can be "infinite" as well as fleeting.

Nono also addresses how fragments interact with one another. In the preliminary list drawn up in the sketches, he specifies "no development, but succession and prolification."[38] The phrase could serve as a modus operandi for the fragmentary. In lieu of the deliberate, incremental progress characteristic of development, fragments multiply. "Prolification" captures the sense of spontaneous, abundant growth spawned by the "succession" of fragments. The growth, though, may be more controlled – dare we say developed? – than Nono's phrase leads us to believe. Speaking to the Bonn audience, the composer mentions how the *scala enigmatica* from the Ave Maria of Verdi's *Quattro pezzi sacri* serves as "Grundmaterial" for the work (Ex. 3.1).[39] Specific intervals drawn from it, particularly the tritone, appear prominently in the fragments, linking one to another. Not only do intervals return but so do whole phrases, sometimes even whole fragments. There is much repetition in the work. We have already encountered two instances of it, the numerous returns of the high stillness and scrawl figures discussed in Chapter 2. As illustrated in those cases, the repetition is rarely exact; the returning material is altered in some way, usually timbrally or harmonically.

---

[38] The original reads "non svillupo, ma successione e prolificazione." The phrase connects to a drawing of four blocks with arrows going within and between the individual blocks, suggesting the swirling and connecting movement of fragments. Archivio Luigi Nono, 44.04.03/12.

[39] "Nono: Streichquartett *Fragmente-Stille, An Diotima*," 158. For a discussion of Nono's use of the scale, see Döpke, "Réflexions fragmentaires," 101–5; Linden, "*Luigi Nonos Weg zum Streichquartett*, 187–93; Spree, *Fragmente-Stille, An Diotima*," 27–32. Just as the Ockeghem quotation was a memorial to Maderna, the use of the Verdi scale is most likely a tribute to Nono's teacher Hermann Scherchen, with whom he studied the Verdi work. The sketches contain a brief note connecting the two men with those two works. Archivio Luigi Nono, folio 44.04.01/01vDx.

Whereas such changes fall short of the rigor and thoroughness implied by development, they do create lines of continuity and connection within the larger field of fragments. "Continuity and connection" is a plan of action that can be placed alongside that of "succession and proliferation." The two may seem at odds, but such tensions thrive in the fragmentary.

The topic of form has been much disputed in the scholarly literature on Nono's String Quartet. Regarding the structure of the piece, some critics place the work in Blanchot's "beyond." For them, there is no form of any kind nor any sweep of unity to bring the fragments together.[40] A few writers do point out an overall structure, albeit not any sort of traditional design. Herman Spree, for instance, sees the layout of fragments creating larger symmetrical patterns based around the numbers 7 and 11.[41] Martin Zenck takes an especially broad view, describing the form as the sum of the fragments.[42] The threads of continuity between the fragments have also become entangled in the scholarly debate. Almost every writer draws attention to the intervallic linkages provided by the *scala enigmatica* and the return of certain phrases; however, they differ over how much connective power the ties exert. Not surprisingly, scholars pursuing detailed analyses, like Spree and Werner Linden, have focused on these materials (particularly the scale and tritone) and seen them as forging cohesion within and between fragments.[43] Jurg Stenzl, on the other hand, holds that the fragments create "no strict linear progression from the first tone to the final chord, rather, an extremely fragile fabric that seems to be open in all directions and tends, time and again, towards a standstill."[44] Other writers acknowledge the connective materials but see them as overwhelmed by the divisiveness of the fragmentary. Guy Gosselin refers to elements of "internal cohesion" but qualifies that the fragments mask them, although with great difficulty.[45]

A different approach to issues of form and continuity can be gained by drawing inspiration from the individual fragment. It, to recall, embodies opposing tendencies, being at once momentary and infinite. In this sense, the single fragment serves as a microcosm of the larger field, which too

---

[40] Heinz-Klaus Metzger sees the "autonomous" fragments as precluding the possibility of synthesis or cohesion, whereas Wolfgang Rathert views the String Quartet as undermining the finality of closure and the seal of unity and completion that closure secures. Heinz-Klaus Metzger, "Wendepunkt Quartett?" in *Luigi Nono, Musik-Konzepte* 20 (1981), 109; Wolfgang Rathert, "Ende, Abschied und Fragment: Zu Ästhetik und Gechichte einer musikalischen Problemstellung," in *Abschied in die Gegenwart: Teleologie und Zustandlichkeit in der Musik*, ed. Otto Kolleritsch (Vienna: Universal Edition, 1998), 231–33.

[41] Spree, "*Fragmente-Stille, An Diotima*," 141.   [42] Zenck, "Dal niente," 21.

[43] Spree, "*Fragmente-Stille, An Diotima*"; Linden, *Luigi Nonos Weg zum Streichquartett*, 168–217.

[44] Quoted in Stäbler, "About Silence," 75.

[45] Gosselin, "Le silence," 86. Nicola Gess also upholds these elements but adds that they are not enough to create any sort of linear link or to diminish the overwhelming sense of dissimilarity bred by the fragments. Gess, "Dichtung und Musik," 26.

contains contradictions. The field responds to the tensions between the fragmentary and the whole, that is, the energy of discontinuity, disruption, and separation whipped up by the former and the push toward continuity and connection sustained by the latter. Both tendencies are active in Nono's String Quartet. The work does not move beyond the whole, as Blanchot envisions the fragmentary doing. It does, though, travel a distance from the ideal. Nonetheless, the dynamics of the whole – as forged by the intervallic linkages and repetitions of phrases – still operate in the piece. The forces are enough to give the whole a presence. For Nono the fragmentary, as a state, depends on that presence. It needs its antithesis to be active, not absent. Only then can the contradictions upon which the work builds emerge.

In talking to the audience in Bonn, Nono grew rapturous about contradictions. He quickly pushed past any musical and textual details and entertained larger questions of human existence. Fragments, according to him, reveal moments of "potential" in life. Such moments naturally assume countless forms, many of them contradictory. So strong and unique are the tensions between them that they can never be resolved, especially through, as he mentions, dialectical synthesis. For Nono, the challenge of life, and of works like the String Quartet, is to "develop" "different possibilities, potentials, strengths, or weak moments," which together "offer a multiplicity of thoughts, of life, of existence." Contradictions, in other words, are part of our lives. What is left for Nono, and for us, to do is to take them and to "develop" them "further."[46]

The String Quartet "develops" a range of tensions, ideas, and elements. As to be expected of a compositional state that exists in "multiplicity," the fragmentary provides numerous opportunities to explore such "possibilities." One pursuit is to expand upon the "potential" of individual fragments. As mentioned in Chapter 2, the repetitions of the high stillness and scrawl figures bring out the unique kinds of silence possessed by each one. The String Quartet also exacerbates tensions by using the lines of repetition to heighten the contradictions between the whole and the fragmentary, and between elements of continuity and discontinuity.

The second half of the work (figs. 26–51) features a series of markings placed beside the Hölderlin headings of certain fragments. So small and innocuous are they that they can easily go unnoticed, but that would be an unfortunate oversight for they point to lines of repetition. Through such orderings as A–F, I–III, α–γ, and 1–4, the markings tick off a series of connected passages. We will begin with the last of these groups, the sequence 1–4 (figs. 44, 47, 49, and 51/52). The four units in the group are not exact repetitions; rather, they restage an idea initiated in fig. 44 (Ex. 3.2). That

---

[46] "Nono: Streichquartett *Fragmente-Stille, An Diotima*," 159.

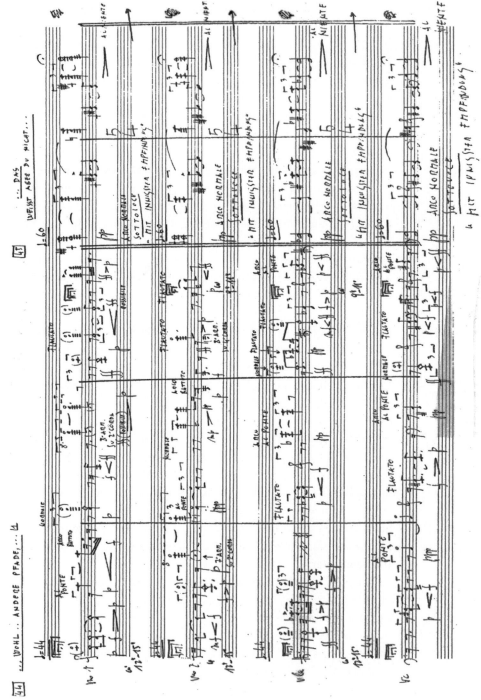

Ex. 3.2 Nono, *Fragmente-Stille, An Diotima*, fig. 44
© Copyright G. Ricordi. Reproduced by permission

figure explores sudden shifts in register. Each of the quartet lines states a single pitch or tritone interval and bounces it between different octaves.[47] In the following three units, the pitch material broadens as pitches are raised a half step (fig. 49) and more outside pitches are introduced (particularly in the viola and cello). The basic plan of leaping between registers, though, holds. The jumps, combined with mercurial changes in bowing techniques and dynamics, create a kaleidoscopic soundworld.

Across the four units, a larger shape emerges. The first figure begins sparsely with the fundamental pitches and intervals. The second, third, and the beginning of the fourth expand and agitate the mix. The end of the fourth unit, which serves as the end of the String Quartet (figs. 51–52), winnows things down to an especially sparse point. The parts return to some of the original material, except for the viola, which now plays the tritone c-f♯ in different octaves (the cello's interval previously), and the cello, which surprisingly plays a perfect fourth (d-g), the last sound in the piece. During this stretch, the relentless octave shifting relaxes. Taking all four units together, a conventional pattern emerges: a block of independent lines grows more dense and agitated, builds to a climax, and then calms down. The pattern conveys a whole, as it has a clear beginning, goal, and end, with each fragment fitting into a certain spot in the design. The sense of conclusion is particularly strong, as the parts, after returning to the original elements, drop out one by one.[48] Nono may have placed the design here to give weight to the ending of the String Quartet. Not much weight, though, as the tension between the whole and the fragmentary undermines the conclusion. Even with the final taper, we still have the open and ambiguous close of a fragment, particularly the unexpected move from the pervasive tritone to a perfect fourth in the concluding cello line. Moreover, the flowing design created by the four passages is interrupted by other fragments, making it hard to hear the overall shape. The growing contradiction between continuity and disruption appropriately reaches a high point at the end of the work. One group of fragments offers what is perhaps the most cohesive and conclusive structure in the work only to have it taken apart by the unsettling force of the fragmentary.

Three other marked sequences appear before the final 1–4 group: A–F (figs. 33, 35, 37, and 39); I–III (figs. 39 and 40); and α–γ (figs. 40 and 42). Unlike the sequence described above, these markings refer to both the Hölderlin fragments and the music. In particular, they point back to the

---

[47] These passages are discussed in detail in Spree, "*Fragmente-Stille, An Diotima*," 125–32.
[48] A similar gesture occurs near the end of the first half of the work with the final statement of the high stillness passage (fig. 24).

poems from which the bits of text were excised. The lines in the A–F group come from "Die Eichbäume"; those in I–III, "Emile vor ihrem Brauttag"; and those in α–γ, "Diotima."[49] Nono is once again looking to a whole, the poems from which the lines were chipped off. It might be more accurate to say that Nono is looking back to a whole. The glance back is not made out of any attempt to reassemble the pieces and make the poems complete again but rather to see what they have become, works ripped apart by the force of the fragmentary. With the Hölderlin poems, the whole is evoked, but now as a site of loss.

The three groups also repeat and extend musical elements.[50] The A–F sequence restates a collection of chords (one of which is taken from fig. 26); the I–III group recalls phrases from fig. 26; and the α–γ chain turns to the tritone-infused lines first heard in figs. 19 and 21.[51] The sequences unfold during a stretch that could be called the hot spot of the fragmentary (figs. 33–45). Disruptions come fast and furious here. One fragment no sooner sounds than another one replaces it. At the same time, though, we have three marked streams of repetition, which, along with other recurring phrases and the pervasive tritone interval, create lines of continuity and suggest a whole. The contradiction between continuity and disruption intensifies. It might all sound like discontinuity, but that is the result of another way that Nono has "developed" the contradiction. Throughout this stretch, the brief moments of connection are severed by other fragments, which are often part of a separate chain. One line of continuity breaks off another line, or, befitting the paradoxes of the fragmentary, continuity becomes discontinuity.

Another point of exploration taken up by the String Quartet is that into the act of expression. Chapter 2 discussed how the work situates the act within the borderland of silence. True to its to-the-point title, the piece also has the act play out in a realm of fragments. In both cases, feelings of diminishment and loss ensue. With the former inquiry, the expressive utterance falls into either the void of silence or the redoubt of inner song. The repetitions within the fragmentary hollow out the utterance, even erase it. Both inquiries concentrate on the sections marked with the score direction "mit innigster Empfindung" taken from Beethoven.

---

[49] The numbers 1–4 mentioned above come from three different poems: "Wohl geh ich täglich" (fig. 44), "Emilie an Klara" (figs. 47 and 51), and "An Diotima" (fig. 49).

[50] The combination of a specific musical passage with fragments drawn from a single poem invites further questions about the text/music relationships in the work; however, there are no apparent answers as to why a certain passage is linked with a specific poem.

[51] In the A–F group, the chord is a cluster covering the pitch classes c–e with microtonal alterations, particularly to the framing major third. The chord first appears as part of a phrase in fig. 26 (chord number 4) and is isolated in fig. 27.

The citation calls to mind Adorno's comments on Beethoven's late fragmentary works. It is worth briefly considering Adorno's observations because he too makes a link between the fragmentary and expression, but connects the two in contrasting ways to Nono. The "force of subjectivity," according to Adorno, "bursts" Beethoven's compositions "asunder," leaving behind a field of fragments. The remaining pieces preserve bits of conventional gestures, which are so hardened as to be impervious to the blast of subjectivity. The subject exists within the emptiness between fragments, "the space it has violently vacated."[52] Nono's work also contains fissures and pockets, but, contrary to Adorno, both the gaps and the fragments harbor the subject. Chapter 2 described how the silent spaces at the end of and between fragments serve as an entrance to a reflective interiority. As discussed below, the "mit innigster Empfindung" passages also convey the presence of the subject.

By itself, the score direction suggests a figure of expressive depth. The third movement of Beethoven's String Quartet no. 15 creates that impression, as the marking appears at the end of the convalescent's impassioned song of thanksgiving. Nono's String Quartet sets no such detailed scene. The borrowed direction, though, similarly enhances moments in which there appears to be a voice expressing some deep sentiment. In fig. 26 (Ex. 2.7), the impression of a voice is created through several means, including the exclusive use of a homophonic texture (the only extended stretch in the work so far) and lyrical phrases produced by normal bowing techniques in contrast to the whirring and crinkling sounds heard earlier. Similar means are used later in another voice-like fragment, the one containing the "Malheur me bat" quotation (Ex. 2.6). The deep emotion being called upon is not exactly clear, but the lyricism of the passage conveys reflection and wistfulness.

The presence of the subject is also suggested by the structure of the fragment. The passage reveals a design, instead of twitching pitches and sounds. Across the first five measures, it consists of four distinct phrases with ascending and descending shapes.[53] The phrases can be heard as shaping two different structures. The first is what can loosely be called a period. There are obviously no cadential points of definition as found in the traditional form, but the passage does have two balanced complementary halves. The "antecedent" begins with an ascending/descending phrase (including the

---

[52] Theodor Adorno, *Beethoven: The Philosophy of Music*, ed. Rolf Tiedemann, trans. Edmund Jephcott (Stanford University Press, 1998), 125–26.

[53] The repeated chord in the sixth measure is not considered here, as it does not reappear in the repetitions of the figure. It has more of a local function in fig. 26, setting up the three repeated chords that begin the next fragment.

lone chord in the first measure), followed by an ascending one, whereas the "consequent" responds with a descending phrase and concludes with a curvilinear one. Another way of approaching the passage is as a palindrome. As seen in the annotated chord numbers (explained below), the five bars break down into two parts, mm. 1–3 and 4–5, which are framed by the same chord (number 1). Another identical chord (number 3) marks the end of the first half and the beginning of the second. The sequence of chords in between, though, is not exactly symmetrical. The two parts are almost the same length, eight chords in the first and nine in the second.[54] Behind both designs can be heard the workings of the subject, a presence that not only has found a new lyricism to impart innermost feelings but also crafts a specific way of shaping the lyrical utterance.

Material from the fragment returns nine times, a significant amount even in a work that restates so many shards. Such extensive repetition does not come as a surprise. Deep emotions are rarely proclaimed once and then forgotten. They press; they demand – all of which leads them to reappear frequently and often in different guises. In nineteenth-century Romanticism, this insistence typically follows the scenario of an emotionally infused theme becoming more intense and expansive up until the climax of a movement. Beethoven's "mit innigster Empfindung" music in his own string quartet is no exception. The direction appears in the third and final statement of the opening theme, by which time the theme has not only reached a new emotional intensity but has also broadened melodically and rhythmically from the first statement.

Nono sets a very different course, or courses. In the work, he uses two different ways of repeating the "mit innigster Empfindung" material, both of which, though, lead to the same outcome. The first is a rather traditional gesture in which a theme, like a spoken emotional utterance, frequently reappears, each time in an altered form. In Nono's String Quartet, five repetitions adhere to this approach. The passages (figs. 34, 36, 38, 43, 45) are all marked with the Beethoven direction and fall under the same Hölderlin heading ("das weisst aber du nicht"). In these fragments, Nono draws upon chords from the original statement in fig. 26 which, upon closer examination, consists of four chords repeated with variations (Ex. 2.7). To be more precise, there are only two basic harmonies. The first and third chords are built upon microtonal pitch classes spanning from e to b quarter-tone flat, whereas the second and fourth chords feature microtonal clusters built around pitch classes from c quarter-tone flat or c to e quarter-tone sharp

---

[54] Symmetrical aspects are also touched upon in Döpke, "Réflexions fragmentaires," 103–5 and Linden, *Luigi Nonos Weg zum Streichquartett*, 213.

Ex. 3.3 Chords of Nono, *Fragmente-Stille, An Diotima*, fig. 26

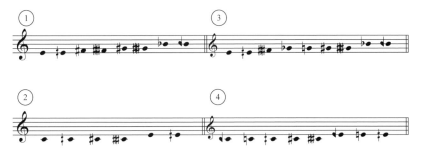

(Ex. 3.3).[55] In the subsequent repetitions, Nono features only the first and third chords, which, in terms of pitch materials, are essentially the same chord. The sonorities in the repetitions are varied in terms of transposition, voicing, and the inclusion of additional pitches. Even with these changes, there is a sense of loss as the full harmonic palette of four chords has been reduced to two, which can be heard as one and the same chord. The multi-phrase design of the original is also gone. In each passage, Nono beads together two to five chords to form a single phrase. The one phrase we are left with skews the contours of the original into abrupt ascents and descents, some between remote registers. The alterations squelch the lyricism first stirred by the call "mit innigster Empfindung."

The course laid down by the repetition of these emotionally charged fragments is one of diminishment. Such an outcome is not a surprise in the astringent, disruptive world of the fragmentary. We could hardly expect the effusive expansion heard in the Beethoven string quartet. Nonetheless, the severity of the diminishment is striking. So much is gone in terms of form, harmony, and lyricism. The deep emotions, though, remain deep – the Beethoven direction has not lost its influence. However, the emotions, always ambiguous, appear to have changed. The fragments now speak of loss, a sentiment surpassing the wistfulness evoked by the original statement.

The second way of repeating the chords and phrases from fig. 26 is through reminiscence. Innermost emotions do not have to be voiced anew every time one turns to them. They can instead be recalled, a look back to a rich expressive moment. Nono states the four individual phrases from fig. 26, separating each of them by groups of other fragments. The phrases are stated exactly, not altered in any way. That is, with one exception: Nono

---

[55] Spree also sees the passage as based upon two "Grundklänge," which are similar to the two basic harmonies pointed out here. Spree relates the two harmonies to the *scala enigmatica*. Spree, "*Fragmente-Stille, An Diotima*," 93.

Ex. 3.4 Nono, *Fragmente-Stille, An Diotima*, fig. 50

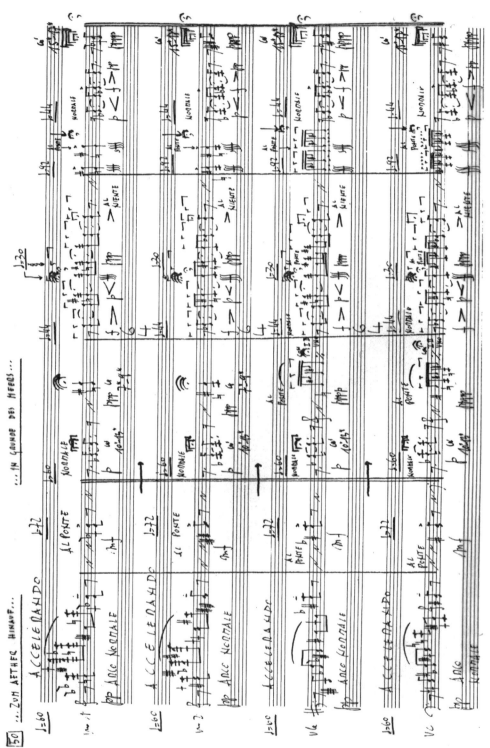

removes the direction "mit innigster Empfindung."[56] The phrases return but now absent the call to infuse them with strong feelings. Without the plea, they become pale memories of a past utterance.

We have already encountered three of the repetitions, the ones marked I–III (figs. 39–40). They state in order the first, third, and second phrases. The fourth is held off until much later (fig. 50, but Nono does not mark it as IV). Some of the repeated groups elaborate upon materials to fuel a sense of forward motion. The repetition in the 1–4 sequence, as described above, leads to the formulation of a whole, though one that never fully comes together. The I–III group, in contrast, does not expand upon the original material nor does it build up any momentum, let alone create a whole. Instead we look back to fig. 26, which has become a broken whole. Indeed, in the original statement, that passage, being relatively self-contained and shaped by an internal structure, comes close to evoking a whole, more so than almost any other single fragment. The structure has now been splintered, and the passage emerges as a series of disjointed bits, just like the other fragments. The scraps of fig. 26, though, are different for they speak of something that once was; something that can only be remembered; something that has become an object of loss.

The loss is complete by the time we get to the statement of the fourth phrase (fig. 50), the last we hear of the "mit innigster Empfindung" music (Ex. 3.4). By this point, both reminiscence and varied restatements have failed to restore the emotional or melodic breadth of the original passage. After the fourth phrase, however, the possibility of such a return arises. The opening chord of fig. 26 reappears to mark the beginning and end of a new segment (the last four bars of fig. 50). As in fig. 26, it functions as the outer poles of an arch form; however, the music between the two points in fig. 50 could not be more different from that in the previous fragment. We return to the "other" lyrical music in the String Quartet, that heard at the beginning of the work. This music emphasizes tritones and augmented octaves, stated without much of the microtonal inflections typical of the fragment in fig. 26. The two lyrical passages (figs. 26 and 50) share one thing in common: symmetry. The "mit innigster Empfindung" passage (fig. 26) almost erected a palindrome. The new passage in fig. 50 completes the form, laying down a symmetrical series of chords, if not rhythms and dynamics, between the two framing harmonies. The raising of an arch form, especially one with the same endpoints, underscores the diminishment of the "mit innigster Empfindung" passage. In a space where it once stood and in design that it

---

[56] In the fourth phrase (fig. 50), the "sotto voce" marking is also removed.

came close to achieving, there is now nothing of the original material. The call for deepest feelings and the music responding to it have vanished.

In the sketches of the String Quartet, Nono called the final two fragments (figs. 50 and 51) a "finale."[57] Such a conclusive structural moment seems out of place in the evanescent world of the fragmentary. Yet the two sections possess weight. The final fragment, to recall, announces the end of the work by having the instruments drop out one by one until only the cello plays. The preceding one (fig. 50) marks a different type of ending – the last breath of the "mit innigster Empfindung" music. The latter outcome is not surprising. From the beginning, the act of expression has been depicted as short-lived. The individual fragment may provide a refuge for deep feelings, but it is only a transient space, and the expressive utterance will end when the fragment collapses. The fate of the utterance within the lone fragment is the same as that across the realm of the fragmentary. Instead of reinforcing the "mit innigster Empfindung" passage, the repetitions efface it. Each one diminishes the original utterance; each one takes a step toward its final depletion. Nono's String Quartet offers an idea of how the act of expression fares in the fragmentary, an experience of emotional intensity giving way to disintegration and loss.

Kurtág

In an essay on Kafka, Adorno describes the difficulties of the critic in peering into the author's fictional worlds. He also describes the impossibility of Kafka's characters peering outside their own worlds. They are "windowless monads," driven by a relentless "inwardness" to a "hermetic" existence.[58] With those characters, Adorno finds yet another case of the modernist subject, a being alienated from the surrounding social sphere. Kurtág draws upon the idea of separation in his *Kafka Fragments* (op. 24, 1985–86). As the title makes clear, he evokes another facet of the modernist subject – fragmentation, an aspect that Adorno surprisingly does not bring to the fore in his essay. Kurtág tightly pairs the two qualities. They shape the subject as unveiled in the work. Moreover, separation is a central dynamic in creating the state of the fragmentary in the piece.

Kafka Fragments, scored for soprano and violin, consists of forty individual movements, or fragments, each of which sets a text by the Czech writer. The fragments range from the minuscule, around twelve seconds in length, to relatively long pieces, some approaching seven minutes. They are

57 Archivio Luigi Nono, 44.23/19vdx.
58 Theodor Adorno, *Prisms*, trans. Samuel and Shierry Weber (London: Neville Spearman, 1967), 252, 261.

Ex. 3.5a Descending motive, Kurtág, *Kafka Fragments*, "Elendes Leben" (double)
© Copyright Editio Musica, Budapest. Reproduced by permission

Ex. 3.5b Descending motive, Kurtág, *Kafka Fragments*, "Eine lange Geschichte"
© Copyright Editio Musica, Budapest. Reproduced by permission

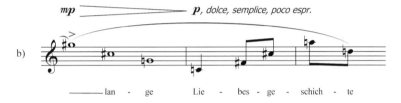

demarcated as individual movements in contrast to the ceaseless flow of
fragments in Nono's String Quartet. The texts come from a diverse group
of Kafka's writings, including diary entries, letters, and stray bits compiled
into posthumous collections.[59] Ripping them from the original sources and
depriving them of any surrounding context, Kurtág presses them into the
service of the fragmentary.

    A succession of vocal movements based on texts by a single author calls
to mind a song cycle. In other words, there could be a whole, the coherence
provided by a genre, to tie together the fragments; or, to be more accurate,
a whole for the fragments to tear apart. The dynamics of separation are so
strong that they interfere with any push toward unity, especially the continuity of a song cycle. Typical of the genre, there are recurring motives between
the movements. For instance, a descending motive appears in some of the
fragments, including the number "Eine lange Geschichte" discussed below
(Ex. 3.5a and 3.5b). It pushes down through the intervals of a perfect fourth,

[59] The sources for the individual fragments can be found in Stephen Blum, "Kurtág's Articulation
      of Kafka's Rhythms," *Studia Musicologica Academiae Scientiarium Hungaricae* 43 (2002), 347–
      48. For discussions of individual fragments and how the work fits into the composer's oeuvre, see
      Klaus Kirchberg, "Bruchstücke einer Konfession: György Kurtág und seine Kafka-Fragmente,"
      Neue Zeitschrift für Musik 149, no. 1 (1988), 23–27, and Rachel Beckles Willson, *Ligeti, Kurtág,
      and Hungarian Music during the Cold War* (Cambridge University Press, 2007), 210–15.

tritone, or perfect fifth.[60] The motive sets off salient words and images but does not appear frequently enough to bind together all forty fragments. It is hard to imagine any motive being tensile enough to unite such a disparate collection. Like Nono, Kurtág keeps up the presence of a whole, if only to undermine it. Whereas Nono's String Quartet emphasizes specific intervals and fans out lines of connection to create a tension between continuity and discontinuity, Kurtág's work plays up dynamics of separation.

The texts selected by Kurtág widen the divide between movements. Unlike in most song cycles, no narrative runs between the individual movements. Nor is there a consistent first-person voice to guide us through the fragments. An "I" does appear, but only here and there and often so sketchily as to make us wonder if it is the same person. The texts in the work, like those in a cycle, do return to certain themes; however, even here the piece affronts the genre. Two main themes are, of all things, separation and fragmentation.[61] Several of the texts deal with the isolation found in contained spaces, be it hiding places, prison cells, or the emotional armor protecting oneself.[62] Many fragments elaborate upon the idea of paths, an image that holds out the hope of connecting distant points, or, as here, fragments.[63] As to be expected, the paths are either covered or difficult to traverse.[64] Adding to the sense of detachment is the different forms of the fragments selected by Kurtág. There are a range of types, including aphorisms, emotional outbursts, fleeting scenes, and excerpts so vague and brief that they could only be called fragments. In his writings, Blanchot similarly scrambled together different kinds of fragments, which contrast in terms of genre (fiction, philosophy, and theory) and tone. The diversity obstructs the continuity from one fragment to the next, as the reader, or the listener in the case of Kurtág, never knows what to expect next. The changes in style also further isolate the individual fragment, which becomes a single type of piece in a larger cluster of different types.

To be alone among so many lonely people is a predicament explored by Kafka. What is so remarkable about his work is the different ways in which he stages isolation. His characters are not just the cliché single figure in the urban hive; rather, each inhabits a unique type of loneliness. The uniqueness

---

[60] The motive can also be followed by an ascending pattern based on the same intervals, as seen in Ex. 3.5b. Examples of the motive can be found in, among other movements, "Es zupfte mich jemand am Kleid" (I/8), "Sonntag, den 19. Juli 1910" (1/11), "Stolz" (I/17), "Elendes Leben (Double)" (III/5), and "Zu spät" (IV/1).

[61] István Balázs mentions the theme of "ars poetica," the process and ordeals of artistic creation. Balázs, "But, chemin, hésitation," in *György Kurtág: Entretiens, textes, écrits sur son oeuvre* (Geneva: Contrechamps, 1995), 179.

[62] See fragments I/3, I/14, and III/3.

[63] See fragments I/2, I/3, II/1, III/7, III/8, III/9.   [64] In III/8, the path can reach a distant point.

emerges from the degree to which the characters are set apart and how they respond to that solitude, some seeking to withdraw further, others to reach out. Among the group: a man trapped on the other side of the insect/human divide and imagining himself as part of his human family's domestic life before finally accepting his seclusion on the other side; a man so solitary that he fights the urge to look outside the window; and a "hunger artist" who retreats into himself through starvation and in doing so attracts crowds of admirers.[65]

As with Kafka's characters, in Kurtág's work we can ask how each fragment is set apart and how much it is removed from the others. These are novel questions to pose, as most accounts of fragmentary works begin by asking how connected the different pieces are, not how separated they are. The routine questions, as Blanchot would suggest, betray our allegiance to the whole and to the values of unity. *Kafka Fragments* compels us to shake off critical habit and focus on what can be called the force of separation. Consistent with the duality of the fragmentary, the impulse closes off fragments but never completely, as the conclusions keep them both distinct from and open to each other. Many of the Kafka texts deal with the force of separation, which is characteristically presented in diverse ways. The settings pick up on these ways and work with and against them to various effects. To explore this variety, we will focus on two different kinds of fragments: the aphorism and the emotional outburst. They are arguably the two most contrasting types: the former a crystallization of wisdom, the latter a splurge of feeling.

The first type, the aphorism, is akin to the maxim, a phrase held up as a general truth or witty observation. Blanchot, to recall, exiled the aphorism from the fragmentary, a realm in which the terse phrases would seem to flourish. To him, the aphorism is self-contained rather than being porous like a true fragment. It is also enamored with the completion and self-sufficiency of the whole. Like a fragment, it seeks separation, but, in its case, the response is to separate altogether, or to roll up like a hedgehog as Schlegel put it. In Kafka's texts, we can hear the speaker of the aphorism trying to escape the surrounding disarray and confusion and to withdraw into a supposedly unbreakable sphere of wisdom. In that space, there are no contrary voices to disturb either the speaker or the wholeness of the aphorism.

Through the soprano and violin parts, Kurtág gives us both the speaker's voice and the contrary ones. The relationship between the two parts takes different forms throughout *Kafka Fragments*. With the aphorism, there is a dialogue between the two, as opposed to the more melody-and-accompaniment type of relationship heard in the majority of

---

[65] See the stories "The Metamorphosis," "The Street Window," and "A Hunger Artist."

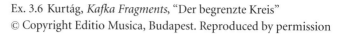

Ex. 3.6 Kurtág, *Kafka Fragments*, "Der begrenzte Kreis"
© Copyright Editio Musica, Budapest. Reproduced by permission

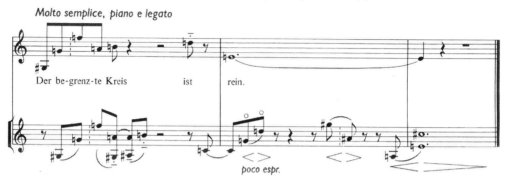

movements. The dialogue usually involves the two working out some sort of scheme that focuses on the truth put forth by the aphorism. Through the scheme, they can either validate the bit of wisdom or, more often than not, upend it.

The confounded aphorism is of particular interest. A good example can be found in the movement built around the short sentence "The closed circle is pure" ("Der begrenzte Kreis," III/6, Ex. 3.6).[66] Once again something closes itself off, with the circle being undoubtedly more tight and impregnable than a hedgehog. The text reiterates a long-held view of the circle as the most perfect shape, a perfection giving it a sense of purity.[67] To complement the venerable shape, Kurtág calls upon the one classic circle at a composer's disposal: the circle of fifths. He not only rounds it fifth by fifth but also takes the points along the curve, the twelve chromatic pitches, and arranges them into new groups, specifically clusters. Both approaches share one aim: to complete the chromatic, which in turn will close the circle, thus making it pure. The circle of fifths and clusters are joined by two other recognizable musical types: the canon and the triad. All four bear strong associations and through them create the double focus typical of the fragment. On

---

[66] "Der begrenzte Kreis ist rein." I have used the English translation by Júlia and Peter Sherwood from the published score of the work: *Kafka-Fragmente* (Budapest: Editio Musica Budapest, 1992). For a different interpretation of the work, see Arnold Whittall, "Plotting the Path, Prolonging the Moment," *Contemporary Music Review* 20, nos. 2 and 3 (2001): 96–97. Kurtág emphasized the logical quality of the text when he associated it with Eusebius in his *Hommage à R. Sch.* (1990), which includes a revised version of the voice/violin fragment.

[67] For a discussion of the purity and perfection of the circle, see Georges Poulet, *The Metamorphosis of the Circle* (Baltimore: Johns Hopkins University Press, 1966). On the utopian views of the circle, see Laurent Gervereau, "Symbolic Collapse: Utopia Challenged by Its Representations," in *Utopia: The Search for the Ideal Society in the Western World*, ed. Roland Schaer, Gregory Claeys, and Lyman Tower Sargent (New York and Oxford: New York Public Library and Oxford University Press, 2000), 357.

the one hand, we peer into the fragment, concentrating on what shape the individual elements assume and how they relate to each other. On the other hand, we contemplate the larger meanings that the elements possess outside of the diminutive world of the fragment. The dual focus can help us to examine how Kurtág uses the dynamics of the fragmentary to bring out the ideas of close/open boundaries and purity/impurity condensed in the text.

The voice and violin begin with a point of imitation, commencing what could become a canon. Although brief, the moment of imitation is enough to prompt us to look beyond the fragment. With the inherent potential for melodic perpetuity, the canon evokes the image of the circle, which is made up of a line that never reaches an end.[68] A canon built upon a subject that melodically curves up and down reinforces the image. Across almost two octaves, the voice and violin pack together a chromatic cluster of pitch classes from f to b. The cluster is almost complete, except for one pitch class – f♯. After a short rest, the voice begins what appears to be another melodic subject, a drop from d″ to e′, which could be heard as an inversion of the opening ascent from g♯ to g′ natural. If so, the voice has misaimed, as it should hit d♯′, not e′. The minor/major seventh discrepancy is significant not just for the sake of contrapuntal accuracy but also for drawing attention to d♯, another pitch class that goes unstated. Whatever the case, the violin has abandoned the idea of a canon. It begins the circle of fifths, setting out from the traditional starting point of c natural. The movement along the circle does not get that far, making it only to e. It is interrupted by the descent from g♯″ to a♯′, which can be heard either as a delayed imitation of the drop from d″ to e′ in the voice (imitation at the tritone) or as an echo of the g♯-a♯ pair in the violin that served as an accompaniment (and a surprise addition) in the first measure. The concluding e′ in both the violin and voice is overlaid with a c♯″, which, along with the just-stated a, creates a surprise ending on an A major triad, the 'perfection' of which, especially in contrast to the surrounding clusters, suggests purity.[69] The pitch classes in the final phrase ("ist rein") divide into two groups; the first, c-e, is the complement of the opening f-b cluster and the second, g-a♯, appears in the violin part. Although too dispersed and mingled to be heard as a cluster, the c-e collection is similar to the initial one in that it is missing a single

---

[68] The revised version in *Hommage à R. Sch.* reinforces the impression of melodic perpetuity. The new version is scored for B♭ clarinet, viola, and piano. The first two instruments take the parts of the soprano and violin respectively, whereas the piano adds a new part, which extends the points of imitation begun by the clarinet and viola.

[69] The emphasis on the pitch classes e, d, and g♯ could be heard as a faint preparation for the final A major triad. Whittall hears the triad being prepared by those pitches. Whittall, "Plotting the Path," 96–97.

pitch class – in this case d♯. Together, the two could complete the chromatic collection, if not for those missing pitch classes.

The text speaks of a closed circle. The music offers an incomplete one. The circle of fifths barely starts before it breaks off, and the larger twelve-tone collection is left short of two notes (d♯, f♯).[70] Nor is the music pure, as it mixes together triads and clusters. The aphorism in the text has been thrown into doubt; however, the fragment, comprised of both text and music, has come into its own. The discord between text and music creates conditions conducive to the fragmentary. Like all fragments, this movement is incomplete, made up of a blocked circle of fifths and a gapped chromatic collection. The ending on the A major triad is also ambiguous. The incompleteness and ambiguity combine to create a characteristically open ending. At the same time, there is an abrupt, decisive close, sharp enough to halt the progress along the circle of fifths. The force of separation is at work, or forces, as we have two opposing dynamics in play. As described above, the aphorism takes separation to an extreme by crafting a self-contained thought. The tendency is met by a counterforce of separation, one that keeps the fragment distinct but not wholly isolated. It is an example of what Blanchot calls "unfinished separations."[71] Unable to close fully, the fragment takes on ambiguities and gaps, making it part of the larger state of the fragmentary, with all of its ambiguities and gaps.

Worlds apart from the laconic aphorisms, yet packed together in the same work with them, are those fragments that come across as emotional outbursts. The pieces present an "I" who expresses a range of emotions, usually in an agitated, forceful manner. The speaker typically reacts to thoughts of women he knows or to the sight of those merely passing by on the street. The utterances captured in the fragments reveal how isolated he is. Even with the women in his life, he comes across as a distant observer, distanced by feelings of unworthiness. Many of the utterances, though,

---

[70] In the revised version in *Hommage à R. Sch.*, Kurtág alters the shape of the circle formed in the fragment. With the new piano line, he includes the missing f♯ in the first phrase, but not the d♯ in the second. At the end of the piece, he adds two fifths, f♯-c♯, c♯-g♯, to the circle begun by the other instruments. The first pair (f♯-c♯) is notably the most distant point along the circle from the c natural starting point used by both the viola and piano (in imitation). The sketches for *Kafka Fragments* in the Paul Sacher Stiftung include an unpublished setting of the text. It might have been intended as a "double" to the published version. Two of the fragments in the work, "Verstecke" and "Elendes Leben," have doubles. Like the doubles, the setting has affinities with the preceding (in this case, the published) movement, including a point of imitation based upon an angular subject and the circle of fifths. The unpublished version does not move step by step along the circle, but it does have the violin play fifths as dyads, although not in the sequential order of the circle. The progress along the circle is incomplete; however, all twelve chromatic scale degrees are stated over the course of the movement, although not in ways linked with the circle of fifths.

[71] Blanchot, *The Writing of the Disaster*, 58.

carry a hope of some sort of romantic or emotional connection, a dream that proves deluded. The utterances can serve as a way of making such a connection or, at least, of resisting separation. They are projected outwards with a momentum that can take them beyond the protagonist's confined interiority. Some declarations and fantasies never make it that far. They are the thoughts left unvoiced, the ones that we will never hear. Others, however, do break through. A few utterances are launched with such energy that they actually reach another person, as in the excerpts taken from letters. Others, though, land in a diary entry, a private sphere but one nonetheless located in the outside world. In all of these cases, the utterances contend with the force of separation, which strives to keep the speaker apart from the surrounding social sphere. Kurtág's settings pick up on this tension, manipulating it in various ways.

In the fragment "Eine lange Geschichte" (IV/2, Ex. 3.7), a brief glance at a woman stirs a rapturous storm: "I look a girl in the eye and it was a very long love story with thunder and kisses and lightning. I live fast."[72] Lost in the romantic tumult, the speaker captures another contradictory aspect of the fragmentary, a moment at once fleeting and spacious. A quick look becomes a "very long love story." To tell that story, the violin, in this and other outburst fragments, serves as a dramatic accompaniment to the voice, as opposed to the independent roles taken up by both parts in the aphorisms. It also offers a sinister accompaniment. Kurtág specifies a scordatura tuning of g c♯′ g♯′ d♯″. As heard in Saint-Saëns's *Danse macabre* and Mahler's Fourth Symphony (second movement), scordatura tunings can have associations of death.[73] Kurtág's tuning is similar to that in the former work, which lowers the e string by a half step but, unlike Kurtág's piece, does not retune the other strings. Mahler, on the other hand, tunes all the strings a step higher. The evocation of death confirms what we already expected: this love story is doomed.[74]

The voice and violin respond to every shift in mood, of which there are many in this short outburst. The nervousness of the glance is captured in convulsive vocal phrases backed up by agitated glissandi in the violin (mm. 1–2). The ensuing epic love story appropriately receives a drawn-out vocal phrase, which is set to the descending motive mentioned above (mm. 3–5). The stormy kiss releases a frenzied repetition of a violin motive,

[72] "Ich sehe einem Mädchen in die Augen, und es war eine sehr lange Liebesgeschichte mit Donner und Küssen und Blitz. Ich lebe rasch." English translation by Júlia and Peter Sherwood from the published score of the work.

[73] They also make possible chords and passagework that would be either very difficult or impossible to play with regular tuning (as in m. 5 "Donner und").

[74] Scordatura tunings do not always evoke death. As mentioned below, Bartók used them to suggest folk music dances.

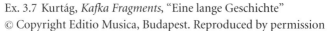

Ex. 3.7 Kurtág, *Kafka Fragments*, "Eine lange Geschichte"
© Copyright Editio Musica, Budapest. Reproduced by permission

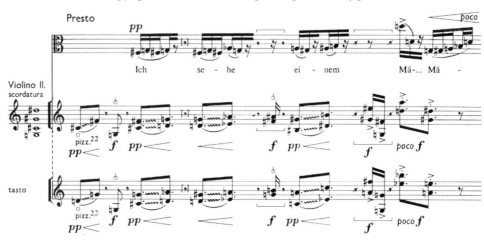

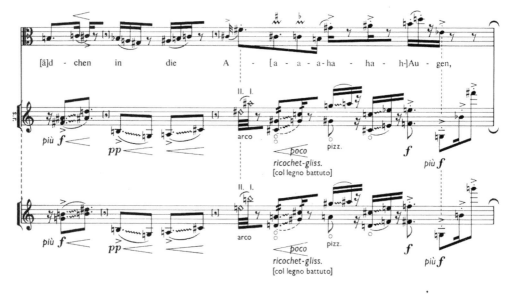

²² (Daumen-Pizzicato)
(thumb-pizzicato)
(hüvelyk-pizzicato)

one that, as we will see, flaunts the death associations (m. 7). Musically
distinguished from each other and separated by pauses, the small sections
come across as fragments within a fragment.

There is one more internal fragment. After the closing line "I live fast," the
violin alone plays a conclusion (mm. 9–12). Such postludes appear in many

Ex. 3.7 (*cont.*)

of the outburst fragments.[75] The passages can be heard as an attempt to
extend emotions beyond the words of the speaker, as in the piano postludes

[75] The sketches for this movement and other outburst fragment movements in the Paul Sacher
Foundation reveal that Kurtág concentrated on the postludes. Earlier versions of the pieces
often have a short instrumental close, or no close at all. In later versions, he built up the longer
postludes, suggesting that he wanted to draw out some emotion or effect.

Ex. 3.7 (cont.)

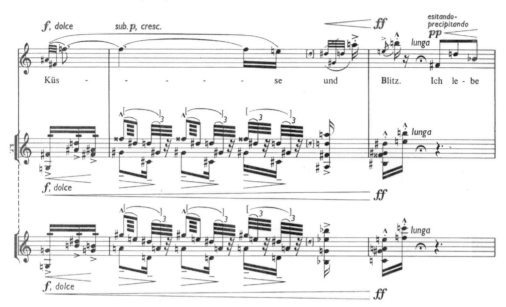

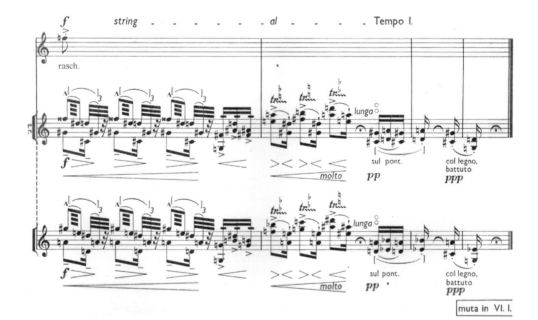

to some of the songs from Schumann's *Dichterliebe*.[76] In particular, the violin draws out the ecstasy of the kisses by returning to the repeated figure used to highlight that feeling. The rapid repetition builds momentum, which may seem a foolhardy thing to do in the fragmentary, so soon will the ending cease all motion. It could also be viewed as a resolute thing to do, as the escalating emotional energy confronts the force of separation head on. Separation, though, will come; it always does. Given the inevitability, the momentum can be heard as an attempt to forestall that moment, to hold off the close of the fragment. As long as the kiss figure repeats, passion is projected outward; the story grows longer.

Both are, of course, cut off. The story cannot be long, the speaker has to be sequestered again. The separation achieved, though, is not decisive. The kiss figure is followed by a brief pause, after which two very quiet short phrases appear. They are variations of phrases heard earlier (beginning of m. 2) in a passage that serves as a transition from the opening skittish exclamations to the grand statement of the "very long love story." With those phrases appearing again, we expect another change, perhaps a return to the rapture of the love story. One never comes, just the quick ending of the piece. Quick it is, as well as vague and open. The ambiguity arises from the sudden change to the quiet phrases and the expectation of some new passage. The energy of the protagonist's emotions keeps the conclusion open. So emphatically are the emotions projected that the abrupt ending is not enough to still them completely. The kiss figure has been stopped but the passion it arouses hangs in the air and drifts beyond the close.

Death also hangs in the air. The postlude features melodic figures that build upon the death associations of scordatura tuning by creating a link with Saint-Saëns's *Danse macabre*. The rapid blur of the kiss figure (mm. 7, 9) consists of a fifth and tritone pair sequence made up from the dyad in the lower line (c♯'-g♯') and the final half of the tremolo line (g♯'-d"). The figure recalls the morbid tuning that opens up the *Danse*: d'-a', a'-e♭".[77] The closing two chords strengthen the link (mm. 11–12). Consisting of parallel fifths a tritone apart, they contain the three pitches of the "deadly" part of the kiss figure (c♯'-g♯'-d"). Away from the morose, the scordatura can

---

[76] A specific connection is made between the use of postludes in the two works. The fragment "Träumend hing die Blume" (II/18) ends with one of the longer instrumental postludes in the work, a correspondence with the Schumann song "Am leuchtenden Sommermorgen," which also deals with flowers and concludes with a long piano postlude. Kurtág appropriately subtitled his fragment "Hommage à Robert Schumann."

[77] Other melodic links can be found in the tremolo line in the kiss figure (in descending sequence: f𝄪"–d♯"–d"–g♯') and the descending motive appearing sporadically throughout the cycle as heard in the vocal phrase on the words "sehr lange Liebesgeschichte" (g♯"-c♯"-g'-c').

also be heard as pointing to another piece: Bartók's *Contrasts*. The third movement of that work features a violin with an alternate tuning (g♯ d′ a′ e♭″) similar to Kurtág's in the lowering of the e string. Bartók begins the movement with the same tuning dyads heard in *Danse macabre*. He simply calls his dance "Sedes" (Fast), a title that can be heard as commenting on the last line of the Kafka text: "I live fast." The two references reveal how vast the realm outside of a fragment is and how we are encouraged to canvas the territory in search of references to make sense of the internal ambiguities. The references also say much about the open endings of fragments. At the moment when Kurtág's fragment is to taper to an end, it expands outward by having us contemplate associations with two earlier pieces and the ideas of death and dance. With such persistent emotions, uncertain conclusions, and external connections, separation, as Blanchot put it, remains "unfinished."

That point was already made by the aphorisms, albeit to contrasting effect. Aphorisms and outbursts could not be more different, yet in this work they reach similar conclusions, endings that are in some way incomplete and ambiguous. Such endings are hardly remarkable. Those qualities after all are hallmarks of the fragmentary. What is remarkable is that these two types of pieces end that way. They should not. Aphorisms withdraw and seal themselves off. Emotional outbursts stream on and on; they do not quickly break apart into fragile bits. The force of separation, with its opposing tendencies, brings the two to similar points. It prevents the aphorism from being totally isolated, and stops the outburst cold, giving it no room to broaden. *Kafka Fragments*, more so than many compositions venturing into the fragmentary, reveals the force of separation at work. That force has to work, as it meets so many opposing pressures, including the independent courses of the aphorisms and outbursts.

The individual fragments are not the only elements shaped by the dynamics of separation: so too is the larger state of the fragmentary. In that state, the single pieces are to be separated, a dynamic that makes them brief and alone, in other words, fragments. Yet at the same time, they emerge open-ended, which prevents them, especially the aphorisms, from being cut off altogether. The duality sustains the field of the fragmentary, as opposed to a field of isolated fragments. The hovering ambiguities and porous endings create a sense of space surrounding the individual fragment. Many fragments concluding in this manner build a collective space. Another contradiction underlies the fragmentary: a space that uses the force of separation to achieve proximity and connection.

Kurtág's placement of emotional outbursts in the fragmentary provides an opportunity to see how he represents the act of expression under such conditions. It is a strikingly different vision from that offered by Nono. In the String Quartet, a declaration of deepest emotions returns several times, as if to build upon those emotions and perpetuate them across the disruptions of the fragmentary. The utterance, though, is gradually effaced to a point of nothingness. In *Kafka Fragments*, the utterance is a singular event. It comes and goes quickly instead of withering away over numerous repetitions. As depicted in the work, the act of expression, no matter of what feeling, sparks intense flashes. All we can ever convey, or experience, are such brief moments. The fragment, for Kurtág, is the apposite means to convey this type of expression. It compresses the utterance, making it even more brief and fraught. Adding to the intensity is the conflict between the effort to extend the emotion and the abrupt close dictated by the force of separation. This conflict has its own expressive value, apart from the specific emotion being conveyed. It creates a general feeling of tension and uncertainty, all of which come to the fore in the endings of the fragments. The characters caught in the fragments know those conflicts and stresses all too well. They constantly confront the sudden conclusions, the moments of separation. They push outward with an emotional utterance in the attempt to overcome isolation. The utterance, though, offers at best a brief reprise. It can be nothing more than a fragment.

Kurtág's work also gives us a different view of the fragmented subject. Evoking that figure, Adorno stresses isolated pieces, saying little about the different types of pieces or the relationship between them. *Kafka Fragments* emphasizes variety, be it the types of fragments or the kinds of emotion. It also reveals the different social and emotional maneuverings of the subject, particularly whether to withdraw within or reach out from an isolated seclusion. Moreover, the work gives us a new conception of the space occupied by the subject: not a field of scattered fragments but rather a state in which pieces are suspended, kept apart yet together by their own incompleteness and separation.

Besides playing a significant role in the inquiry into the act of expression, the fragmentary lends itself to another inquiry, that into the relationship between part and whole. Modernist music has come up with various ways of interrelating smaller units, parts, and larger forms or designs, wholes. The fragmentary is one such way. As with Blanchot's conception of fragmentary writing, the relationship has served as a means of contesting the much-contested ideals of unity, continuity, and completion. In closing, this chapter pulls back and looks at changes in the relationship during the last decades of the twentieth century and the initial years of the twenty-first.

As is so often the case in accounts of late modernism, the discussion begins with 1950s–60s serialism. If anything, it seems that this particular line of inquiry would have been neglected in that music, which did not subvert unity, as the play between part and whole is wont to do. Quite the contrary, serial composers extolled unity, seeking ever deeper levels in integral serial and pure electronic works. In such pieces, one whole guarantees another; the row, a precompositional code of set relationships, yields the work, the realization of those relationships. At the same time, many compositions create a fractious flow of discontinuous parts, which appear to contravene ideals of unity. Such disjunction can be found in the leaps between modules in Stockhausen's *Klavierstück XI* and Boulez's *Structures II*, in which the direction and sequence of the leaps is determined by the performer. The two works may sound like they are made of distinct, unrelated parts, but the parts are, of course, related, as they originate in a precompositional design. Unity is uplifted even more, as the unruly music adheres to an authoritative scheme. It is lifted even higher with the balance of opposites so prized in post–World War Two modernism. The Stockhausen and Boulez works, for example, bring together rigorous systems and chance procedures. The relationship between part and whole fascinated serial composers, who played off the tension between the two, yet ultimately brought them together so that the parts were made one with the whole.

The next step in this quick overview is 1960s collage idioms. By reaching out to the tonal past and mixing old and new, works using collage idioms strongly rejected the hermeticism of integral serialism. They also drastically changed the terms of the relationship between part and whole set by that music. The parts – quotations and bits of past and contemporary styles – forcefully stand out. Amid the frenzy of the scraps, no whole, a preconceived form or system, immediately appears. This is not to say that there are no lines of unity underpinning such works. It is important to remember that many of the composers turning to collage idioms had been committed to serialism in the 1950s and early 1960s. Venturing into a seemingly anarchic style, they held fast to the idea of binding internal connections. For instance, Rochberg's *Music for the Magic Theater* and Berio's *Sinfonia* create elaborate linkages between quotations and new passages.[78] The connections, though, tend to be local, uniting a particular stretch of music. In these moments, a whole, a nexus of connections, solidifies, yet it ultimately breaks apart

[78] In *Hymnen*, Stockhausen pursued intermodulation as a way of uniting the different anthem fragments and the surrounding electronic sounds. As he describes it, the approach has the scope of a system, although not the rigor of integral serialism. Metzer, *Quotation*, 141–42.

as the music restlessly moves on to another passage and a new patch of connection. Through the frequent disruptions, the whole comes across as something perpetually on the verge of being.

It also emerges as something that once was. Collage compositions evoke a second type of whole, the work from which a quotation originates. The latter is a whole in the sense of having once been complete before a bit was excised from it. A new type of connection is being made, that between a quotation and its source, a work that is now fractured and incomplete. The Rochberg and Berio pieces underscore the point by quoting, or, more accurately, building upon, movements by other composers, Mozart and Mahler respectively. In each work, we hear most of the original movements, but not all of them, as they are either abruptly cut off or broken apart by borrowings or new passages. With this second kind of whole, we can appreciate the varied and intricate ways in which collage compositions have shaped the relationship between part and whole. In these works, the parts may be more prominent than the whole, but the latter still has a presence, albeit a distant one. The whole is out there beyond the parts, as either a possibility or a loss.

Another compelling take on the relationship between part and whole can be found in the music of John Zorn. Of particular interest are Zorn's "aural cinema" pieces, which pay homage to directors, like *Godard* (1984), or, as with *Spillane* (1986), a writer whose books have spawned numerous films.[79] Both works are also "filing card" compositions, so called because the directions for the styles and/or sound effects to be produced are put down on a single card, which is placed in a set sequence with other cards. The performers face the virtuosic task of creating a range of styles and sounds in rapid succession, with some bits lasting no more than a few seconds. The "cinema" works in many ways represent a sequel to 1960s collage idioms. They too mix together bits of familiar materials, although not so much quotations as allusions to different styles. In both, the parts dominate, but with different results for the whole. Through the use of quotations, the collage compositions suggest a distant whole, whereas Zorn's works have the parts create a whole. The "fragments" in *Spillane*, for instance, build up a narrative.[80] The styles chosen by Zorn are loaded with associations of place, feeling, and effect and when strung together they can lay out a series of events or moods, such as those found in a private eye B-movie. In

---

[79] John Zorn, liner notes, *Godard/Spillane*, Tzadik 7324 (1999).

[80] Zorn adopts the term "fragments" during an interview with Edward Strickland. *American Composers: Dialogues on Contemporary Music*, ed. Edward Strickland (Bloomington: Indiana University Press, 1991), 133.

Godard, the individual pieces, some more obviously than others, relate to the works and aesthetics of the director, whose creative persona serves as a focal point.

A narrative and a persona are very different types of wholes than the removed and fractured kinds evoked by collage works. A story, for instance, has immediacy and sweep, as the listener is constantly putting together the different stylistic plot lines and waiting to see what happens next. Zorn also believes that the extra-musical constructions produce a strong sense of unity: "Using a dramatic subject (Godard, Spillane, Duras, Duchamp) as a unifying device is a revelation. It insures that all the musical moments, regardless of form or content, will be held together by relating in some way to the subject's life or work."[81] Another revelation is that a composer so taken by the commotion of disparate parts could be so beholden to, and assured of, the ideal of unity. With him, fragments cannot only be unified, but they can also beget unity. How different from Blanchot, who saw the fragmentary as breaking free from any suggestions of unity or the whole: "fragmentation is pulling to pieces (the tearing) of that which never has preexisted (really or ideally) as a whole, nor can it ever be reassembled in any future presence whatever."[82]

A work that comes close to Blanchot's "pulling to pieces" is Ferneyhough's *Les froissements des ailes de Gabriel* (scored for solo guitar and chamber orchestra). The piece functions as the second scene in *Shadowtime* (2004), a "thought opera" based on the life and work of Walter Benjamin. Two thoughts elaborated upon by the opera are those of time and angels, ideas that come together in Benjamin's memorable image of the angel of history. History is the time of mortals (the force battering the angel). Ferneyhough suggests the time of angels. He draws inspiration from the medieval idea that angels are "deaf to time" yet must act within it when dealing with mortals. One way for them to measure time would be with the steady beating of wings, the "basic unit" of their earthly chronometry.[83]

To evoke angelic time, Ferneyhough calls upon the fragment. The scene consists of 128 segments, which last anywhere from two to fifteen seconds.[84] The fragments were composed independently from the work as part of a "thirteen-page originary structure." Ferneyhough used a "random selection process" to pick units from the structure and to determine the order in which they unfold. The aleatorically derived sequence results in sudden

---

[81] Zorn, liner notes.   [82] Blanchot, *The Writing of the Disaster*, 60.
[83] Brian Ferneyhough, email correspondence with the author, March 31, 2006.
[84] *Shadowtime*, program book, Lincoln Center Festival, July 21, 2005.

juxtapositions in instrumentation, dynamics, and texture, all of which serve to "rigorously negate" "linear logic."[85] The overall rhythmic and melodic hyperactivity, however, often blurs the breaks between fragments, creating the impression of continuity.[86] Such spells, though, cannot overcome what Blanchot describes as the "experience" of discontinuity, interruption, and separation.

Ferneyhough exploits the dynamics of the fragmentary to different effects. Like the flapping of an angel's wings, the fragments mark time by dividing it into units. They also mask time, suggesting the timeless-ness that they supposedly overcome. Disconnected from the surrounding bits, each fragment creates a short-lived present, moments that stall for-ward motion and slough off a sense of past since there is no connection with the preceding units. As Ferneyhough notes, "time in music fails if it disappears without remainder into the musical experience."[87] In addition, his version of the fragmentary, like Blanchot's, claims a spot well beyond the rule of the whole. The work creates no whole, other than a random sequence of 128 fragments. The sequence, as the composer claims, forestalls the "linear logic" of continuity and coherence. Moreover, there is no whole that exists outside of the work. The originary structure is just a repository of fragments, another type of collection that similarly shuns notions of unity.[88]

Besides the inquiry into the relationship between part and whole, another historical narrative can be built around the works discussed here, a narrative retold often in accounts of late twentieth-century arts. The compositions can be viewed as caught in the split between modernism and postmod-ernism. The Rochberg, Berio, and Zorn works have been corralled into the postmodern camp by scholars, while Nono, Kurtág, and Ferneyhough have been considered as paragons (or, to some, the last stand) of modernism.[89]

---

[85] The above observations were taken from the email correspondence (March 31, 2006) with Ferneyhough.

[86] The analysis of the work undertaken here did not reveal any prominent melodic motives or pitch collections to tie together the fragments; however, a thorough analysis of the pitch content of the work may reveal some connections. Such an analysis is beyond the scope of this discussion.

[87] *Shadowtime*, program book.

[88] In his discussion of the opera, Whittall relates the dialectic between the fragmentary and continuity (a "central pillar of Ferneyhough's compositional aesthetic") to similar notions in Benjamin's thought. Whittall, "Connections and Constellations," *Musical Times*, 144 (Summer 2003), 27.

[89] Robert Fink has discussed postmodern qualities of the Rochberg piece. Fink, "Going Flat: Post-hierarchical Music Theory and the Musical Surface," in *Rethinking Music*, ed. Nicholas Cook and Mark Everist (Oxford University Press, 1999), 128–32. Keith Potter has mentioned both modernist and postmodernist elements in *Sinfonia*. Potter, "The Current Musical Scene," in *Modern Times: From World War I to the Present*, ed. Robert P. Morgan (Basingstoke: Macmillan,

Much effort has been spent on elucidating the differences between the two. This study offers what could be a point of contrast, the ways in which the two approach the relationship between part and whole. Modernist works typically have one term overwhelm the other. The whole absorbs the parts in 1950s serialism, whereas, in the Nono and Kurtág pieces, the parts undermine the whole or, as in Ferneyhough's operatic scene, outright displace it. Postmodern compositions, on the other hand, keep both sides in play. They enjoy the means and effects of fragmentation but cling to the whole. The parts have a much stronger presence than the whole, but the latter is still there. It is either a possibility created by momentary connections or something situated outside of the piece, like a preexisting composition, the source of the quotations, or a potential work, such as the imaginary movies scored by Zorn. Many theories of postmodernism would reject such a view. The evocation of a whole and lines of unity, no matter how faint, contradicts the theoretical tenet of an endlessly fragmented world. In that world, fragments are related to each other only through "difference," and not through some lost or possible whole.[90]

The contradiction does not so much upend theories of postmodernism as reveal the limitations of a categorical history, such as that based on the divide between modernism and postmodernism. Accounts of the split emphasize, even distort, differences, while overlooking affinities and exchanges between individual works on the opposing sides of the schism. Chapter 2 made a similar point in regard to expression. The inquiry into the state of the fragmentary offers a similar rejoinder to the categorical approach. There is indeed a split between the collage works of the 1960s and the ideals of post–World War Two serialism. The former critiqued the latter, particularly the faith placed in the inclusiveness of structure and the rejection of the tonal past. At the same time, the two are joined in a colloquy around the aesthetics of the fragment, one extended by the works of Nono, Kurtág, and Ferneyhough. There are, of course, different views about the relationship between part and whole, but all of the compositions get at the fragment through that relationship. With a shared interest, the modernist and postmodernist

---

1993), 363–64. Susan McClary places her analysis of Zorn's *Spillane* in a larger discussion of postmodernist aesthetics. McClary, *Conventional Wisdom: The Content of Musical Form* (Berkeley: University of California Press, 2000), 145–52.

90 See Jameson, *Postmodernism*, 30–31. In his discussion of Bob Perelman's poem "China," Jameson mentions how the "unity" of the poem can be found in the "absent book" lying outside of the text. Susan McClary offers an interpretation of *Spillane* that also departs from the tenets of theories of postmodernism. She mentions how the signifiers in the work, particularly the opening scream of a woman in distress, are not the empty cultural referents that postmodernist critics often describe but rather sounds with troubling cultural meanings. McClary, *Conventional Wisdom*, 145–52.

pieces can be seen as participating in the inquiry into the fragmentary. A categorical approach would miss out on both that colloquy and the continuing inquiry. Instead of a decisive break, there is tension, created by the collage compositions working with and against modernist ideals. As strongly as those compositions pull away, they remain captivated by an object that had long captivated modernist composers, the fragment.

4 Lament

To "take back" a masterpiece. That has to be one of the most audacious claims made by a modernist work. In Thomas Mann's novel *Doctor Faustus*, Adrian Leverkühn's final composition, a *Lamentation*, "revokes" Beethoven's Ninth Symphony.[1] The work plies personal and national despair with new compositional means to create a music that renders the "Ode to Joy" vainglorious. Alongside the challenge to Beethoven, another bold encounter with the past can go unnoticed: in the same work, Leverkühn not only undermines the past but also embraces it. He seeks a union that comes across as a surprise, if not inconceivable. His last piece brings together the lament and modernism: the former, an age-old and, according to Mann, original form of expression; the latter, the visions foreseen by Leverkühn. Mann has little to say about how exactly the union works; indeed, he tellingly gives more details about the ways in which the piece "takes back" the Beethoven symphony (DF, 486, 488). Instead of specifics, the author wants us to imagine the possibility of the two coming together and the expressive riches created from the binding of centuries.

Leverkühn's *Lamentation* is far from a one-time historical collision. Composers throughout the twentieth and twenty-first centuries have turned to the archaic genre and re-created it in new ways. Whittall has described the lament as a recurring topic in modernism, one elaborated upon by such composers as Bartók, Britten, Birtwistle, and Ligeti.[2] This chapter builds upon Whittall's study. It adds some names to his list of composers but, above all, it sets these laments within a specific context, the various modernist explorations of expression. In *Doctor Faustus*, the lament drives such an undertaking, what Mann calls the "liberation" or "reconstruction" of expression, a shift as far-reaching as that which ushered in the Baroque period (DF, 486, 488). No such grand designs are schemed here (it is hard to be as grand as Mann), but this study does see the lament as pushing a particular "reconstruction," the search for more directly expressive idioms beginning around 1980. Many composers since that time have turned to the lament. The choice hardly comes as a surprise, for the genre pulsates

---

[1] Thomas Mann, *Doctor Faustus*, trans. H. T. Lowe-Porter (New York: Alfred A. Knopf, 1963), 478, 490. All subsequent references to the novel will be made in the text.
[2] Whittall, *Exploring Twentieth-century Music*.

with expressive effects and associations. It has also served as a departure point in the modernist inquiry into expression. As used by late modernist composers, the genre instigates a group of questions raised repeatedly in the inquiry: whether or not to use established expressive models or voices, what is the expressive potential of modernist idioms, and how to figure the relationship between expression and structure.

To answer these questions, we need to clarify what a lament is around the turn of the twenty-first century. Whereas Whittall looks at works either entitled "lament" or generally evocative of mournfulness, the focus here is more restrictive, set on a group of pieces that take on voices and/or dynamics of historical lament repertoires. The ligatures between old forms and modernist idioms can create, as depicted by Mann, a new type of lament, what can be called the modernist lament. The term comes across as a contradiction. The newest of sounds and an archaic cry of sorrow, it seems, would only rebuff each other. Yet, as heard in recent works, the two interact, even cooperate. They build a common ground, and it is that ground that forms the modernist lament, not so much a style as a musical-expressive space from which it is possible to survey aspects of both the modern and the venerable genre.

Before we can get to the modernist lament, we need to begin with the lament. By lament, this study refers to a wide range of works or rituals, including ancient Greek mourning rites, Eastern European folk songs, and Baroque basso ostinato arias. The intent is not to construct a universal lament paradigm covering all traditions but rather to draw attention to expressive dynamics shared by different repertoires, particularly those dynamics that have been exploited by modernist composers.

One such feature is how a lament begins.[3] Before a lament, there is woe and anguish. The lament, though, does not commence until a new voice is

---

[3] This discussion draws upon a variety of sources, covering a range of lament traditions, particularly Baroque opera, ancient and modern Greece, and Eastern European folk idioms. Notable sources include James Porter, "Lament," *The New Grove Dictionary of Music and Musicians*, ed. Stanley Sadie and John Tyrell (London: Macmillan, 2001), vol. XIV, 181–88; Lauri Honko, "The Lament: Problems of Genre, Structure, and Reproduction," in *Genre, Structure, and Reproduction in Oral Literature*, ed. L. Honko and V. Voigt (Budapest: Akadémia Kiadó, 1980), 21–40; Ellen Rosand, *Opera in Seventeenth-Century Venice: The Creation of a Genre* (Berkeley: University of California Press, 1991), 361–86; Margaret Alexiou, *The Ritual Lament in Greek Tradition*, second edn, revised by Dimitrios Yatromanolakis and Panagiotis Roilos (Lanham, MD: Rowman & Littlefield, 2002); C. Nadia Seremetakis, *The Last Word: Women, Death, and Divination in Inner Mani* (University of Chicago Press, 1991); Gail Holst-Warhaft, *Dangerous Voices: Women's Laments and Greek Literature* (New York and London: Routledge, 1992); Charles Segal, "Oral Tradition Song, Ritual and Commemoration in Early Greek Poetry and Tragedy," *Oral Tradition*, 4/3 (Oct 1989), 330–59; Irene Kertész Wilkinson, "Between Life and Death: The Funeral and Mourning Rituals of the Southeastern Hungarian Vlach Roma," in *Music, Sensation, and Sensuality*, ed. Linda Phyllis Austern (New York and London: Routledge, 2002), 181–97; Gail Kligman, *The Wedding of the Dead: Ritual, Poetics, and Popular Culture in Transylvania* (Berkeley: University of California Press, 1998); Irina Paladi, " 'Dragă a mea mămuţi': Eine rumänische Totenklage für

taken up, a voice of ritual, formulas, and convention. To thrash in sorrow is not to lament. Intense feeling must be mediated through, become obedient to, prescribed means of expression, like a set formal structure or ritual pattern. It is only when the speaker subordinates his or her emotions to those means that a lament begins. For example, at the end of the *Iliad*, Andromache and Hecuba greet the dead body of Hector by pulling out their hair and throwing their bodies at the funeral cart, but they, along with Helen, cut off the frenzy to begin a proper lamentation. Although each possesses a singular grief – that of wife, mother, and sister-in-law – they pour that grief into the same tripartite poetic structure. On the Baroque opera stage, such different characters as queens, gods, and nymphs lock their anguish to descending chromatic bass lines, an emblem of sorrow in the seventeenth century. Drawn from different times and traditions, the two examples reenact a specific moment: a character taking on the ritual voice of lament. It is a voice that transcends one's individual emotions and gives them a broad, communal resonance, be it that of mythic mourning or a treasured operatic moment.

The voice also creates distinct tensions. One strong conflict emerges between the force of personal expression and the fixity of the governing forms. Those structures can bind. The passions driving one to lament do not always yield to those forms, creating clashes between the two. Baroque opera, to return to one of the above examples, dramatizes this tension. Characters frequently push away from the regularity of the basso ostinato through overlapping vocal phrases or, in some cases, by abruptly switching to recitative. Lament is also shaped by a dynamic of transgression. The genre draws attention to boundaries, lines that are most often crossed in some sort of disruptive, agonized way. Feelings are so strong that these lines, which hold in everyday life, cannot remain intact. Folk and ancient laments fixate on the divide between speech and song. In both, the line is frequently traversed, but the movement across is far from smooth and routine. With each crossing, we experience tension as speech swells into song or melodies disintegrate into speech. Sometimes the voices are transformed into sounds that appear to be neither speech nor song, something like a

die Mutter," in *Compositionswissenschaft: Festschrift Reinhold und Roswitha Schlötterer zum 70. Geburtstag*, ed. Bernd Edelmann and Sabine Kurth (Augsburg: Wissner, 1999), 363–67; Ursula Michel, "Musik im Totenbrauchtum Rumäniens," in *Weltmusik 3* (Cologne: Feedback Papers, 1986), 103–20; Gisela Suliteanu, "The Traditional System of Melopeic Prose of the Funeral Songs Recited by the Jewish Women of the Socialist Republic of Rumania," *Folklore Research Center Studies* 3 (1972), 291–349; Dániel Péter Biró, "Reading the Song: On the Development of Musical Syntax, Notation, and Compositional Autonomy: A Comparative Study of Hungarian Siratok, Hebrew Bible Cantillation and Ninth-century Plainchant from St. Gallen" (Ph.D. thesis, Princeton University, 2004).

wail. These strange sounds also transgress the perceived natural sonic order
that establishes taxonomies of sound and patterns of sonic behavior. Such
ruptures, though, are usually brief. The rule of the formal patterns, not to
mention that of the sonic order, returns. A lament begins with those voices
and patterns and must end with them as well.

From this account, we can begin to see the appeal that the dynamics of the lament have had for modernist composers. The genre encourages types of sonic behavior indulged in by modernist styles, particularly
wild transformations of sound and the transgression of established boundaries. Both the lament and musical modernism also share a preoccupation
with aspects of expression and structure. Indeed, the interaction between
the two sides in the lament plays into strengths of modernist composition. On the one hand, pronounced dissonances and textural clashes (all
elements won by modernism) can bolster emotional projection to new
degrees of intensity. On the other hand, rigorous structural schemes, an
ongoing interest in twentieth-century composition, can be devised to control the emotions fueling a lament. Throughout the twentieth century,
composers writing laments have brought out the two sides to different
degrees.

Ligeti

As far as childhood musical memories go, Ligeti's are rather dark. Looking
back at his youth in Transylvania, he recalls professional mourners chanting laments in the homes of the deceased.[4] As a topic for a composition
seminar, it is rather specialized. During his years at the Musikhochschule
in Hamburg, the composer taught a class in the Baroque basso ostinato
lament.[5] As these two examples show, the genre of the lament has returned
throughout Ligeti's life. Or, to be more exact, Ligeti has returned frequently to the lament. The genre surfaces in different ways throughout
his oeuvre. Early pieces written while the composer was still in Hungary
include lament movements ("Siralmas nékem" from *Idegen földön*, 1945–
46 and *Musica Ricercata*, mvts. 2 and 5, 1951–53), whereas the major work
from the 1970s, *Le grand macabre* (1974–77), features a delightful parody
of the genre, appropriate for a work about the farcical futility of death.[6]
Traces of the genre appear in such pieces as the Kyrie from the Requiem

---

[4] Ligeti, "Stilisierte Emotion: György Ligeti in Gespräch mit Denys Bouliane," *MusikTexte* 28/29
(1989), 59–60; Richard Steinitz, *György Ligeti: Music of the Imagination* (Boston: Northeastern
University Press, 2003), 9.
[5] Steinitz, *Ligeti*, 271.
[6] Mescalina sings the lament to a not-so-dead Astradomors (Scene 2, fig. 153).

(1963–65) and the Double Concerto (1972).[7] Beginning in the early 1980s, Ligeti wrote four works that have movements either entitled "Lament" or that strongly evoke the genre: the Horn Trio (mvt. 4, 1982), Piano Concerto (mvt. 2, 1985–88), Violin Concerto (mvt. 4, 1990–92), and the Viola Sonata (mvt. 5, 1994). The first of these, the Trio movement, will be taken up in this chapter.[8] The lament movements have received some attention, especially the figures (passacaglia and lamento motif) used by the composer to summon the genre. No one, however, has asked how the movements function as laments. It is a pertinent question, as the movements do not just borrow lament figures but also work within the dynamics of the genre, particularly those of transformation and transgression. Through that involvement, they create striking examples of the modernist lament.

After a four-year stretch in which he completed no new works, the 1980s brought in a period of creative exuberance for Ligeti. During that decade and the next, he wrote a series of major pieces, including the Horn Trio (the piece that broke the compositional silence), the first two books of piano etudes (1984–85, 1988–93), the Piano Concerto, and the Violin Concerto. These works and others explore a range of compositional influences and ideas. The lament was one such inspiration. Ligeti also turned to non-Western idioms, including Balinese gamelan and African drumming traditions, and responded to the music of composers who grabbed his attention, notably Conlon Nancarrow.

The lament plays a role in one of the significant changes in Ligeti's music during this time, the rise of a forthright emotionality. Writing on the fourth movement of the Horn Trio, Josef Häusler has remarked: "Never before has Ligeti so uninhibitedly conveyed pain, grief, and anguish."[9] Richard Toop concurs: "[the Trio lament] was arguably the most directly emotional music Ligeti had ever written."[10] This is not to suggest, as both scholars would be quick to point out, that Ligeti's music prior to the Trio is inexpressive. Far from it, as works from the 1960s (such as the Second String Quartet and Requiem) concoct what the composer called "cooled expressionism," the effect of immobilizing and muting "superexpressive"

---

[7]   Ligeti mentions the evocation of the lament in *Musica Ricercata* and the First String Quartet. Ligeti, "Stilisierte Emotion," 59. In a forthcoming monograph, Amy Bauer traces the various forms the lament has taken in Ligeti's music throughout his career, including the works mentioned above.

[8]   Analyses of the Trio lament movement can be found in Ulrich Dibelius, "Ligetis Horntrio," *Melos* 46 (1984), 55–57; Stephen Taylor, "The Lamento Motif: Metamorphoses in Ligeti's Late Style" (DMA thesis, Cornell University, 1994), 22–49; Taylor, "Passacaglia and Lament in Ligeti's Recent Music," *Tijdschrift voor Muziektheorie* 9, no. 1 (2004), 2–6; and Willson, *Ligeti, Kurtág,* 178–82.

[9]   Quoted in Taylor, "The Lamento Motif," 25.

[10] Richard Toop, *György Ligeti* (London: Phaidon, 1999), 189.

gestures.[11] In the 1980s, the coolness thaws. Pieces are characterized by a frankness of expression, particularly in terms of the types of emotions supported, such stark feelings as "pain, grief, and anguish." The direct terms required means unthinkable in the "cooled" works, particularly the use of lyrical melodic lines and swathes of triadic harmonies.

With those elements, Ligeti aimed to separate himself from both modernist and traditional factions. According to the composer, the desire "épater l'avant-garde" was an inspiration behind the Trio.[12] For him, the ideals of Darmstadt and other modernist circles had calcified. The use of ABA forms and more traditional melodic and harmonic writing in the work would not only be a "provocative, conservative" jab at the "avant-garde," but it would also reveal the potential of elements that those circles had stridently denied.[13] Not surprisingly, the avant-garde jabbed back by attacking Ligeti in symposia and speeches.[14] The use of these elements would appear to align Ligeti with the neo-Romantics, but he was equally critical of that movement.[15] Speaking in 1983, he asserted: "there is a new generation, which I do not belong to – the 'new expressionists'" (a label that could apply to the neo-Romantics).[16] To him, the new generation was part of a "retro" tendency of the time, which was just as much of a dead end as the 1950s–1960s modernist scenes.

Ligeti claimed that the working out of "stylistic problems" inspired the Trio.[17] A specific problem is never cited, but, given the departures taken in the work, one immediately comes to mind: how to use older forms, triadic harmonies, and longer, more flexible melodic lines in new ways. Ligeti wanted to fashion these elements as part of what he called a "modernism of today."[18] In particular, he pulls off an interesting sleight of hand with triadic harmonies. He exploits the harmonic richness of the chords while subverting them and refusing them any sort of sway, which triads tend to claim.[19] We are left in a harmonic no-man's-land, which Ligeti captures with

---

[11] Ligeti, *György Ligeti in Conversation*, 15–19.
[12] Constantin Floros, *György Ligeti: Jenseits von Avantgarde und Postmoderne* (Vienna: Verlag Lafite, 1996), 164.
[13] Floros, *György Ligeti*, 164.
[14] Steinitz, *Ligeti*, 251. Contrary to the modernist attacks on Ligeti, Pierre Boulez did not consider the use of the ternary form in the third movement as necessarily regressive. According to him, the conventional structure is "diverted" from its original functions by the innovative rhythmic and textural idioms. Boulez, "Moderne/Postmoderne" in *Points de repère II/Regards sur autrui*, ed. Jean-Jacques Nattiez and Sophie Galaise (Paris: Christian Bourgois, 2005), 476–77.
[15] Toop, *Ligeti*, 183, 189.
[16] Dibelius, "Ligetis Horntrio," 45.   [17] Dibelius, "Ligetis Horntrio," 45.
[18] Ligeti, "Ma position comme compositeur aujourd'hui," *Contrechamps* 12/13 (1990), 8.
[19] For a discussion of how triadic sonorities are undermined in Ligeti's later music, see Mike Searby, "Ligeti's 'Third Way': 'Non-Atonal' Elements in the Horn Trio," *Tempo* 216 (April 2001), 17–22 and Eric Drott, "The Role of Triadic Harmony in Ligeti's Recent Music," *Music Analysis* 22 (2003), 283–314.

Ex. 4.1 Passacaglia theme and pedal tone, Ligeti, Horn Trio, mvt. 4, mm. 1–5

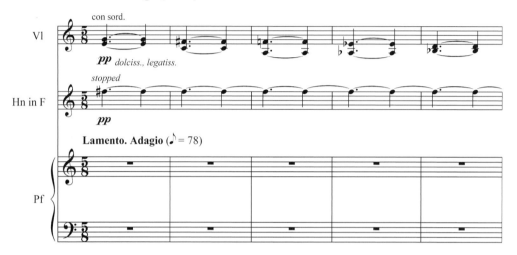

evocative phrases characterized by awkward negatives such as "non-diatonic
diatonicism" and "non-atonal."[20]

A "modernism of today" also involved taking up the archaic voices and
dynamics of the lament. To begin a lament, Ligeti raises not a voice but
rather voices.[21] Such plurality is rare in laments, which typically present
a single voice honed by repeated use in rituals. The Trio movement puts
forth three different lament voices: a passacaglia, a pedal tone, and descending chromatic melodic lines.[22] The first two appear in the opening measures (Ex. 4.1). The violin plays a passacaglia theme, one that emulates the
descending chromatic tetrachord of the Baroque lamento bass. Emulates
but not imitates, as the figure departs in key ways from the historical model,
particularly in the use of two voices with the descending chromatic line

---

20 Dibelius, "Ligetis Horntrio," 45 and Searby, "Ligeti's 'Third Way,' " 19.
21 To begin this lament proved rather difficult for Ligeti. The sketches for the movement in the
    Paul Sacher Stiftung reveal three aborted openings. Each focuses on one of the three lament
    figures – passacaglia, drone, lamento motif – discussed below. The figures appear in very different
    forms from those they would assume in the final version of the work.
22 The Trio movement is the only one of the four to use all three voices consistently. The Violin
    Concerto movement features all three, but the lamento motif appears only in fragments after
    a single very long, and almost imperceptible, statement. There is no consistent use of a pedal
    tone in the movement. The fact that Ligeti used all three voices prominently in the Horn Trio
    movement suggests that he wanted to evoke the genre in very clear terms and relied upon all
    three lament voices in his possession to do so.

Ex. 4.2 a) Horn fifths figure b) First three chords of the passacaglia theme

a)

b)

placed in the upper voice and harmonized from below, in the asymmetrical
sorrow produced by a five-measure phrase in 5/8, and in a chromaticism
that goes well beyond a few sighs, involving ten of the twelve chromatics
(the unstated pitch classes are c♯ and b). The theme makes another askew
reference to the past. The first three measures recall the horn fifths figure in
Beethoven's *Les adieux* piano sonata (no. 26), a motive appearing in preceding movements as well (Ex. 4.2). The figure and the ostinato as a whole are
wrenched by Ligeti's unconventional voice-leading, particularly the tritone
moving to a minor sixth. Elements of tonality – the prominence of thirds,
sixths, and fifths as well as references to past tonal figures – appear but no
overall sense of tonality emerges. The passacaglia offers a succinct example
of "non-diatonic diatonicism."

The second lament voice can be heard in the b-natural pedal tone played
by the horn. A pedal tone by itself does not signify the lament, as do tetrachord passacaglia themes or descending chromatic melodic lines. However,
when combined with a specific lament voice, a pedal tone can intensify that
voice, becoming an integral part of the form. The role of the pedal tone then
all depends on context, and it appears that Ligeti has one particular context
in mind: Eastern European folk laments, particularly the different Romanian songs – bocet, hora lungă, and doina – that he heard as a child and that
he mentioned occasionally in discussing his music.[23] In the sketches for the

---

[23] See Ligeti, "Stilisierte Emotion," 59–60. In pointing out references to folk materials, it is impor-
      tant to remember Ligeti's insistence that the use of Romanian and Hungarian elements in his
      post-1980s pieces is "absolutely non-folkloric." In the preface to the Viola Sonata, he clarifies
      such claims: "It [the first movement, *Hora lungă*] evokes the spirit of Romanian folk music,
      which, together with Hungarian folk music, and that of the Gipsies, made a strong impression
      on me during my childhood. However, I do not write folklore, or use folkloristic quotations, it
      is rather allusions which are made." The comments point to Ligeti's conflicted attitudes about
      using folk materials at this time. On the one hand, he uses the materials more openly than he
      had in decades. On the other hand, he effaces them in his music and distances himself from
      any sort of direct contact with those melodies in his commentaries on his works. The conflict
      may stem from Ligeti's attempt to distinguish his new pieces from the kind of folkloristic works

Ex. 4.3 Excerpt from the sketches for the Viola Sonata, "regional slow lament," György Ligeti Collection, Paul Sacher Stiftung

lament movement of the Viola Sonata, the composer jotted down what he labeled a "regional slow lament," which features two staggered, descending chromatic lines supported by a pedal on the low C string (Ex. 4.3).[24] He never identifies a particular region, but the figure points to the possible role of drones in Eastern European traditions. A possible, but it appears not so common a role: the literature on Romanian lament styles says little about the use of drones; however, field recordings from the 1930s (the period of Ligeti's childhood, when he would have heard performances of the genre) reveal the sporadic use of bagpipes and vocal drones.[25] The prevalence of drones in lament performances, though, is ultimately beside the point. What matters is that they are a definitive part of Ligeti's conception of the genre, a point reinforced by the sketch for the Viola Sonata.[26] What stands out here is how he has reduced the lament to a basic figure, giving us what amounts to a middle-ground linear analysis. The reduction reveals what he considered to be the crucial elements of the genre: descending chromatic lines over a pedal.

The last of the three lament voices is what the composer has called the "lamento motif" (Ex. 4.4). As described by Richard Steinitz, it appears in several works, not all of them marked as laments.[27] The motif takes more

that were expected of composers during his years in communist Hungary. Ligeti, "Ma position comme compositeur aujourd'hui," 9 and *Sonate für Viola Solo* (Mainz: Schott, 2001), preface.

[24] The Hungarian phrase on the sketch manuscript is "helyi (lassú) lamento." There is no clearly corresponding passage in the lament movement of the Viola Sonata.

[25] Sources I have consulted include Béla Bartók, *Rumanian Folk Music*, ed. Benjamin Suchoff, vol. II *Vocal Melodies* (The Hague: Martinus Nijhoff, 1967); Paladi, "'Dragă a mea mămuţi'"; Michel, "Musik im Totenbrauchtum Rumäniens"; Emilia Comişel, "Coordonate ale formei libere în creaţia folclorică," *Studii de muzicologie* 14 (1979), 167–86. Paladi mentions that the accompaniment of a pan flute can give the impression of a drone. "'Dragă a mea mămuţi'," 366. A performance of a bocet from the Bukovina region of Romania done sometime between 1933 and 1943 features the voice accompanied by a bagpipe, which plays a drone part, and a pan flute. The recording has been reissued on *Village Music from Romania*, VDE CD-538 (1988). The song does not come from the Transylvania region in which Ligeti grew up but rather the neighboring Bukovina region. Nonetheless, it does point to the use of drones in Romanian folk lament performances.

[26] *Le grand macabre* makes the same point. In this parody (Scene 2, fig. 153), Mescalina sings rapid-fire descending melodic lines above a dissonant cluster drone (d–e♭–f♭) pungently played by the regal.

[27] Steinitz, *Ligeti*, 294–99. The motif can appear in mournful works that are not cast as laments, such as the piano étude "Automne à Varsovie." In the Piano and Violin Concertos, Ligeti pairs each of the lament movements with a following movement (the third movement of the Piano

Ex. 4.4 Lamento motif, Ligeti, Horn Trio, mvt. 4, mm. 14–20

or less the same shape in all of its appearances, three phrases in which the melody descends largely by half step, with each of the descents covering a longer range. This figure too harkens back to Eastern European repertoires, many of which feature expanding melodic lines often grouped in threes.[28] The Viola Sonata sketch suggests that this figure too is a reduction of folk lament melodies, one that concentrates on the basic melodic shape (descent) and intervals while stripping away the characteristic ornamentation, melodic elaboration, and rhythmic repetition. The reduction reveals the affinities that Ligeti has pointed out between the bocet and basso ostinato lament, similarities that, in the Trio, create collusion between two distant lament traditions.[29]

Although rooted in traditions and specific roles, the three lament voices adopted by the composer prove labile. No sooner do they sound than they begin to grow and change, some to the point of being unrecognizable. The transformations are central to the movement, particularly in regard to form. Indeed, the form of Ligeti's lament derives more from the transformations than from the structural properties of any of the lament voices, even that of the passacaglia. The Trio and other lament movements follow the same basic design, that of an escalating momentum fueled by the changes in the voices that reaches a tumultuous climax roughly three quarters of the way through the movement (Figure 4.1).[30] A quiet and removed postlude

Concerto and the fourth of the Violin Concerto) that draws upon the lamento motif but avoids the trappings of the lament, particularly the slow tempo. The lamento motif, instead, is placed in a *perpetuum mobile* in which it is one of many lines spinning more and more out of control. The lamento motif also appears in the sixth movement (Capriccio) of the *Hamburg Concerto* (1998–99), which does not have a strong lament character.

[28] Bartók mentions the prevalence of "four-section" structures in the bocet repertoire, but he also points out songs having "three-section" structures. Bartók, *Rumanian Folk Music*, vol. II, 26.

[29] Ligeti, "Stilisierte Emotion," 59. The two may also create redundancy. For that reason, Ligeti would pair them in only one future work, the Violin Concerto. Even here, though, the bond between the two is not that close. The passacaglia is an ascending figure (not so reminiscent of the Baroque lament tradition), whereas the lamento motif is played in incredibly long durations that make it difficult to hear as a whole figure. Moreover, the motif is presented in only one complete statement.

[30] The fifth movement in the *Musica Ricercata* follows more or less the same design, revealing that even in this early part of his career Ligeti saw laments building to points of forceful outbursts.

Main body of the lament (mm. 1–77)

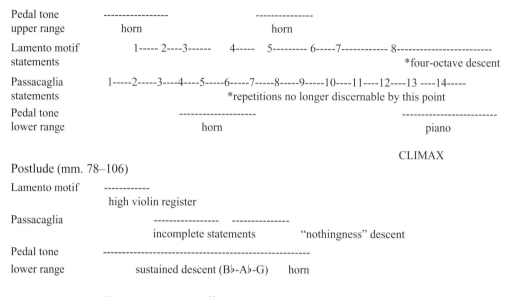

Figure 4.1 Diagram of lament voices, Ligeti, Horn Trio, mvt. 4

(mm. 78–106) follows and closes the movement with recollections of how the lament voices sounded before the roiling transformations.[31]

The changes particularly unsettle the passacaglia. In Baroque lament arias, one statement of the basso ostinato clearly follows another, each adding to an unrelenting sorrow. In Ligeti's movement, the sorrow does not relent, but the clarity of the individual passacaglia statements does. The passacaglia theme returns fourteen times, but by the sixth time, if not earlier, the repetitions can no longer be discerned.[32] Even with the second statement, Ligeti begins to change the register of pitches and to split the dyads between two different instruments (violin and piano LH), with similar alterations multiplying in the following repetitions. Beginning with the fifth statement, the ostinato thickens harmonically, as more and more notes are added to the dyads. Large clusters pack around the clear intervals of the theme. The fourteenth, and last, statement consists of white-key, black-key, and tight chromatic collections (mm. 66–70). With these accretions, not only are the repetitions blocked out but so also are the defining sequence of intervals and the allusions to the Baroque and horn-fifths figures. Only the rigid

---

[31] There is no coda in the Violin Concerto movement.

[32] Compare this with the treatment of the passacaglia in preceding works such as *Le grand macabre*, *Hungarian Rock*, and *Passacaglia ungherese*. In those pieces, the passacaglia themes become obscured by layered materials but they remain more or less intact.

Ex. 4.5 Ligeti, Horn Trio, mvt. 4, mm. 87–92

five-measure pattern keeps the ostinato from being altogether dispersed. Instead of a faithful tally of sorrow, Ligeti's passacaglia becomes a moving, changing force. In pushing to the climax, it amasses harmonic weight, grows louder, and climbs up to the outer edge of the keyboard. In the postlude, the passacaglia theme returns twice and looks back to its original form; however, neither of the two statements is intact (Ex. 4.5).

Drones are by nature inflexible voices. Ligeti's pedal tone is anything but inflexible. It constantly changes pitch, register, dynamics, and roles. In its first appearance, the pedal tone sits pianissimo above the passacaglia theme, a rather strange place for a drone (Ex. 4.1). As the intensity of the lament builds, the pedal tone grows louder and drops down into the piano LH, way down as it reaches two of the bottom notes (C_1 and B_2) on the keyboard (Ex. 4.6). At that same moment, the passacaglia approaches the other end of the instrument. Fanning out, the two parts shape one of the wedges frequently encountered in Ligeti's works. In the postlude, the pedal tone returns to the horn, plumbing that instrument's lower register as well (Ex. 4.5). It proves to be the one voice that does not break apart during the closing section. Three long tones are sustained, one slurred into the next. The pitches form a small melodic descent ($B\flat_1$–A_1–G_1), which, if one looks back to the rest of the movement, can be heard as part of a longer descent (in terms of pitch not register). The line begins with the $c\sharp''$ in the horn (m. 33),

Ex. 4.6 Ligeti, Horn Trio, mvt. 4, mm. 74–76

continues in the piano LH (C_1–B_2) and reaches an end in the horn's final three notes.[33] The pedal tone is one type of lament voice; however, during the course of the movement, it becomes another type of lament voice, the descending chromatic line.

The third voice, the lamento motif, is just as unsettled as the other two. In particular, the distinct shape, the three descending phrases, breaks apart during the growing agitation. The form holds for what could be heard as four statements of the motif (mm. 6–11, 14–19, 19–25, 27–33), but, by the time of what would be the fifth statement, it gives way to longer descents, lines that push down an octave and beyond and string together several small phrases.[34] The piano and violin let loose the first of these descents (mm. 35–48). When the horn finally and dramatically enters in a melodic role (as opposed to playing pedal tones), it and the violin interlock phrases to create another descent (mm. 49–56), which occurs simultaneously with a series of precipitous drops in the piano (mm. 52–56). The culmination of this frenzy is the longest descent of the movement (mm. 64–77), a fall of over four octaves in the piano from $c\sharp''$ to A_2, the lowest note on the keyboard and one step below the already nether-region pedal tone. As the descent deepens, the energy of the line begins to sputter (Ex. 4.6). The lower the line goes, the more fragmented and disjointed it becomes until there is nothing more than two- or single-note attacks, a far cry from the elegant three-phrase structure of the lamento motif. At this point, the motif appears all but lost. It returns, though, at the beginning of the postlude. Set in a celestial violin register way above the crumbling pits just heard, it is restored to its original form of three successive phrases. And then it is lost once more; the motif never

[33] Taylor sees a similar descent unfurling throughout the movement. "The Lamento Motif," 45.
[34] Taylor points out seven overall descents ("The Lamento Motif," 40). A growing rhythmic energy sustains these descents. The energy derives in large part from the use of smaller rhythmic values than heard in the first few statements of the lamento motif.

sounds again – unless one hears a continuation of it in the slow three-note descent in the horn.

The transformations of the three voices are crucial not only to the shape of the movement but also to its functioning as a lament. To recall, the genre can reach points of extravagant sonic metamorphosis. Ligeti's transformations prove just as strange, even monstrous. That the transformations approach the fantastic is clear enough, but what the voices are changed into is not so obvious. The listener can interpret the alterations as he or she wishes. Ligeti, though, provided his own images. His commentary on the movement evokes the act of transformation, underscoring how prominently it figures in his conception of the lament. According to him, the slender passacaglia grows so immense that it becomes a "gigantic imaginary drum," a wondrous image and sound. Its deafening thuds reverberate within an "echo" chamber, that is – according to the composer – what the horn's soft pedal tones have become at the beginning of the postlude. Regarding the lamento motif, Ligeti says only that it undergoes a "dramatic increase in growth," nowhere more so than the last and longest descent, the one covering over four octaves (mm. 64–77).[35] He may not identify a particular transformation but his works suggest one. Many of the composer's pieces set long strings or machinelike lines in play only to have them stutter and break apart, characteristics of what has been called the composer's *meccanico* idiom. As with those lines, the final plunge of the lamento motif relentlessly propels down the keyboard but by the end it splinters. With this in mind, we can hear the transformation as complete. Three tear-like phrases of sorrow are now some sort of frenetic mechanism, which is no sooner set in motion than it falters and comes to a halt.

Ligeti also commits the sonic transgressions typical of the genre. At the dramatically delayed moment when the horn finally takes up the lamento motif (mm. 51–72), it fills the voice with splayed tones. The instrument violates the sonic order of equal temperament by pushing into non-tempered tunings.[36] As used in this work and others, the tunings evoke the sound of natural horns, particularly those heard in Romanian folk traditions.[37] Calling up those instruments, Ligeti commits another transgression. He violates the refined realm of the concert hall by welcoming the uproarious sounds of rural horns.

[35] Quoted in Dibelius, "Ligetis Horntrio," 57.
[36] Ligeti has explored the tuning of the horn in other works, notably the *Hamburg Concerto*.
[37] *"Träumen Sie in Farbe?": György Ligeti im Gespräch mit Eckhard Roelcke* (Vienna: Zsolnay, 2003), 196. A 1930s field recording of a "funeral ritual" from the Bukovina region features a solo natural horn. The CD reissue provides no information on this ritual, but the possibility emerges that the horn part in the lament could be a reference to a folk tradition. Ligeti, however, uses the horn in such a way in non-lament pieces. *Village Music from Romania*, VDE CD-538 (1988). On the death association of the horn in Romanian folk traditions, see Willson, *Ligeti, Kurtág*, 181.

In some laments, the transformations and transgressions are so forceful
that they unleash "acoustic violence." C. Nadia Seremetakis uses that phrase
to describe the vociferous wailing that can explode in laments performed by
women in the Inner Mani region of modern Greece.[38] The frenzied climax
of Ligeti's movement suggests such violence, a suggestion strengthened by
the score directions: "cresc. molto with utmost ferocity, black . . . even more
ferociously cresc. estremissimo."[39] In the most ferocious moments of their
laments, Mani women gather together to bring back the singer from such
a remote emotional point and to control the violence. Another singer will
begin a different lament and nudge it antiphonally into the wailing so as
to reassert the formal and expressive restraints of the genre, bonds which
had been obliterated by the outburst. A lament can never end lost in such
a storm. Just as it begins with the adoption of a lament voice, so must it
finish with that voice (or another one, as in the Mani example), and with
the defining structures of the voice intact.

The Trio movement offers another way to conclude a lament, a far from
conventional way. The acoustic violence is never curtailed. On the contrary, it runs its course, reaching a tumultuous *fff* and pushing to the outer
edges of the keyboard. Only when the violence is culminated does it stop.
The structural schemes of the voices never intervene. If anything, they
have been distorted and broken by the fury. That is how they reappear in
the postlude. We hear faded lines of voices that once were. Ligeti underscores this idea of loss in his description of the movement. In yet another
metaphor of transformation, he compares the postlude to a "photograph
of a landscape," a landscape that, after the picture is taken, "has dissipated
into nothingness."[40] Something as permanent as a landscape or as vibrant
as a lament voice can disappear, leaving us with only dim reproductions
and reminiscences. Ligeti's description captures another transformation,
this one of the genre itself. The change centers on the evocation of loss.
Laments, of course, intensify that feeling, but it is usually the loss of a person not that of the lament voices and structures. In the postlude, we become
aware of the "dissipation" of those elements, all part of a vanished expressive
"landscape." Ligeti creates a new twist on the lament by making the genre
the object of loss.

The postlude takes us into a strange space, strange in that this space is
not part of a lament. Laments end definitively, doing so within either the
terms of the structural schemes, say the last statement of a basso ostinato,

---

[38] Seremetakis, *The Last Word*, 119.
[39] A similar moment in the Piano Concerto lament is marked "con violenza."
[40] Quoted in Taylor, "The Lamento Motif," 27.

Ex. 4.7 Ligeti, Horn Trio, mvt. 4, mm. 100–106

or within the context of a ritual or ceremony. They typically don't have a postlude, especially one that, as in the Trio movement, invites the listener to reflect upon what has happened to the expressive and formal elements in the piece. The movement concludes with shards of the structural schemes. The incompleteness keeps us in a suspended space, no longer part of the emotional heat of the lament but still part of the movement. In the postlude, we are made aware of how powerless the voices are to end the lament and to free us from this ambiguous afterwards. The only thing that can do so is to erase the voices altogether, something else that typically does not occur in a lament. The final cluster chord in the piano takes that ultimate and surprising step (Ex. 4.7). From the cluster, it is impossible to form any of the five passacaglia harmonies, the primary reason being the b and c♯, the two pitch classes not stated in the passacaglia.[41] The passacaglia had earlier been turned into a series of cluster chords, its dyads crowded in those massive sonorities. Now there are no traces of the passacaglia in the final cluster chord. The last sound of the movement, the cluster not only erases the passacaglia chords but also the melodic descent of the lamento motif. One by one the pianist lifts his or her fingers from the chord, creating a descent of and into nothingness as each lifted key clears the resonance of the cluster until there is silence.

---

[41] It is possible to create the opening e-g dyad with the horn pedal, but the emphasis is on the cluster chord itself. Clusters have been closely associated with the passacaglia, which was transformed into a series of such chords. Also obstructing the formation of the passacaglia is the near whole-tone makeup of the cluster. Harmonic sonorities, and melodic motion, throughout the piece have been largely chromatic.

Expression

Having discussed Ligeti's Trio movement as a lament, it is now time to place his lament in the context of the modernist inquiry into expression. The Adagio engages several points raised in the inquiry. In particular, it probes the expressive act of taking up a voice. The act in itself makes a larger statement about modernism. As is well known, modernist idioms can be highly referential, evoking, or raising the voice, of existing styles or pieces. Of course, they can also be withdrawn and isolated, avoiding clear connections to other types of pieces or larger social issues. The references, when made, can be used to different effects, including expressive ones. Works such as Ligeti's laments, draw upon idioms with established emotional associations and use them to make an expressive impact. The reliance on outside associations often stems from concerns over the expressive vagueness or limitations of modernist elements. Ambiguity is the result of the fact that many elements, having departed from traditional syntax, have no ready expressive role or meaning. For instance, the massive clusters in Ligeti's 1960s works were a new sound and open to expressive interpretation and role playing, as seen in the use of the sounds in a Requiem and cinematic outer space tableaux, or both at once as in Kubrick's *2001: A Space Odyssey*.[42] As for limitations, the dissonant compounds of new music can form a narrow expressive palette, confined to what Rochberg called "overintense extremes."[43] For him, quotations, the ultimate referential voice, were a way out of those extremes by using Beethoven, for instance, to speak of grandeur, passion, and other emotions supposedly inaccessible to modernist styles. Although an outside voice, the lament is not used for expressive ventriloquism (in the manner of Rochberg's quotations); rather, it is a traditional expressive forum, the voices and dynamics of which a composer can utilize, even if, as with Ligeti, in ways that violate the traditions of the genre.

Consistent with the modernist proclivity to inquiry, Ligeti's lament movement explores both the expressive act of raising a voice and the modernist reliance on outside voices.[44] The movement is very much invested in the act of taking up an established voice, as it takes up the voices of the lament, and

---

[42] For a discussion of the interpretative issues raised by the inclusion of *Atmosphères* in the film, see Arved Ashby, "Modernism Goes to the Movies," in *The Pleasure of Modernist Music: Listening, Meaning, Intention, Ideology*, ed. Arved Ashby (Rochester, NY: University of Rochester Press, 2004), 359–67.

[43] Rochberg, *The Aesthetics of Survival*, 239.

[44] Ligeti can be heard exploring the act of raising a voice in *Aventures* (1962). The work is a pasticcio of expressive gestures gone awry. The singers begin some sort of vocal statement or gesture only for it to veer off in a wrong direction, a path that often leads to strange, unexpected sounds.

with them a genre dependent on a model of expression based on the raising of a voice. The lament, along with such genres as the ode and the ceremonial drama, adheres to a model in which performers call upon and repeat traditional materials, such as classic tales or specific melodic phrases. The materials usually include moments or voices rich in expressive associations, such as a particular dramatic scene or a sorrowful melody. The repetition of these forms over time deepens both the associations and the moments. By taking up the form and those features, the performer enters into an already rich expressive sphere. As in the lament, the raising of a particular voice initiates and channels emotional expression.

Ligeti's lament movements may draw upon this model, but they complicate it. In a lament, the issuing of the voice is spontaneous and the performance follows more or less a course established by the governing structures or ritual. In Ligeti's lament, the voices emerge but are eventually broken into pieces and transformed beyond recognition. Instead of proceeding on a course established by a set structure, they become caught up in a mounting agitation. The difficulties raise the question: how much can one rely on outside voices, or how much can one speak through them? If such voices are needed, and the movement suggests that they are, they can prove unstable and vulnerable. This is especially the case when the outside voices are brought into a modernist realm, which possesses its own distinct, rival voices, such compositional elements as packed clusters, remote registers, and unbridled melodic strings. In the Trio, those elements subdue the outside voices, making it difficult for them to assume their original breadth. As much as the voices are needed and cultivated, the movement seems to argue, there is a limit to how much they can expand, in terms of both expression and form, in a modernist setting.

The Trio movement gets beyond those limitations by creating additional expressive dynamics and associations. In doing so, it brings up a question that arises in the modernist inquiry: what is the expressive potential of modernist elements, these new sounds and harmonies? Ligeti finds an expressive role for modernist elements within the lament. He does so through the act of transformation central to the genre. The lament voices in the Trio movement may become, to use Ligeti's phrase, "a gigantic imaginary drum," yet, at the same time, they turn into clusters, resonant pedal tones in extreme registers, and frenetic melodic activity. In other words, they become modernist voices, ones that, to draw again upon Ligeti's description, convey "ferocity." The transformation reverses the sonic course of the lament. In performances of the genre, lament voices emerge from the noise of wailing. Ancient accounts of the origins of the genre depict a similar birth. Pindar, for instance, described how Athena "wove" the lament from the mournful

shrieks of the Gorgons.[45] Lament voices are the refined expressive voices
born from din. In the Trio, "ferocious" voices emerge from the refined
lament. They, however, do not completely displace the lament voices, which
appear at the end of the movement, albeit in pieces. They instead join the
lament. The movement has given the modernist elements an expressive
context and viability. They are voices that can thrive within a lament, work
within its dynamics, fortify its expressive moments, and fill it with new
sounds.

Ligeti's lament touches upon another topic pursued in the modernist
inquiry: the relationship between expression and structure. The relationship, it goes without saying, is not just a modernist concern. It is central
to all sorts of musical creation. Some styles and genres, like the lament,
foreground the relationship by disciplining emotion through prescribed
forms. This type of severe control fascinated Ligeti. In a 1987 interview,
he described how such restraint can create a powerfully expressive music
and cited examples in Central African drumming and the Korean dramatic
genre P'ansori.[46] Surprisingly, he never mentions the lament. The lament
movements he wrote at the time, though, challenge the formal discipline
characteristic of the genre. As seen in the Trio movement, Ligeti skews the
relationship between expression and structure by building an emotional
momentum that fractures and contorts the forms of the lament genre. For
Ligeti, the lament opened up a musical world in which expressive impulses
escape the boundaries set for them by an established structure. The movement offers an example of how the inquiry into expression is not just
analytical; rather, the probing of an inquiry, here the exploration of the
limits and powers of voices – both traditional and modernist – can generate
expressive results, which, in Ligeti's case, is a turbulent momentum.

In writing this type of lament and this type of emotionally intense music,
Ligeti was not alone. The lament movements, as mentioned above, can be
heard as part of the turn to a more directly expressive idiom that began in
the 1980s. Many composers made the turn through the lament. Among the
composers taking up the genre are Kurtág, Schnittke, Gubaidulina, Turnage,
Golijov, Birtwistle, Ferneyhough, Harbison, Pärt, and Saariaho. With their
works, the lament has become an important vein of expression in recent

---

[45] See Pindar's Twelfth Pythian Ode. A discussion of the Pindar text can be found in Charles Segal,
    "The Gorgon and the Nightingale: The Voice of Female Lament and Pindar's Twelfth *Pythian
    Ode*," in *Embodied Voices: Female Vocality in Western Culture*, ed. Leslie C. Dunn and Nancy A.
    Jones (Cambridge University Press, 1994), 17–34.
[46] Ligeti, "Stilisierte Emotion," 61. Ligeti also mentions examples from European traditions,
    including the poetry of Hölderlin (whose work Ligeti set during the early 1980s), which "styl-
    izes" emotions through the use of archaic meters, and the music of Ravel, which creates precise
    grids for expression.

music. What is remarkable is how many of these composers similarly exploit the emotional power of the lament. As with Ligeti, they stage the genre so that an expressive drive breaks down the continuity of a set form, often, similar to Ligeti's works, through scenes of acoustic violence. The following analyses reveal how laments by Kurtág and Saariaho play out this scenario.

The Lamentoso movement of Kurtág's orchestral piece *Stele* (1994), like Ligeti's works, evokes the lament through a passacaglia-like descending chromatic bass phrase. Kurtág, though, begins his lament at a much more intense level. Unlike the quiet, mournful opening of the Ligeti Trio movement, the orchestral lament starts "wild, rushed, impatient."[47] It begins almost at a climax and from there it reaches not one climax, but two. In the first, the passacaglia voice succumbs to a frenzied textural buildup. Resilient, it starts over, even more harried, only to buckle once again. Something happens that never happens in a Ligeti lament, or almost any lament: acoustic violence repeats.[48]

Saariaho's *L'amour de loin* (2000) presents an operatic rendition of the modernist lament. In the Baroque, the genre was at home on the stage.[49] With its return there in Saariaho's work, it proves to be still comfortable in the theater, but it takes on a different expressive form. The opera draws upon the life, or legend, of the troubadour Jaufré Rudel, whose songs idealize a "distant" love, that of a woman who the poet is never to meet. Unlike his historical counterpart, the operatic Jaufré, with the help of a mysterious Pilgrim, sets out to see her. During the long sea journey, he grows anxious about the encounter and sings a lament in which he fears that meeting her will mar the purity of their love and lead to doom (Act IV, scene iii).

The libretto calls Jaufré's lament a "complainte." The French genre belongs to the larger medieval planctus family. Troubadours did perform complaintes and other lament-type pieces, but no song in the genre by Jaufré survives.[50] The complainte as a genre has survived, but primarily as a historical relic, a song more read about than heard. As such, it does not offer a recognizable lament voice, unlike the Baroque passacaglia, a more alive and familiar relic. Saariaho, though, uses the genre to fashion a

---

[47] The opening directions read "Lamentoso – disperato, con moto. Nicht zu schnell, aber wild, gehetzt, ungeduldig."

[48] An extended analytical discussion of the entire piece can be found in Richard Toop, "*Stele* – A Gravestone as End or Beginning? György Kurtág's Long March toward the Orchestra," *Contemporary Music Review*, 20, nos. 2 and 3 (2001), 129–49.

[49] Saariaho has evoked the lament in other works, including "Miranda's Lament" and "Mort" (from *Oltra Mar*).

[50] In an index of planctus-type works (including the complainte), Janthia Yearley lists 52 surviving works in Provençal, none by Jaufré. Yearley, "A Bibliography of Planctus in Latin, Provençal, French, German, English, Italian, Catalan and Galician-Portuguese from the Time of Bede to the Early Fifteenth Century," *Journal of the Plainsong and Medieval Music Society* 4 (1981), 12–52.

voice suitable to a modern lament, one which harkens back to its medieval inspiration.

The complainte, like many types of medieval chanson, builds upon a group of melodic phrases, which are arranged in a specific order, one coordinated with the poetic structure (AAB, ABAC, for instance).[51] Saariaho crafts three melodic phrases (A, B, C) and links them together in a structural chain longer and more intricate than that found in the Middle Ages: ABABCACACAC. The key point is not that Saariaho departs from a specific medieval form but that she adheres to the type of repetitions defining those forms. The consistent, narrow melodic repetition heard in the aria is rare in the composer's music, suggesting that she was using the approach to connect to the complainte, or medieval song in general.[52] It is a loose connection, though, as the chromatic melodies belong to the modernist period. The three phrases (A, B, C) are all built around dyads a fifth apart, with each of the pairs being presented in a melodic sequence made up largely of semitones and tritones (Ex. 4.8). Phrase A features three melodic fifths (c–g, f♯–c♯′, g–d′) set in an ascending pattern of tritone and half step, creating a collection in which the first three notes and the last three form the same pitch-class set (3–5). In some statements of the phrase, Saariaho approaches the c with a B♮ leading tone, thereby creating one more fifth in the collection (B–f♯). Phrases B and C follow a different design (with the latter being an exact statement of the former transposed up a half step). Both present pairs of fifths a half-step apart. Some statements lift the lower two notes (c♯–d, d–e♭) an octave higher to extend the melodic range. When all three figures are combined, we can see that the pitches of the B and C phrases fill in the tritones of A, leaving only two half-steps unstated in each tritone span (e–f, b–c′, which also form pairs of fifths).

Whereas the chromatic intervals are more the stuff of the modernist lament than of the medieval complainte, the incessant repetition of the phrases accords with both. Melodic repetition plays a prominent role in many lament repertoires. As seen in the Baroque basso ostinato, it can be a symbol of unending sorrow. At the same time, it can be a structural constraint. Grief becomes locked in the phrases. Confined there, it can neither fly off in different directions with each emotional outburst nor suddenly take a new form; rather, it must submit to the steady course of repetition, just as mourning adheres to the ceremony of a ritual. In Saariaho's lament,

[51] On formal structures in troubadour music, see Elizabeth Aubrey, *The Music of the Troubadours* (Bloomington and Indianapolis: Indiana University Press, 1996), 132–97.

[52] Saariaho does successively repeat melodic phrases in a loose way, as heard in the "concerto"-type pieces such as . . . *à la fumée* and *Amers*, but these works do not feature the involved formal structures built around consistent repetitions as used in the aria.

Ex. 4.8 Saariaho, *L'amour de loin*, Act IV, scene iii
Libretto by Amin Maalouf. Music by Kaija Saariaho. Libretto © Copyright 2000
Amin Maalouf. Rights licensed to Chester Music Limited, London W1T 3LJ. Music
© Copyright 2000 Chester Music Limited, London W1T 3LJ. All rights reserved.
International copyright secured. Reprinted by permission

Jaufré channels his despair into the three phrases, using the restatements to intensify a deepening dread. The repetitions also hold his sorrow back from growing excessive, but only to a certain point. The dynamics of transgression and transformation eventually disrupt the continuity of the structural repetition and lead the complainte into an outburst.

Before the climax of the lament, there is already violence and strain. The scene opens with a storm at sea, which inspires both the sorrow behind the lament and the melody of Jaufré's song. Saariaho evokes the churning clouds and ocean with a frenzied dense orchestral cluster. Over a pedal b♭, most of the orchestra plays driving sixteenth-note phrases. Each division of the beat creates a complete or near-complete chromatic cluster. From the vertical to the linear, the individual instruments present repeated chromatic lines, many of them featuring two- or three-note flecks heard in the lament phrases. In the wake of the tempest, Jaufré begins his complainte with the A phrase (m. 391) only to be interrupted by a chorus of sailors, who add to the medieval flavor with a melody harmonized in fourths and fifths.[53] He resumes the lament and once again stops, this time to convey to the Pilgrim his fears that his beloved Countess may have heard that he has set out on a journey to find her. He voices his anxieties with the C phrase and she responds with the same phrase, offering him little comfort (mm. 441–83).

After the last interruption, Jaufré extends the complainte, making his way through the intricate melodic form (ABABCACACAC) (mm. 485–573). For most of the aria, the structural repetition withstands the pressing despair. The phrases, in terms of range and interval patterns, remain relatively intact. In the last four statements of the A and C phrases, though, the increasingly fraught Jaufré pushes past the upper range of the phrase and hits an f♯'. The expressive impact created by the end of the lament derives not so much from the C phrase being breached, but from the presence of the C phrase at this point. Its return creates a moment of transgression. The phrase has been associated with the otherworldly in two previous appearances, during the Pilgrim's description of angels bearing mysterious messages and at the moment Jaufré conjures up the voice of a genie (mm. 508–10). When Jaufré picks up the phrase at the conclusion of the aria, he builds upon this association and adds to it suggestions of death. In his final cries, he has visions of reaching out to the forbidden fruit in the Garden of Eden and being burned by an "incandescent star." As heard in some lament traditions, he has slipped beyond the everyday world and entered an unknown realm of mystery and death. Lament once again stretches a tether between our world and some next realm.[54]

The spiritual, emotional transgression sets up a culminating musical transformation. As soon as Jaufré finishes the aria, the opening storm returns. The orchestra releases the turbulent texture and burst of individual lines heard at the beginning of the scene. As mentioned earlier, some of the lines in the opening sonic mass draw upon lament phrases, a connection suggesting that Jaufré's complainte has been born from a storm

---

[53] This analysis does not have the time to focus on the orchestral accompaniment of the lament, other than to note that it consists of individual melodic lines many of which feature motives from the lament phrases.

[54] Kligman, *The Wedding of the Dead.*

and will eventually become one. That the lament and storm stand beside each other in the same scene is worthy of note. Both serve as distinct numbers in eighteenth-century opera, where they never meet, being dramatically and musically so removed from each other. Storms usually inspire either prayers for or celebrations of deliverance from nature's wrath; laments most often follow death.[55] At the very beginning of the twenty-first century, the two meet and merge. The transformation from storm to lament and back to storm does not signify a new sort of operatic dramaturgy; rather, it puts into stark terms the late modernist understanding of the lament. The genre stirs expressive turmoil and force. In other words, it becomes a storm. Transformations are to be expected in a lament, but a meteorological metamorphosis is fantastic even by the standards of the genre.

The final storm in Saariaho's opera matches the violent endings in the Ligeti and Kurtág works. All three pieces escalate an expressive momentum that pushes beyond the strictness and continuity of the forms established early on. The works not only violate those structures but also stress the genre of the lament to such a degree that it takes on new, contorted forms, like the "drum" and "echo chamber" at the close of Ligeti's movement, the repeated acoustic violence in Kurtág's composition, and the tempest in Saariaho's. The dramatic outcomes in each piece say much about the types of direct expressive statements that composers since the 1980s have sought. Searching for veins of expression suitable for this moment in the history of modernism, some composers settled on outright intensity, a power born from and surpassing that of the lament.

So accustomed are we to the "overintense extremes" of new music that we might find it hard to think of a modernist lament ending in any other way. Yet the union between new idioms and the age-old genre can assumes various forms, some the antithesis of that described above. Two examples include Boulez's *Rituel in memoriam Bruno Maderna* (1975) and the *Lamentation* from *Doctor Faustus*. Both pieces bring together the lament and structural ideals of modernism, the twelve-tone system and its expanded serial offshoots. In the two works, governing structural schemes do not falter in the face of a building emotionality but rather create their own expressive realms.

Boulez's *Rituel* enacts an "imaginary ceremony," one devoted to "remembrance" and "extinction."[56] The composer gives the ceremony no specific name other than what it is, a ritual. It remains unique and enigmatic: a new

---

[55] Two examples include Gluck's *Iphigénie en Tauride* and Mozart's *Idomeneo*. In the former, the storm that swells up in the Overture leads to supplications for delivery from the tempest. In the latter, those at sea and on shore pray to Neptune to end the storm.

[56] Other pieces by Boulez have mourning associations, including . . . *explosante-fixe* . . . (to commemorate the death of Stravinsky) and *Répons*, which features a "funeral-march" like section. Dominique Jameux, *Pierre Boulez*, trans. Susan Bradshaw (London: Faber & Faber, 1991), 365.

rite performed only with the piece and nowhere else. Lament would seem
to be one way to grasp the composition, so practiced is it in loss, memory,
and the obedience paid to structure. Yet the work resists designation as a
lament, or any specific genre. Its resistance, though, makes the lament all
the more relevant, for the piece appears to be designed to prevent a lament
from forming. Lament is a type of ritual to be avoided, in part because
of intense emotionality and the threats posed to structural exactitude. If
the compositions of Ligeti, Saariaho, and others have expressive dynamics
override the forms and even the genre of the lament, *Rituel* erects structural
schemes resilient to the expressive flux of the genre.

Boulez's ceremony is intricate. Not surprisingly, many scholars have
sought to decode the elaborate rite by uncovering the layered interrelation-
ships and the calculated coherence that they sustain.[57] There is not room
enough here to lay out these designs, only space enough to give an outline
of the rite. The work is built around pairs of responses and verses, which
add up to fifteen separate sections. The former, the odd-numbered sections marked *très lent*, put down weighty chords followed by terse melodic
phrases, whereas the latter, the even-numbered sections marked *modéré*,
create an unsynchronized heterophony by overlapping the melodies presented by eight different groups in the orchestra. During the course of the
piece, the orchestral groups are added one by one, and the melodic lines in
the verses grow longer and more florid. The fifteenth section, which takes
up almost one third of the work, begins with all eight groups sustaining a
chord but steadily scales back until only two are playing at the close.

Rituel erects the architecture of what could be an impassioned lament.
As in the Ligeti and Kurtág works, the texture grows denser, the melodic
lines sprawl, and energy builds to a climax after which there is a reduction.
The similarities end there. In *Rituel*, the form does not animate a rushing
emotionality. It could hold the swell of a lament, but it does not. How could
it when several elements conspire against such an outcome? The dynamics
create the most forceful obstruction. Instead of the push to *fortissimo* and
beyond heard in the Ligeti and Kurtág pieces, the dynamics, especially
in the verses, constantly change. The markings follow an organized series
consisting of different degrees (*p, mp, mf, f, ff*). With the constantly shifting
dynamics, we hear a structural logic at work, not a mounting emotional

---

[57] Analytical studies of the work can be found in Ivanka Stoïanova, "Narrativisme, téléologie et
invariance dans l'oeuvre musicale," *Musique en jeu* 25 (1976), 15–31; Paul Griffiths, *Boulez*
(London: Oxford University Press, 1978), 58–60; Michael Beiche, "Serielles Denken in 'Rituel'
von Pierre Boulez," *Archiv für Musikwissenschaft* 38 (1981), 24–56; Michael Denhoff, "'Rituel'
von Pierre Boulez: Anmerkungen zur Raum – und Zeit – Konzeption," in *Festschrift Emil
Platen zum sechzigsten Geburtstag*, ed. M. Gutierrez-Denhoff (Bonn, 1986), 208–19; Goldman,
"Exploding/Fixed," 144–67.

plea. The same holds for the other elements, which adhere to the rule of a preconceived plan instead of any sort of expressive spontaneity. Dictating the logic is the number seven, which is the basis for different facets of the work, including rhythm, harmony (the chief seven-note chord), and melody (a seven-note row).

The piece also holds to a general structural principle, one averse to the mechanics of the lament. Boulez notes that "the same formulas," the responses and verses, return over and over, but each time changed in "profile and perspective." In other words, certain gestures – say, the opening oboe phrase, the seven-note chord – reappear more or less the same yet slightly different depending on how they are manipulated by the ruling structural schemes and their position within an individual section. In *Rituel*, transformation ultimately underscores sameness, whereas in a lament, transformation pushes to wholly new places, as a voice becomes something else altogether. Transgression, the destruction of a governing scheme or natural order, is one of the places to which metamorphosed lament voices head. Neither dynamic is possible in *Rituel*. The "formulas" remain unvarying, and the structural scheme all-encompassing. Nor does the work give quarter to a building emotionality and the tensions between expression and structure that such intensity can create. There are, as Jonathan Goldman points out, "dense orchestral powers," but they remain "motionless."[58] With all these features stilled, *Rituel* stops the momentum of a lament from ever building.

This is not to say that *Rituel* is an inexpressive work. It has expressive qualities, but they remain difficult to encapsulate. An austere mournfulness and a rigorous inevitability are two impressions that come to mind. These qualities are achieved through an elaborate structural scheme, which is elevated in this piece, lifted up to the status of a ceremony. That a composer connected to the most visionary formal designs of the 1950s and 1960s raised a precompositional design to such a plane comes as little surprise. Like a ceremony, the structure of the work is something inviolate and sacred. Mourning defers to it, and through the constant acting out and repetition of the structural plan, we do too, becoming participants in the ritual.

If Boulez weighs structural control over expressive momentum and Ligeti and other composers tilt the scales in the opposite direction, Mann achieves a third way. Leverkühn's *Lamentation* pushes both sides to extremes. It is at once the composer's most thoroughly organized and expressive piece. The work refines "a formal treatment strict to the last degree" and releases the "most frightful lament ever set up on earth" (DF, 485, 487). The concord

---

[58] Goldman, "Exploding/Fixed," 146.

of the two, as Mann acknowledges, comes across as a paradox (DF, 485). Pitched at such superlative degrees, one side, it seems, would preclude the other. Yet the union can be attained and done so through structure. With the twelve-tone system devised by Leverkühn, construction reaches a summit, supposedly sitting above all other facets of the work. It, though, ultimately serves as a stepping point to something higher, expression. Mann formulates the relationship between the two terms in different ways but, in each case, expression lies beyond structure, either representing the productive result created by construction or existing on a different plane.[59] "Expressiveness," for instance, is "the issue of the whole construction" (DF, 491). Mann also describes the *Lamentation* as making a "breakthrough," a reference to a phrase taken from his conversations with Adorno (DF, 485).[60] The latter poised modernist music on the point of "a breakthrough beyond construction to expression." In other words, modern music could use new structural means to reach a new type and level of expressiveness. Finally, Mann even incorporates this view of expression into the compositional labor of twelve-tone music. With "the previously organized material" and "already given structure" established by the system, Leverkühn can move on to expressive detail and "yield himself to subjectivity" (DF, 488).

The twelve-tone system provided Mann with a new way of fashioning the connection between structure and expression. The lament offered him an older model of the relationship, one that he ultimately rejects. The genre serves many roles in the novel, including a cry of personal and national agony and a despairing double to the "Ode to Joy." It is also a historical precedent. Mann makes three references to early seventeenth-century lament works. Two pieces are mentioned in passing, a chromatic chaconne by Jacopo Melani and Monteverdi's *Lamento della Ninfa* (DF, 484, 486).[61] The third composition, Monteverdi's *Lamento d'Ariadne*, comes up several times. For Mann, the piece is a historical counterpart to the *Lamentation*.[62] With the

---

[59] For a different view of the relationship, one drawing upon Adorno's conceptions of mimesis and rationality, see Christa Bürger, "Expression and Construction in Adorno and Thomas Mann," in *Thinking Art: Beyond Traditional Aesthetics*, ed. Andrew Benjamin and Peter Osborne (London: Institute of Contemporary Arts, 1991), 131–43.

[60] Thomas Mann, *Tagebücher 28.5.1946–31.12.1948*, ed. Inge Jens (Frankfurt: S. Fischer, 1989), 66, 952.

[61] Mann may be evoking the latter work with his reference to "the softly echoing plaintive song of nymphs" (DF, 486).

[62] The piece also accentuates the lament as Adrian Leverkühn's personal cry of despair. "Adrian" is clearly a metathesis of "Ariadne" (Berthold Hoeckner, *Programming the Absolute: Nineteenth-century German Music and the Hermeneutics of the Moment*, Princeton University Press, 2002, 238). The relationship between Adrian and an early Baroque operatic character singing a lament is brought out in the scene in which his friends (including Serenus Zeitblom, the chronicler of the biography making up the novel) see the composer sitting at the piano with the score of the *Lamentation*. As in a Baroque lament scene, they are the observers and commentators who gather around the lamenter. Like Ariadne or any other lamenter, Leverkühn only begins his emotional plea when he has such an audience. The composer, though, no sooner starts his

lament, Monteverdi sought a "liberation of expression," a revolutionary step to be equaled three-hundred some years later by the "reconstruction of expressiveness" in Leverkühn's final piece (DF, 486, 488). Mann has little to say about how Monteverdi exactly liberates expression. We do know that Mann drew upon Ernst Krenek's book *Music Here and Now*, particularly the connection Krenek made between Monteverdi, the composer forging the transition from modality to the new tonal system, and Schoenberg, who charted a path from tonality to atonal idioms.[63] Krenek does describe what could be called a "liberation of expression" in Monteverdi's music. The Italian composer turned to the new tonal system in part for its structural and expressive possibilities but at the same time moved beyond its "boundaries" in pursuing expression. No sooner was a new structural means established than it was surpassed.

Whereas Krenek may have influenced Mann's view of Monteverdi, his model of liberation ultimately has little bearing on Leverkühn's *Lamentation*. The structure of the grand work remains intact; it is not "poisoned" from within, to borrow Krenek's way of describing the effect of expression on Monteverdi's use of the tonal system. The absence of such a threat raises questions about the genre of Leverkühn's final opus. Scholars have examined different facets of the work – its Utopian claims, the influence of Adorno, the promise seen in the twelve-tone system, the eulogy offered for German culture – but no one has stopped to ask – as has been done with every piece discussed in this chapter – how does the *Lamentation* function as a lament.[64] To do so offers new insights into the work, especially Mann's visionary design of the relationship between structure and expression.

Mann goes to great lengths to set up the work as a lament. He establishes a Baroque pedigree and draws upon a repertoire of expressive gestures taken from earlier lament styles, including suspensions, chromatic melodies, echo effects, and sighs. Nowhere does he evoke the expressive energies animating the Baroque lament, or any style of lament for that matter. Such forces as the tension between expressive impulse and structural control, the

---

lament than he collapses. He plays a "strongly dissonant chord" on the piano and releases a wail, instead of song (DF, 503). The lament, once again, disappears, as we get the setup for the genre and then only a wail, not the ritualistic song provided by the genre. Laments are intended to discipline wails, to transport them into a song of sorrow.

[63] Mann, *Tagebücher*, 481. The connection between the two books is also discussed in Gunilla Bergsten, *Thomas Mann's "Doctor Faustus": The Sources and Structure of the Novel*, trans. Krishna Winston (University of Chicago Press, 1969), 184. Ernst Krenek, *Music Here and Now*, trans. Barthold Fles (New York: Russell & Russell, 1967), 119–20.

[64] These issues and a host of others are discussed in the abundant literature on the novel. Some significant studies include Bürger, "Expression and Construction"; Bergsten, *Thomas Mann's "Doctor Faustus"*; Berthold Hoeckner, *Programming the Absolute*, 237–52; Michael Bedlow, *Thomas Mann, "Doctor Faustus"* (Cambridge University Press, 1994); Patrick Carney, *Faust As Musician: A Study of Thomas Mann's Novel "Doctor Faustus"* (New York: New Directions, 1973).

transformation of lament voices, and transgression seem out of place, if not impossible, in a lament that Mann describes as "very certainly non-dynamic, lacking in development, without drama" (DF, 487). It is a strange description of the genre but perhaps not of Mann's conception of the lament. In some ways, his piece resembles Boulez's *Rituel*. Both works are ruled by structure, specifically the same two types of construction: serial or twelve-tone designs and variation form. Boulez's composition calculates different serial schemes around the number seven and Leverkühn's piece employs the twelve-tone system. The former repeats "formulas" with slight changes, whereas the latter sets up a variation form (the antithesis of that used by Beethoven in the "Ode to Joy") in which themes and sections emerge from a common source, like the rings created by throwing a stone into water, each one individual but "always the same" (DF, 487). With both principles taken "to the last degree," there is no possibility of any of the stresses, disruptions, or strange metamorphoses heard in a conventional lament.[65] As in Boulez's piece, the genre has been thwarted.

Going beyond Boulez, it is also erased. Mann loads his work with gestures suggesting the genre but then takes the unusual step of effacing them. In the composition, these elements are not merely "imitated" but rather they are "distilled" or "refined into fundamental types of emotional significance and crystallized" (DF, 488). Earlier pieces by Leverkühn draw upon outside styles, but they partake in "caricature" and "parody," meaning obvious and ironic allusions (DF, 410, 489). The *Lamentation* is "without parody." Having "refined" the lament voices, it is "stylistically purer" than the previous compositions (DF, 489). Stylistic purity complements structural purity. The work achieves an "absoluteness" of form, a structure of wholeness and perfection that does not allow for the slightest outside element, not even a "free note" (DF, 488).

To fit into such a pure world, the lament voices borrowed by Mann must be stripped of their associations. The process diverts the course of transformation so typical of the genre. In both a conventional lament and Leverkühn's work, the voices change into something else. Whereas the former may distend the voices until they become a new type of sound, one monstrously expressive, the latter reduces them, so that they become something enigmatic. We no longer hear the voices, just their essences. What these "crystals" are, how they sound, and what expressive effects they create remains unclear, even in Mann's vivid prose. All we know is that the most obvious signs of the lament have been diminished.

---

[65] Mann does mention an "outburst," but it appears that it is accommodated in the structure of the work (DF, 489).

    As the work progresses, Mann's account, our score, refers less and less to the lament and other Baroque topics. By the time the chorus drops out to begin the final "purely orchestral" section, there are two broad tributes to the expressiveness of the lament but none of the specific references to lament voices that appeared earlier in the piece (DF, 489). Tellingly in the last paragraph, which makes up the concluding movement of the work, Mann twice raises the need for a voice to convey a darkening despair as well as a remote hope. He finds a voice, but it is not that of the lament, which had earlier responded to that call. A single pitch played by a solo cello instead provides the needed voice, a pitch proffered not by the venerable genre but by the "uncompromising" structure of the piece (DF, 491).

    If the lament disappears, then why evoke it? As mentioned before, the genre carries so much symbolic weight, an antithesis to the "Ode of Joy" and a funeral rite for both Leverkühn and Germany. Mann also enlists the expressive significance of the lament. He upholds it as "the first and original manifestation" of expressiveness and as bearing unmatched emotional power. With this in mind, we can begin to see how the lament figures into Mann's view of the relationship between structure and expression. To recall, Mann, departing from Adorno, creates a modern work that achieves "a breakthrough beyond construction" to a new type of expression. Whereas the means of construction could be specified and historically supported with references to Schoenberg's twelve-tone system, the expressive plane lying beyond construction could not be easily pinned down. It was the new sphere imagined by both Adorno and Mann. For the former, the realm stood apart from the lament. Indeed, the genre, with associations of unrestrained personal emotion, was something to be avoided. According to Adorno, the "most recent works" (like Schoenberg's Fourth Quartet) "pose the question of how construction can become expression without pitifully yielding to a lamenting subjectivity?"[66] In Mann's novel, construction does give in to lament, or, more precisely, it leads into what the novelist calls a lament. He repeatedly tells us how powerful the *Lamentation* is, the most expressive territory upon which Leverkühn and new music in general have ever alighted. One way to describe the realm would be to refer to the lament, the original and most forceful form of expression. The new expressive sphere has little to do with the dynamics of the genre, but it still possesses an emotional force, the closest thing to which we know being the lament. The genre offers an approximation, one that, with its historical associations and expressive abundance, proves rich enough to match the new space. Moving into an untouched expressive sphere, Mann found a name

[66] Adorno, *Philosophy of New Music*, 77.

and purpose for the realm by turning back to the origins of expression, the lament.

Mann's *Lamentation* and the laments created by late modernist composers may set the relationship between structure and expression along different lines but they have one thing in common: the two end in depletion. The *Lamentation* distills the borrowed lament voices into nothingness, whereas the late twentieth-century pieces, such as Ligeti's movements, wear down the voices. In Mann's work, the structural scheme dictates. It demands the purification of the lament and pushes into a new expressive sphere. For Ligeti and other composers turning to the genre in the 1980s, expressive force dominates. They remain truer to the lament voices than Mann does, giving us fuller statements of the voices rather than enigmatic essences. The voices, though, ultimately become fractured in the growing tumult. The *Lamentation* and late modernist pieces may end with depleted lament voices but they leave us in very different places, endpoints that say much about the priorities and aspirations of two different periods in the history of modernism. Mann's novel leads us to a new, and hard-to-imagine, expressive space, one preordained by the logic of the twelve-tone system. The *Lamentation* speaks to the writer's ambivalence about the system, at once a promising new formal approach and a symbol of rigid control. The late modernist compositions share none of that ambivalence. Emerging after the heyday of serialism, they reject both the promise and the control. By re-creating an archaic genre in modernist terms, they claim an expressive realm that is familiar – familiar in the sense of being elemental, as raw and basic as the lament itself.

5 Sonic flux

That modernist composers were the first to venture deep into the realm of sound should come as no surprise. Two pressing needs drove them there. As Douglas Kahn has written, they crossed the line separating music and sound "to bring back unexploited resources, restock the coffers of musical materiality, and rejuvenate Western art music."[1] The noises of the Futurists and the sound masses of Varèse were surely fresh resources. By traversing the border, composers could not only lay claim to the new but also undermine the old, the established ideas of what is music. Each foray had the dual effect of revealing the borderline, one that was held to be so fundamental as to go unnoticed, and effacing it so that it would become not so prominent or inviolate. With the line trampled upon, music faced the disorder of its supposed opposite, an exposure that threatened the syntax and figures of common practice idioms and revealed them to be nothing more than strands of sound.[2]

As bold of a challenge as the exploration of sound was, it has not received as much attention as that paid to other compositional parameters, notably those of tonality and rhythm.[3] The imparity stems from the challenges of discussing sound. The concept is broad, if not amorphous, and its elements are not as neatly quantifiable as those of pitch or rhythm. This chapter aims to enrich the literature by approaching sound through the topics of compositional states and expression. The former, as we have seen, offers insights into the modernist emphasis placed on artistic material. Sound is perhaps the most tangible of musical materials, as it comes across as either a mass or an object (to use two images that appear often in discussions of sound) that can be molded. In particular, it can be manipulated to evoke

---

[1] Douglas Kahn, *Noise, Water, Meat: A History of Sound in the Arts* (Cambridge, MA: MIT Press, 1999), 69.

[2] Jacques Attali views the interaction with sound as increasing the power of music to subdue aspects of sound. Though he does not deal with the modernist encounter with sound, his book brings up the concept of noise. My study employs the word "sound" as a broad heading that can include such concepts as noise. The emphasis on sound is not to discount the powerful subversive, disorienting effects that the welter called noise can have. Attali, *Noise*, trans. Brian Massumi (Minneapolis: University of Minnesota Press, 1985), 3–6.

[3] A few studies in music scholarship have considered broad aspects of sound, particularly the "musicalized" sounds covered below. Notable studies include Kahn, *Noise, Water, Meat*; Brian Ferneyhough, "Shaping Sound," in *Sound*, ed. Patricia Kruth and Henry Stobart (Cambridge University Press, 2000), 151–72; and *Audio Cultures: Readings in Modern Music*, ed. Christoph Cox and Daniel Warner (New York: Continuum, 2005).

the ideals of specific states, like that of flux discussed here. Expression is a topic rarely broached in regard to sound, which seems too raw and crude to have any nuanced expressive impact. Yet sound, both blunt and subtle, has served as one more tool in the modernist inquiry into expression.

A crucial historiographical task to be pursued further in studies of modernist music is to isolate the different conceptions of sound cultivated by musicians; only then can we get a clearer idea of the many meanings held by the term. Clarification is necessary, as sound, by nature and definition, can be a general, if not motley, entity. Henry Cowell, for instance, defined it as "comprising all that can be heard."[4] The definition does little good in guiding us through the specific uses of sound in late modernist compositions, or even in Cowell's own works. We should instead let the pieces lead us to a definition of sound, or, more accurately, definitions. Sound is not a single auditory phenomenon but rather an array of phenomena. By engaging some of those phenomena, individual pieces put forward different ideas of what sound can be. Four areas should be considered in identifying the approaches to sound taken in a work: the types of sounds used, the manner in which they are employed, the contexts in which they are heard, and the properties of sound emphasized.

The sounds engaged by modernist works fall under two large headings: those of the everyday world, sounds that can be specifically identified, such as a car horn or crowd noise, and more purely sonic entities that are composed, a giant chromatic cluster or highly variegated texture, for instance. According to Kahn, the former necessitated another boundary on the sonic map. Honking horns, crying babies, and rushing water were all noises won by pushing beyond the line separating music and sound. Such goods could not be left where they were found; they were always to be brought back into some sort of musical context. Upon arrival, though, the cargo proved difficult to unload. The sounds possess a stubborn specificity, always pointing back to where they came from. Their real-life origins initially attracted composers, but the persistent recollections of those sources could detract from a musical presentation. The threat was downplayed by "musicalizing" the sounds, a process that involved transforming them so as to obscure, if not altogether erase, the original identities and make them more malleable to compositional treatment.[5] Even the composers who envisioned a future for music in worldly sounds subjected their materials to that

---

[4] For Cowell, sound encompasses the opposition crucial to him, that between music and noise. The distinction between the two is an acoustic one, that between periodic and non-periodic vibrations. Henry Cowell, "The Joys of Noise," in *Essential Cowell: Selected Writings on Music*, ed. Dick Higgins (Kingston, NY: Documentext, 2001), 250.

[5] Kahn, *Noise, Water, Meat*, 68–71, 101–116.

process. Luigi Russolo, for instance, dictated that the "noise sounds" drawn from modern life be rendered into "abstract material," and, in his writings on *musique concrète*, Pierre Schaeffer similarly advocated that the recorded sounds be altered so as to ease the transition "from the purely 'sonorous' to the purely 'musical.'"[6] Through such prescriptions, composers drew a new line, that between sound and "musical sound."[7] The new boundary may have replaced the old one, or shifted the line, but it still relied on the same distinctions. Sound remains isolated, set apart not only from music but also from new versions of itself, the transformed noises. The realm of music, on the other hand, expands, taking in and controlling new materials. Moreover, the status of music is reaffirmed, a self-contained, and removed, art defined by rigorous thought and promises of transcendence.[8]

Kahn does not discuss the second type of sound, that of composed sonorities. This chapter deals with works engaged with that category. To turn Kahn's phrase, those pieces along with a range of modernist works create "sonic music." Sounds are not brought from the outside but rather forged from within. Specific noises are passed over for general properties. Over the course of centuries, sound has been associated with a wide range of characteristics, many of them viewed as antithetical to music, including instability, irrationality, motion, power, nature, and flux. Modernist composers have evoked the phenomenon of sound by emphasizing one or more of these qualities. The possibilities of new idioms have allowed them to realize the properties with unprecedented force. They can push listeners into the midst of crashing masses or mutating clusters. All of these scenes, of course, play out within the context of a composition. Within that context, the relationship between music and sound is not as one-sided as it can be with sounds drawn from everyday life. Sound does not have to be altered to serve the premises of music; rather, music emulates qualities of sound. Moreover, music needs sound for its energies and dynamics. Through sound, music can be re-created.

The compositions by Saariaho, Lachenmann, and Neuwirth discussed in this chapter concentrate on two properties: motion and transformation. Sound is often conceived of as being in constant motion, a perception that results in part from the idea of it being unstable and uncontainable. Traditional musical idioms, of course, move too, as is to be expected of a rhythmic, temporal art. With sound, though, the movement is far-ranging and pronounced, as sound streams across space or other types of sounds.

---

[6] Luigi Russolo, *The Art of Noises*, trans. Barclay Brown (New York: Pendragon Press, 1986), 86–87. Pierre Schaeffer, "Acousmatics," in *Audio Cultures*, 76–81.
[7] Kahn, *Noise, Water, Meat*, 69.   [8] Kahn, *Noise, Water, Meat*, 70, 101.

Sound cannot stay in one place, nor can it stay in one form. It always changes. A sound begins as one type of entity, but its elements – color, weight, harmony, or texture – do not keep the same for long, turning the sonority into another type of sound, and then yet another type. Transformation can be continuous.[9]

Through both qualities, composers have developed a compositional state, that of flux. Given the prominence of the two properties in conceptions of sound, it could be argued that any sound-based work opens up this state, making it less than the well-defined and specialized forums characteristic of states. What distinguishes works involved with sonic flux is the degree to which both qualities are accentuated. They become central events in a piece, even a modus operandi. The first composer to establish the conditions of the state was Varèse. He "liberated" sound not only as material for composition but also as a raw force for composers to commandeer. As he described his music, sonic masses constantly move, colliding with and penetrating each other.[10] Moreover, materials, such as lines or blocks, appear in one sonic setting and take on new forms when emerging in different surroundings.[11] Given Varèse's significant influence on music since World War Two, it is not surprising that other composers have explored the state of flux.[12] Stockhausen's *Gesang der Jünglinge*, for example, sustains the dynamics of this state. It shuttles sounds through loudspeakers and across the sonic continuum, while making the boy's voice more and more like electronic timbres. Ligeti's orchestral cluster works from the 1960s release undulating sound masses that appear to move as they change color, thickness, and shape. The ideals of motion and transformation were central to the early conceptions of spectralism. Grisey penned what could be a definition of this state. Sound, or "forces," he wrote "are infinitely mobile and fluctuating; they are alive like cells with a birth, life, and death, and above all tend towards a continual transformation of their own energy."[13]

The properties of sound can sustain a state, but they can also inhabit what are called here archetypal figures. The difference between the two is one of scale. States stretch out over complete works or movements, whereas the archetypal figures appear in local contexts, anything from a single measure

[9] For a discussion of different approaches to transformation in electronic music, see Denis Smalley, "Defining Transformation," *Interface* 22 (1993), 279–300.

[10] Edgard Varèse, "The Liberation of Sound," in *Contemporary Composers on Contemporary Music*, ed. Elliott Schwartz, Barney Childs, and Jim Fox (New York: Da Capo, 1998), 196–208.

[11] A good example is the opening E♭ clarinet melody in *Intégrales*.

[12] On the influence of Varèse after World War Two, see Robert P. Morgan, "Rewriting Music History: Second Thoughts on Ives and Varèse," *Musical Newsletter* 3, no. 1 (1973), 3–12; 3, no. 2 (1973), 14–23.

[13] Gérard Grisey, "*Tempus ex Machina*: A Composer's Reflections on Musical Time," *Contemporary Music Review* 2 (1987), 239–75.

to, as in the Lachenmann opera analyzed below, several scenes. Archetypal figures almost always arise within the context of the state of sonic flux, which is no surprise given that they too focus on fundamental qualities of sound. The figures are archetypal in that they condense those qualities, particularly motion and transformation, into distinct forms and have recurred frequently enough in works to become basic shapes. The glissando, as discussed in regard to Harvey's *Mortuos plango, vivos voco*, is one such figure. Helmholtz isolated the glissando in the wail of sirens, attention that made it a significant shape in the scientific history of sound.[14] With his use of sirens, Varèse gave the glissando an unprecedented role in the musical exploration of sound. Typical of the effacement of the real-world resonances of sounds, his works downplay suggestions of fire and danger. They instead turn the sirens into prominent and incisive lines in a larger choir of flux.[15] The glissando, the voice of the siren, moves along a curvilinear line, always inching up or down in range, never staying put. With the microtonal slides, it constantly changes, not just in terms of pitch, the fixing of which it flouts, but also in terms of identity. When the figure is writ large, as in the Neuwirth opera studied here, it can be a high piercing sound one moment and a grumble the next, the perfect means for Neuwirth to suggest the metamorphosis of one character into another person.

Another common figure, one that appears in Lachenmann's opera, is that of sonic diminishment, the gradual decline from a full sound mass to nothingness. It offers a straightforward way to channel the energies of sound, something as basic as a giant decrescendo. The figure builds upon the idea of sound being in constant motion, as here a passage moves between extreme points of fullness and emptiness. A corresponding figure is the open-ended crescendo, which, as in the music of Varèse, accumulates energy and volume before throwing sounds out into space. The last archetype to be discussed is the sonic continuum. We have already encountered it in *Gesang der Jünglinge*, and will do so again in pieces by Saariaho. As heard in those works, the figure builds upon both the properties of motion, the traveling back and forth along the line, and transformation, the blurring of identities that occurs while moving across the space, especially in the nebulous middle area.

Sound has also played a role in the modernist inquiry into expression. Such a role may come as a surprise given that the expressive dimensions of sound have received little attention. Even Adorno, who was fascinated

---

[14] Kahn, *Noise, Water, Meat*, 83–91.
[15] In a discussion of Varèse's *Ionisation*, Ferneyhough mentions how the composer "contrives to subsume" the "outside world" elements of the sirens "to their musically assimilable component features: duration, volume, pitch-contour, and the like." Ferneyhough, "Shaping Sound," 156.

by the expressive implications of compositional strategies, was quiet about those arising from the cultivation of sound. In fact, he had very little to say about sound, which he often reduced to timbre, seeing it either as superficial or irrational. It was only late in his career that he paid more attention to sound, perhaps in response to the greater role played by it in contemporary composition.[16] In a 1966 talk entitled "Funktion der Farbe in der Musik," he returned frequently to current works, particularly Ligeti's *Atmosphères*. The piece fascinated him in how close it came to achieving the paradox of being music without pitch, so far do individual pitches disappear into the overall effects of color and sound.[17] As to the expressive sides of this and other recent works immersed in sound, hardly a word is said.[18]

The act of expression and sound may at first appear to have little bearing upon each other. The former involves the raising of a voice, a gesture associated with the individual, be it the performer or a character. Sound grows in mass, mingled sonorities, which, if anything, threaten to overwhelm a voice. As Adorno found out with *Atmosphères*, it can be difficult to detect a single pitch or line in a world in which the overall impression is one of accumulation and crowded activity. Yet these differences make the pair so vital. The two create an opposition crucial to sound-based works, that between voice and sound. The opposition appears prominently in pieces by Varèse, which have single melodic lines repeat over and over amid the collision of sound masses, and in *Gesang der Jünglinge*, which releases a boy's voice into the world of vacillating electronic timbres.

The differences and tensions between voice and sound come down to two basic areas. The first, as touched upon above, is the contrast between the individual part and the mass. Voice, be it vocal or instrumental, presents a single melodic line usually set off in a thin or unobtrusive texture. Such clarity enhances the lyricism and sense of address characteristic of the voice. Sound, made up of human voices, instrumental timbres, or real-world noises, typically involves clotted mixes in which there is little individual detail. The second area involves meaning. Discussing the distinctions between the two, Mladen Dolar argues that "what defines the voice as special among the

---

[16] On Adorno's critical aversion to sound, see Julian Johnson, "'The Elliptical Geometry of Utopia': New Music Since Adorno," in *Apparitions: New Perspectives on Adorno and Twentieth-century Music*, ed. Berthold Hoeckner (New York and London: Routledge, 2006), 78–84. Ferneyhough has discussed how the treatment of sound throughout the twentieth century works within and against Adornian ideals of advanced material. Ferneyhough, "Shaping Sound," 151–72.

[17] Theodor Adorno, "Funktion der Farbe in der Musik," *Darmstadt-Dokumente I*, ed. Heinz-Klaus Metzger and Rainer Riehn (Munich: Edition Text + Kritik, 1999), 311.

[18] Adorno does mention how the mixture of instrumental sounds typical of nineteenth- and twentieth-century orchestration could serve to elucidate formal moments and create expressive effects. "Funktion der Farbe in der Musik," 291.

infinite array of acoustic phenomena is its inner relationship with meaning." "The voice," he adds, "is something which points to meaning, it is as if there is an arrow in it which raises the expectation of meaning, the voice is an opening toward meaning." In a musical context, meaning can emerge from the texts carried by melodic lines and the different associations surrounding a voice, including the general, like that of the human and the individual, or the more specific depending on context, as with the evocation of childhood and innocence in *Gesang der Jünglinge*. Sounds, on the other hand, can possess meaning, but it is something that we ascribe to them. Dolar contends that sounds "seem to be deprived of it [meaning] 'in themselves,' independent of our ascription, while the voice has an intimate connection with meaning."[19] A point not pursued by Dolar but relevant to late modernist music is the observation that sound resists meaning because it often comes across as a welter, something so dense and changeable as to be irrational. To recall Shakespeare's description of human existence, life is a play made up of "sound and fury," which "signify nothing." Yet, as discussed below, modernist composers have long explored what sound can signify, if anything at all, and how clearly it can do so. Lachenmann and Neuwirth's operas, as will be seen, deal with the meanings that sound can possess or the ones that we can give to them.

The opposition between voice and sound is crucial to a particular line of inquiry into the act of expression: how the act unfolds in the world of mutable sound. Much attention is paid to how the act begins. The raising of a voice is the means by which the act is initiated, but to do so, to find the material or even room for a voice, in a fluctuating sonic environment can prove challenging. Once raised, the voice must endure the vicissitudes of the state. As with the fragmentary and silence, the strains and ensuing expressive tensions form part of the inquiry. There is, though, a question specific to the realm of sound: what happens to the voice, especially the subject raising the voice, when the surroundings are in constant transformation. As the works discussed below demonstrate, the encounter between the voice and sonic flux creates a range of expressive possibilities. Key to the encounter are the archetypal figures. Epitomes of sound, they come to the fore and interact with the voice in different ways; sometimes they eclipse the voice and at other times, in an outcome appropriate for a realm of metamorphosis, they become a voice.

---

[19] Dolar, *A Voice and Nothing More*, 14. Dolar argues that the voice at a certain point does not contribute to the transmission of meaning, its material and presence being so unique and vague as to resist definition. It is important to keep in mind that Dolar's concept of voice largely involves speech.

Saariaho

Even as a child, Saariaho considered sound to be a slippery thing. She was fascinated by how sounds could change and take on new forms, as when speech becomes song.[20] Equally captivating for her as both child and adult has been the sensation produced when music surpasses its limits and is prolonged through noise.[21] Alert to the smallest sonic shifts, Saariaho has not surprisingly approached sound as a state of flux. It also comes as little surprise that the music of Varèse, the first composer to draw out that unstable state, has been a constant point of reference for her.[22] Another significant influence is the spectralist works of Grisey and Murail, especially the idea of interpolation, which she defines as "the gradual change from one state to another."[23] Having moved to Paris in 1982 to study at IRCAM, she became more familiar with the aesthetics of spectralism and utilized the technology there to probe the materials of sound. Her pieces from the 1980s adhere closely to spectralist ideals, as they feature sonic objects created from the molding of harmonic spectra and follow the constant evolution of those sonorities.

So quickly do styles change that Saariaho went from being a student to a successor of spectralism. Focusing on works from the 1990s, musicologist Damien Pousset has designated Saariaho, Philippe Hurel, and Marc-André Dalbavie as belonging to a post-spectralist movement.[24] Their works fulfill basic premises of spectralism, particularly the cultivation of spectra-based sonorities, but respond to new inspirations. Saariaho's works during the 1990s, for instance, set into relief individual melodic lines, a departure from the dense, mutating sonorities of early spectralist compositions. The interest in the individual voice has yielded two types of pieces. Saariaho has written many concertolike compositions for solo instruments and ensemble. So "competitive" is the relationship between the two sides that Pousset has labeled the pieces "stile concertato."[25] The second group of works is for human voice and ensemble, pieces that served the composer well as a testing ground for the opera *L'amour de loin* (2000).

The prominence of solo melodic lines coincides with another shift away from early spectralist composition. For Pousset, the works of the three

---

[20] Pierre Michel, "Entretien avec Kaija Saariaho," *Kaija Saariaho* (Paris: Éditions IRCAM, 1994), 15.

[21] Michel, "Entretien," 15.   [22] Michel, "Entretien," 15.

[23] Anders Beyer, *The Voice of Music: Conversations with Composers of Our Time* (Aldershot: Ashgate, 2000), 304.

[24] Damien Pousset, "The Works of Kaija Saariaho, Philippe Hurel, and Marc-André Dalbavie – Stile Concertato, Stile Concitato, Stile Rappresentativo," *Contemporary Music Review* 19, no. 3 (2000), 67–110.

[25] Pousset, "The Works of Kaija Saariaho," 109.

composers create a "more dramatized discourse," characterized by "theatri-
cality" and the "accentuation of expressive gestures."[26] The ever-changing
relationship between the solo instruments or voices and the ensembles
adds another dimension to that drama, as does the lyricism imparted by
the soloists' lines. Saariaho's titles provide focal points for all the drama.
Throughout her career, she has given pieces titles that conjure vivid images
or instigate the beginnings of vague narratives. Some of the more suggestive
ones include *Vers le blanc*, *From the Grammar of Dreams*, and *Château de
l'âme*.

Just as evocative are the titles of two significant works in the turn to a
post-spectralist style, *Du cristal* and . . . *à la fumée* (1990). The two pieces can
be performed separately or as a diptych. The former is for large orchestra
and the latter features alto flute and cello soloists with orchestra. Saariaho
has called the pair a "transition" in her oeuvre.[27] To be more specific, the
transition occurs between the two pieces. *Du cristal* marks "the end of a
road," the last work in a period preoccupied with spectral and harmonic
analysis, whereas . . . *à la fumée* is the first of the concertolike works from
the decade.[28] With the latter, Saariaho set the challenge for herself of using
the "materials" of *Du cristal* "completely differently."[29] The differences are
not just those of genre, solely orchestral versus concertolike compositions,
but also structural. Saariaho describes . . . *à la fumée* as open to "more unexpected formal developments," in contrast to a sequence of "linear events."[30]
Pousset furthers this idea by describing *Du cristal* as a work bearing a "completed" form characterized by integration, unity, and fusion and . . . *à la
fumée* as being about dissolution, dispersion, and dynamic motion.[31] Both
descriptions elaborate upon ideas conveyed in Saariaho's pictorial titles,
which are drawn from the evocative title of Henri Atlan's book *Entre le
cristal et la fumée*. For him, the two are extreme states. The former possesses

---

[26] Pousset, "The Works of Kaija Saariaho," 108–9.

[27] Michel, "Entretien," 17. Ivanka Stoïanova places the two works in the context of the changes
occurring in Saariaho's oeuvre, especially her conceptions of the ideals of spectralism. Stoïanova,
"Kaija Saariaho: Spektrale Komposition und symphonisches Denken," in *Frau Musica (Nova):
Komponieren heute*, ed. Martina Homma (Sinzig: Studio-Verlag, 2000), 331–49.

[28] *Du cristal* also marks a beginning in that Saariaho used the work to explore the idea of magnifying
the physicality of performance in a piece for a hundred musicians. Michel, "Entretien," 17–18.

[29] Beyer, *The Voice of Music*, 308. The challenge would continue with *Cendres* (1998), which draws
upon materials from . . . *à la fumée*.

[30] Michel, "Entretien," 18.

[31] Pousset, "The Works of Kaija Saariaho," 100. Stoïanova also builds upon the contrasts in the
titles of the pieces. For her, *Du cristal* creates symmetry through its different sound elements. She
never describes that symmetry in any detail. . . . *à la fumée*, on the other hand, is not so clearly
organized; rather, it develops a temporary spatial form through the sharp contrasts in materials.
Moreover, she mentions how the former builds upon the structural logic of spectralism, that
of creating larger formal elements through the microscopic elements of a sonority, whereas the
latter largely does away with that premise. Stoïanova, "Kaija Saariaho," 338–40.

a "perfectly repetitive symmetrical order" and the latter exists as "a variety infinitely complex and unexpected in its details."[32]

The opposition between physical states is one way to hear the diptych. Saariaho's titular prepositions offer another. As she wrote, the materials of *Du cristal* are transformed in . . . *à la fumée*. Through the revisions, we move *from* (du) exactness *to* (à) amorphousness. The diptych not only executes a transformation but, as put up front in the titles, it is also about transformation. One result of the metamorphosis is the emergence of the individual melodic lines in . . . *à la fumée*. The two qualities, transformation and the prominence of solo melodic lines, make the diptych an apposite piece for this study. So too does the emphasis placed on expression in post-spectralist composition. For Julian Anderson, the diptych possesses a "grander expressive sweep" than previous works, created by "explosive passages of greater violence" and rhythmic vacillations.[33] Another perspective can be gained by introducing the act of expression. Through the solo parts, the works bring the act to the fore, where it must adapt to the ever-changing realm of sound.

To discuss how the act of expression plays out in the two works, we should begin with how Saariaho imagines the world of sound. The title of the diptych is again telling. It conveys the movement between extreme points along a continuum of physical states. For Saariaho, sound is a continuum. As seen in the discussion of early electronic music, other modernist composers have comprehended sound in similar ways. The idea of a continuum rewards many of the modernist interests in sound, which accounts for the reason that the continuum has become an archetype. Modernist composers have reached out to a broader range of sounds than ever used, or heard, before, everything from new electronic sonorities to street noises. Perhaps the only way to map such an array was to place it along the expanse of a continuum. Having set up the line, composers have not surprisingly emphasized the movement from one end to another. In a continuum, the motion of sound becomes a prominent force, sweeping up and carrying along the listener. Transformation has provided one means of movement. It can be, as with Saariaho's crystals and smoke, the way to travel between extreme ends. Saariaho's works along with Stockhausen's *Gesang der Jünglinge* also reveal how transformation can flourish in the broad middle space, where the sounds at the endpoint mix and blur, creating new, and not entirely recognizable, sonorities.

Saariaho has plotted much of her music and theoretical thought along a continuum that she refers to as a "sound/noise axis." She distinguishes

---

[32] Henri Atlan, *Entre le cristal et la fumée* (Paris: Seuil, 1979), 5.
[33] Julian Anderson, "Seductive Solitary," *Musical Times* 133 (December 1992), 618.

between sound and noise largely by degrees of clarity. The far points of sound include sonorities with little acoustical or textural interference, things like "the ringing of a bell or a human voice singing in the Western tradition." Smooth textures also fall on this side of the line. Noise includes rough, unstable sonorities. Saariaho signals out the noises created by extended techniques, such things as the sound of breathing in the flute headpiece and strings playing *sul ponticello.* Gnarled textures also gather at this far end.[34] Her works are in constant motion along the continuum, typically moving through transformation. *Lichtbogen* (1985–86), for instance, foregrounds the gradual transition from "one pure sound – here a string harmonic (natural or artificial) into a very noisy sound."[35] The axis can be transposed to other parameters. Saariaho uses it to replace the dynamics of consonance/dissonance in tonal music.[36] In her scheme, the "dissonance" of noise creates "tension" that demands to be "resolved" to a more stable sound. A single instrument can also be laid upon the axis.[37] As we will see with the alto flute and cello in . . . *à la fumée,* an instrument can encompass extremes, producing the fracas of extended techniques one moment and a simple melodic line the next.

The archetypal sonic continuum offers one way to approach the diptych; the established genre of the concerto presents another. As mentioned above, . . . *à la fumée* is the first of a group of concertolike works. The pieces are by no means traditional concertos, but they have some affinities with the genre. Most obvious is the appearance of soloists who wield a virtuosity and lyricism that distinguish them from the ensemble. The soloists also engage in the standard role playing of the genre, sometimes working closely with, or even from within, the ensemble and at other times standing apart as the two parties vie against each other with different materials. In Saariaho's works, though, the relationship between the two is not so well defined, the result of the sonic world in which the concerto finds itself. When sound incessantly changes and the music zips back and forth across a broad continuum, it becomes impossible to insist upon specific positions and roles. The soloists and ensemble frequently occupy the ambiguous middle ground in the continuum, a space in which the relationship between the two is not easily clarified and the lines between them are not distinct.

The concerto not only provides a genre context for . . . *à la fumée* but it also serves as a starting point in understanding how the act of expression unfolds during the piece. In a conventional concerto, the emergence of the

---

[34] Kaija Saariaho, "Timbre and Harmony: Interpolations of Timbral Structures," *Contemporary Music Review* 2 (1987), 94.
[35] Saariaho, "Timbre and Harmony," 129.
[36] Saariaho, "Timbre and Harmony," 94.   [37] Saariaho, "Timbre and Harmony," 94.

soloist is a heightened moment. One way to appreciate the moment is to hear it as the raising of a voice. Concertos do not present the entrance of the soloist in such basic terms, but a concerto caught in the realm of changing sound may do so. To recall, the distinction between voice, the independent melodic line, and mass is crucial to sound-based works in general and Saariaho's idea of a sound/noise axis in particular. Some pieces, like . . . *à la fumée* and Lachenmann's opera, concentrate on how a voice emerges from the shifting masses. In doing so, they draw attention to the initial and most fundamental component of the act of expression, the raising of a voice. We not only hear a voice appear but we also listen to it take on expressive weight and roles, both of which are gained through the interaction with the surrounding world of mutable sound.

In discussing *Du cristal* and . . . *à la fumée*, two issues will be pursued: the raising of the solo voices and how the voices assume an expressive presence through the medium of flux. The two pieces are intricate and long, around thirty minutes back to back. Given the brief space available here, an analysis must be restricted to specific sections. The passages to be discussed include the opening and closing sections of each work. The sections merit attention because they, as to be expected of such locations, either establish or bring to a culmination key dynamics. Moreover, there are linkages between the passages, both within and across the individual pieces.

Such connections raise larger questions about form, that of the two separate works and the diptych. As mentioned earlier, Saariaho used materials from *Du cristal* in composing . . . *à la fumée*. The recycling creates linkages between them, none more prominent than the low e♭ trill in the solo cello that ends the former and begins the latter. The mirrored trill has led Martha Brech to propose a symmetrical relationship between the works.[38] Yet, whereas there are shared events between the pieces, the sequence of recall in . . . *à la fumée* is nowhere specific enough to pin down a palindrome, nor would one expect to find it in the scattered state of smoke. The formal structures of the individual pieces are not much more clearly defined. Pousset states that *Du cristal*, true to its name, features a symmetrical ABA′ design. The work does shape a loose ternary form in which, as Pousset points out, the second A section distorts materials from the first part. The return of the A material, however, does not follow a clear retrograde pattern or adhere to "classical requirements of symmetry."[39] Perhaps the best way to approach the individual works and the pair as a whole is not through either

---

[38] Martha Brech, "Kaija Saariaho's Diptych *Du cristal* and . . . *à la fumée*: An Analytical Approach," in *Topics–Texts–Tensions: Essays in Music Theory on Paavo Heininen, Joona Kokkonen, Magnus Lindberg, Usko Mrilaninen*, ed. Tom Mäkelä (Magdeburg: Otto-von-Guericke University, 1999), 26–50. Brech also discusses a proportional relationship between the two works.

[39] Pousset, "The Works of Kaija Saariaho," 100–101.

Ex. 5.1 Opening sonorities in Saariaho, *Du cristal*

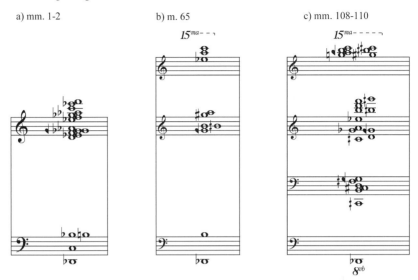

preconceived ideas of symmetry, no matter how tantalizing the shared trill and images of crystals may be, or pre-established forms but rather through the dynamics of transformation. Distinct passages and sound types return throughout the individual works and duo. Each time they return, they are altered so as to give us new versions of the material. The metamorphoses create parallel passages that are too numerous and sometimes too askew to be accommodated in all but the most general form, for example the loose ternary structure of *Du cristal*. The parallels are the result more of the pervasive transformations of the realm of sound than of the building of a set form.

The opening A section (mm. 1–126) of *Du cristal* initiates a tension that runs throughout the diptych. It poises dense sonic masses against independent melodic lines. The masses of the A section are all built upon a db played in the double basses.[40] As seen in the first block (mm. 1–10), the sonority does not closely replicate the natural harmonic series as is common in earlier spectralist pieces (Ex. 5.1a). There is, though, some overlap between the two, especially the microtonal beading in the upper register. In two subsequent statements (mm. 65, 108), the spectral profile changes considerably (Exx. 5.1b and 5.1c). Despite the differences, the db foundation provides enough consistency to make it possible to hear the blocks as a recurring element. In her analysis of the concertolike work *Amers*, Ivanka Stoïanova describes how a sonority based upon an eb trill

---

[40] The foundation tone is also taken up by the tuba, piano, and harp at times.

Ex. 5.2a Melodic lines in the opening passages of Saariaho, *Du cristal*, solo violin, mm. 20–26

Composed by Kaija Saariaho. Copyright © 1990 Edition Wilhelm Hansen Helsinki OY. All rights reserved. International copyright secured. Reprinted by permission

Ex. 5.2b Melodic lines in the opening passages of Saariaho, *Du cristal*, oboes 1–3, mm. 27–29

Composed by Kaija Saariaho. Copyright © 1990 Edition Wilhelm Hansen Helsinki OY. All rights reserved. International copyright secured. Reprinted by permission

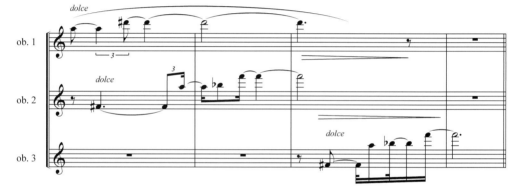

in the cello (the same trill used in the diptych) plays a similar role as a "centralizing presence."[41]

As serried as the masses can be, their thickness inevitably wavers, undone by melodic stirrings. In the first block (m. 20), solo parts in the strings play melodic lines as opposed to sustained notes. The melodies are far from lyrical, consisting of only two or four pitches, but the impetus toward lyricism is strong enough to earn the stunted lines the direction "sempre intenso, espressivo" (Ex. 5.2a). With such encouragement, the impetus grows more forceful as the woodwinds begin to play phrases, which, along with the solo string parts, expand in range and length (Ex. 5.2b). No matter how active, though, the lines still unfold within a larger sonic block. The block thins out as the lines take shape, but the latter can never escape it.[42]

As the melodic activity increases, the mass reasserts itself. In m. 65, another d♭-based sonority settles into place. The return establishes the two

[41]   Ivanka Stoïanova, "Une oeuvre de synthèse: Analyse d'*Amers*," in *Kaija Saariaho*, 51.
[42]   Stoïanova mentions the intertwined melodic lines in the fluctuating sonic masses, but she never sees the lines pushing to break free from the mass. Stoïanova, "Kaija Saariaho," 339.

roles to be played by the blocks. On the one hand, they provide points of
coherence; on the other hand, they check the growth of the burgeoning
melodic lines. In the adamantine world of *Du cristal*, dense masses rule, not
melodic filigree. The block in m. 65, though, is not nearly as thick as that
heard at the outset of the piece (Exx. 5.1a and 5.1b). It is scored for just
strings, which play in harmonics and at dynamic levels from *piano* to *mezzo
piano*. Nonetheless, the mass is strong enough to halt the melodic motion
that began within the first block. The tension between solid sonorities and
melodic lines, though, resumes as new lines form. Unlike in the previous
block, the new lines do not arise imperceptibly from the strings and winds.
The synthesizer, glockenspiel, vibraphone, and piano now take up lyrical
parts. Saariaho has referred to these melodies of "clear and metallic timbres"
as being "infinite," in the sense that they soar seemingly unconstrained by
"gravitation" or "direction."[43] The lines float more freely than the wind and
string parts heard previously, giving the melodic impetus greater strength.
Once again, though, the sonic mass reclaims the melodic lines; this time
with a loud, thick full-orchestral sonority built upon d♭ (m. 108, Ex. 5.1c).
The block holds, even with ripples of the "infinite" melody, until the close
of the A section.

The tension between blocks and lines continues to play out in the B
section (mm. 127–299), which is largely set apart by the absence of the d♭-
based sonorities.[44] The "grandioso" statement of a d♭-based block marks the
return of the A section (mm. 300–373). It revisits and transforms materials
heard earlier. The materials, though, do not reappear in the same order
in which they were first stated nor are they presented in the reverse order
that would create crystalline symmetry. The returning elements include
the "infinite" melodies (A section, mm. 94–106, A′ section, mm. 303–
14) and whirls of wind lines within a block sustained by strings (A, mm.
37–52, A′, mm. 316–29). The quiet strings-only harmonics version of the
d♭-based sonority heard earlier in the first A section (m. 65) also comes
back in an altered form (m. 342). The order of the elements in the first A
section is wind figures, harmonics chord, and "infinite" melody, whereas
in the closing one it is "infinite" melody, wind figures, and harmonics
chord. In the A′ section, the harmonics chord begins the process of sonic
diminishment that will close the piece. Untouched by internal melodic lines,
the sonority dwindles to a cluster of trills atop the d♭ in the bass, which too
drops out, leaving behind the e♭ trill in the solo cello that will open ... *à la
fumée.*

---

[43] Michel, "Entretien," 23.
[44] The section, though, does feature sonorities built upon a c quarter-tone sharp.

Ex. 5.3a–c E♭-trill based sonorities in Saariaho, . . . *à la fumée*

a) mm. 1-8   b) mm. 10-15   c) mm. 16-21

The beginning of . . . *à la fumée* illustrates how the constant transformation of materials turns the diptych into a hall of mirrors. Passages reflect each other, to the extent that one section can offer different views of two or more previous sections. With the e♭ trill, the opening of . . . *à la fumée* can be heard as a revision of the end of *Du cristal*. It can also be heard as commenting on the initial section of *Du cristal*, which does not even include the trill sonority. The close reflection between the conclusion of *Du cristal* and the start of . . . *à la fumée* demonstrates how specific the revisions can be. If the former completes a process of sonic diminishment, the latter expands upon its sonic materials. The e♭ trill is the only remainder of the once-imposing blocks that filled *Du cristal*. It now becomes the foundation of the sonorities that will swell throughout . . . *à la fumée*. In an opening passage (mm. 1–23), the e♭ trill is stated three times, with each appearance producing richer and more colorful sonorities (Exx. 5.3a–5.3c). Saariaho was so fascinated by the trill that she did several spectral analyses of it, having it played normally, with heavy bow pressure, and *sul ponticello* (Ex. 5.4).[45] The opening three sonorities of . . . *à la fumée* draw upon the spectral data, although none adhere exactly to the overtone series of the trill (Ex. 5.3a–5.3c).

As the trill sonorities build, so too do the melodic lines crossing the blocks. The lyrical threads provoke the tension between sonic masses and independent melodic lines that shaped *Du cristal*. The renewal of that pressure at the beginning of . . . *à la fumée* can be heard as a commentary on the opening of the preceding piece. The tension takes on a special significance at the outset of a work, as it establishes a dynamic that will unfold throughout the rest of the piece. Hearing it pick up once again at the opening of . . . *à la fumée*, we

---

[45] She used the trill in two later pieces, *Amers* (1992) and *Près* (1992).

Ex. 5.4 Spectral analysis of the eb-trill based sonority
Adapted from Ivanka Stoïanova, "Une oeuvre de synthèse: Analyse d'*Amers*," in
Kaija Saariaho (Paris: IRCAM, 1994), 54

cannot help but think of what happened earlier in the initial moments of
Du cristal. This time Saariaho sets out on a different course, the terms and
outcomes of which would be unimaginable in the first composition.

In the initial section of *Du cristal,* the db-based sonority returns twice to
reestablish the governing harmonic area and halt the growth of the melodic
lines. The first section of... *à la fumée* (mm. 1–78, before the entrance
of the soloists) begins with the waves of three eb-trill based sonorities
mentioned above, but they soon disappear as does their harmonic sway.
The piece moves on to two new sonorities. The first (m. 25) is built upon
a g quarter-tone flat and has some overlap with the trill sonorities. The
following sonority (m. 56) is erected on a c♯–g dyad and is far removed
from the opening blocks. Like the eb-trill sonority, the subsequent two do
little to contain the proliferating melodic lines. To make the connection
between the openings of the pieces clearer, Saariaho draws upon the two
types of lines that popped out at the beginning of *Du cristal,* the wind and
brass swirls and the "infinite" melodies. Far from being thwarted, the lines
now grow to the point that they evolve to a next stage, the emergence of the
two soloists (mm. 79–84). With those parts, the melodic impetus becomes
uninhibited and will dominate sections of the work. The tension between
sonic mass and melody, though, has by no means been defused. If anything
it has intensified. The soloists give the melodic lines new force and range,
but the blocks still cut off melodies, both those within the ensemble and
those played by the soloists.

The entrance of the soloists marks the entrance of the concerto genre. No
sooner does the genre enter the diptych than it finds itself on the unfamiliar,
and unstable, ground of sonic flux. Far from being dislocated, the soloists
thrive on that new terrain. Indeed they quickly create a sonic archetype
figure, the continuum. They not only create it but they also rule it. They can
traverse the space with ease and transform all sorts of sounds while roaming
it. The command of the continuum is just as much part of their virtuosity,

Ex. 5.5 a) Soloists' lines from Saariaho, . . . *à la fumée*, mm. 83–90

b) Soloists' lines from Saariaho, . . . *à la fumée*, mm. 132–40

Composed by Kaija Saariaho. Copyright © 1991 Edition Wilhelm Hansen Helsinki OY. All rights reserved. International copyright secured. Reprinted by permission

a)

b)

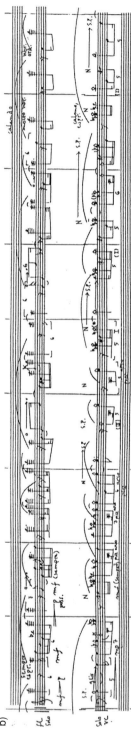

their elite status in a concerto, as is the ability to play complex, demanding parts.

When the soloists first appear, there is little to separate them from the ensemble. The alto flute extends a figuration pattern played by the harp and then settles on a long trill, while the cello also holds a trill. To recall, the trill figure has a strong connection with the sonic blocks, the opening one of which is based on the low e♭ trill. The alto flute and cello trills may be on different pitches (f′ and C, respectively), but they suggest that a new mass could be forming as happened earlier. The two grow more melodic, however, crafting elaborate lines with broad curves and sudden changes. They also grow independent of the ensemble sonorities, which if anything support rather than contain them.

Through the soloists, we become increasingly aware of the piece operating in a sonic continuum. It stretches out between the points of sound and melody, the latter being the spot conducive to the independent lines suggestive of the voice. This mapping of the continuum revises the terminology, but not terrain, of Saariaho's noise/sound axis. Her conception of noise, to recall, encompasses the packed, volatile masses discussed here, whereas she uses sound to refer to thinner sonorities, even single lines, as in her example of a human voice. The tensions between the masses and individual lines in *Du cristal* and the beginning of *. . . à la fumée* hinted at such a space, but the latter could never escape the pull of the masses, thus leaving no substantial gap between them. The soloists, though, free the lines and create a gap. Indeed, in their first extended passage (mm. 79–167), the two go well beyond a gap and instead clear the space of the continuum.

The soloists begin well over on the side of sound. Their initial material not only repeats the trills from the earlier sonic masses, but they also indulge in the extended techniques that epitomize "noise" for Saariaho. Almost every note is altered in some way, inflected by such gestures as different bowing techniques and harmonics for the cello and overblowing and the speaking of syllables into the mouthpiece for the alto flute. The soloists' initial lines are more about the "noise" created by the use of extended techniques than melody, especially considering that the two parts typically repeat short phrases consisting of no more than two or four notes (Ex. 5.5a).[46] From this point on, the soloists begin to drive to the other side of the spectrum. The lines grow longer and the pitches are increasingly left untouched. The culmination point (mm. 124–52) is a series of lyrically shaped lines, especially in the alto flute (Ex. 5.5b). During this stretch, the

---

[46] Each solo instrument also builds its lines around a loose collection of pitch classes. The alto flute uses d, f♯, g, a♭, a♮, b♭. The cello uses b, c, e♭, f, f♯, g.

sonic mass is tellingly at its thinnest, as if being unable to form at such a remote point on the melodic side of the continuum. The soloists having neared one end, their impulse is to head back in the opposite direction, which they do by shortening the phrases and loading on the extended techniques. The ensemble emphasizes the return to the sound side by putting down a series of heavy masses, which alternate with curt lines from the soloists. Previously the crush of the blocks would reinforce the subordinate status of melody relative to sound. The soloists, however, have freed melody from that role. It is no longer something to be quashed, but rather one end in a larger continuum.

The entrance of the soloists can also be heard in terms of the inquiry into the act of expression. Their appearance, as mentioned earlier, suggests the most fundamental component of the act, the raising of a voice. It is not just that the two parts emerge that gives such an impression but rather how they emerge. With their opening extended trills (mm. 80–84), they come across as no different from the sonic masses, seeming to be stray filaments of a larger block. Through short melodies and strange sounds, though, they grow into unique and broader voices and in time become quite voluble. This is the type of stability and growth expected of a voice once it appears.

Modernist works have exploited those expectations by placing the voice in stringent surroundings, where its continuity, or even initial appearance, is in constant peril. Similar dangers, it would seem, await the newly raised voice in the state of sonic flux, which could so warp the voice as to prevent it from ever taking form or have it dissolve into the fluidity created by the ever-changing sonic masses. Indeed, voices do meet such fates, as we will see in Lachenmann's opera, but not in . . . à la fumée. If anything the voices raised by the two soloists adapt to and flourish within the world of mutable sound. With their ability to command the continuum, the two achieve an expressive presence. The voices are not undermined by ceaseless metamorphosis but rather are sustained and enriched by it. Never staying in one form for too long, the two solo voices exist in a state of flux. They cannot be pinned down to any one type of sound or to any one spot on the continuum. The act of raising a voice no longer depends on stability; rather, it is caught up in unrelenting transformation. Flux becomes an expressive position.[47]

---

[47] According to Anne Sivuoja-Gunaratnam, the earlier work *Stilleben* (1988) also emphasizes the mutability of the expressive subject. It "ascribes a nomadic logic, where the subject is in movement or in transition between places, times, and identities." Sivuoja-Gunaratnam, "Rhetoric of Transition in Kaija Saariaho's Music," in *Musical Signification, Between Rhetoric and Pragmatics*, ed. Gino Stefani, Eero Tarasti, and Luca Marconi (Bologna: Cooperativa Libraria Universitaria Editrice Bologna, 1998), 540.

What more fitting way to close the diptych than to bring the soloists and the orchestra to their most changeable points yet. Typical of the persistent metamorphoses in the work, the closing section of . . . *à la fumée* (mm. 430–95) can be heard as an alternative version of a preceding passage, particularly the initial extended solo section (mm. 79–167). It begins with the alto flute and harp whirring around with figurations similar to those heard when the instruments first appeared. The soloists also employ many of the same extended techniques heard at the outset of the earlier section. As before, they sit on the far edge of the sound side on the continuum. Whereas previously the two set out for the opposing melodic side, they now only go as far as the middle of the spectrum, shaping lines that have melodic profiles but that are still distorted by extended techniques. They exist in limbo between sound and melody, and that is where they will remain for the rest of the piece. The orchestra adds to the mix by presenting its two most contrasting materials: a mass made up of melodic lines and solid chordal blocks. In the former (mm. 476–79), the swirling inner parts are poised to break free and take us closer to the side of melody. As earlier in the diptych, block chords check any such liberation. Two emphatically attacked sonorities, alterations of the opening chords built upon a g quarter-tone flat and an eb (no trill), follow the mingled mass, cutting it off and punctuating the nebulous lines of the soloists (mm. 493–95).

In the closing measures, the soloists occupy the middle of the spectrum and the ensemble stretches across its own extremes. Three distinct strands of sound are left suspended, and we are placed on three different spots on the continuum at once. As with other spots in that space, the sounds are still changing and could presumably continue to do so. The final soft notes played by the soloists, the last sounds of the piece, seem as if they are the starting point for another round of transformations. By venturing so far into the state of sonic flux, the diptych alters our perceptions. Here is a space in which finality is achieved in perpetual metamorphosis and ambiguity. Here is a space where the act of expression is to raise a voice, not one that will hold to one identity but rather one that is ever ready to become something else, even its opposite, sound.

Lachenmann

In Lachenmann's works, sounds arrive changed; issued from an instrument whose tones we know so well, they come strange and unknown. Bow hitting string creates a noise alien to the sonic friction that we have experienced time and time again. The composer's sounds are born in a moment of defamiliarization.[48] These moments have captivated Lachenmann, as has the general idea of the technique described by Shklovsky. This is a composer for whom the only reason "to make music" is "to hear, in a new way, what you knew before."[49] Not surprisingly, the idea of defamiliarization underlies many of his central aesthetic concepts.[50] It especially shapes his views of sound, how it behaves, and what it can do.

Of particular interest is the composer's hallmark technique of *musique concrète instrumentale*. The name refers to Schaeffer's school of electroacoustic composition. Lachenmann intensively used the technique in works from *temA* (1968) to *Accanto* (1976) and has modified it in subsequent pieces, in which it serves as one part of other "hierarchies of sound."[51] He later regretted the choice of name, saying that it was "perhaps an error."[52] It was an illuminating error, though, as the comparison with Schaeffer throws light on aspects of Lachenmann's handling of sound. Lachenmann's adjectival tag *concrète instrumentale* clarifies an obvious difference in terms of media. Schaeffer deals in recorded real-life sounds, Lachenmann in acoustic sounds created by conventional instruments. Beyond the chosen medium, the more compelling contrast is how Lachenmann's technique reverses the trajectory of Schaeffer's. The latter tracks a course from "the purely 'sonorous' to the purely 'musical.'"[53] Schaeffer begins with real-life sounds (train noises, shouting) and transforms them to such a degree that they lose any resemblance to the original sound and its meanings and associations. A new "sonic object" emerges from the process, one that in its abstract guise could attain the status of music. His alterations create an "acousmatic" experience, in which we, like Pythagoras's students who listened to their master sight unseen behind a screen, are unable to perceive the source of the sound that we hear.[54] Or so it goes in theory. As listeners of Schaeffer's works know full well, many of the sounds are easily identifiable, and not all are rigorously transformed. Nonetheless, there is an effort to get beyond the banality of real-world sounds and to make them into something more independently rich.

---

[48] David Ryan, "Composer in Interview: Helmut Lachenmann," *Tempo* 210 (October 1999), 21.

[49] Paul Steenhuisen, "Interview with Helmut Lachenmann – Toronto, 2003," *Contemporary Music Review* 23, nos. 3/4 (2004), 10.

[50] Ross Feller, "Resistant Strains of Postmodernism: The Music of Helmut Lachenmann and Brian Ferneyhough," in *Postmodern Music/Postmodern Thought*, ed. Judy Lochhead and Joseph Auner (New York and London: Routledge, 2002), 254.

[51] Lachenmann, "Paradies auf Zeit: Gespräch mit Peter Szendy," in *Musik als existentielle Erfahrung*, ed. Josef Häusler (Wiesbaden: Breitkopf & Härtel, 1996), 211–12. The Lachenmann essay collection will hereafter be referred to as *MEE*.

[52] Lachenmann, "Paradies auf Zeit," 211–12.

[53] Pierre Schaeffer, "Acousmatics," 81.　　[54] Schaeffer, "Acousmatics," 77.

Lachenmann begins with musical sounds, or musical means of creating sounds, and "demusicalizes" them. Whereas Schaeffer tried to pull us from the noises of the street to music, Lachenmann leads us from music to unfamiliar sounds. The two also differ in terms of the object of transformation. Schaeffer operates on a finished sound, a sonic event that has been completed and preserved on tape. Lachenmann, on the other hand, alters the means of producing a sound. He isolates aspects of production that are typically blocked out in appreciating the conventional tone of an instrument. A tremendous amount of physical "energy" is needed to create that tone, particularly the labor involved in technique and the handling of an instrument.[55] Lachenmann concentrates on two kinds of energy: that required to create a sound and that sparked by a sound emerging and projecting outwards. He redirects and intensifies both currents. The musicians approach their instruments in unusual and often strenuous ways, which place the performance in an unsettled field of exertion. The sound events come alive with force and unpredictability. Produced by unfamiliar means, they assume unfamiliar shapes and veer off in unfamiliar directions.

Musique concrète instrumentale alters a sound from the inside out. It begins by exposing the "anatomy" of a sound: in other words, the basic core, like that of the scrape of a bow against a string or the flow of breath.[56] Changes to the interior essence can form a new expressive "outer skin," as the changed sound takes on expressive roles far different from those typically associated with its more conventional origins.[57] The legato lyricism sustained by smooth bowing on the cello, for instance, can give way to bursts of toneless, buzzing noises created by digging the bow into the strings. It is worth pausing over Lachenmann's anatomy lesson, for it reveals how closely his conception of sound taps into the dynamics of transformation and expression explored here. The transformations begin at the most elemental level, the interior of a sound, and expand from there. One alteration begets another until we hear chains of metamorphoses, a sweep that has significant expressive force.

Not only does Lachenmann alter the surface of a sound but he also works upon the cultural meanings surrounding it. He has developed two concepts to group the disparate ideas in those outer rings. "Aura" captures

---

[55] Lachenmann, "Hören ist wehrlos – ohne Hören: Über Möglichkeiten und Schwierigkeiten," in *MEE*, 124–25. On the concept of energy in Lachenmann's soundworld, see Martin Kaltenecker, *Avec Helmut Lachenmann* (Paris: Van Dieren, 2001), 56–61.

[56] Steenhuisen, "Interview," 10. Lachenmann, "Pression für einen Cellisten (1969/70)," in *MEE*, 381–82.

[57] Rainer Nonnenmann, "Music with Images – The Development of Helmut Lachenmann's Sound Composition Between Concretion and Transcendence," *Contemporary Music Review* 24, no. 1 (2005), 7.

the associations and memories that have accrued to a sound over time.[58] The "aesthetic apparatus" enforces "the ruling aesthetic needs and norms."[59] Key to this concept is what he calls the "instrumentarium," which consists of traditional instruments, the techniques involved in the creation of the "beautiful philharmonic sound," the genres and ensembles designed to highlight that sound, and the institutions and markets devoted to promoting it.[60] Both the "aura" and "aesthetic apparatus" submit to the same process of defamiliarization at work on the individual sound. In composing his Second String Quartet, Lachenmann realized that the "medium" had to be "rendered alien."[61] Yet not completely alien, as the Quartet and other pieces keep us aware of the medium in its conventional forms: only then can we appreciate how significantly it has been changed. Lachenmann values the "ambivalence" between the old and new, the flashes of the quartet ensemble we know amid the frenzy of strange performance motions and sounds.[62] How different from Schaeffer's conception of *musique concrète*, which sought to have the listener forget "every reference to instrumental causes or preexisting musical significations."[63]

Both composers hold to Shklovsky's notion that the practices of defamiliarization, the strange depictions and transformations, are a means to a more significant end. By having the listener get beyond the familiar, they heighten the process of perception.[64] Schaeffer stretches out the acousmatic curtain to create not so much new "phenomena" as "new conditions of observation."[65] *Musique concrète* enlivens the "perspective consciousness."[66] Along similar lines, Lachenmann has stated that "the problem is not to search for new sounds, but for a new way of listening, of perception."[67] For him, perception begins with listening and then transcends it: "the concept of perception is more adventurous and existential than that of listening."[68] The existential, an important idea in Lachenmann's thought, denotes an elevated and broad realm of experience. Listeners confront the possibilities of the new created by the unfamiliar sounds; at the same time they have a more keen awareness of the history and associations of the familiar sounds that have been displaced. Perception brings not only knowledge but also liberation.[69] Once so attuned, listeners can free themselves from the binds of habit. In particular, the restrictions of the aesthetic apparatus – what sounds can be

---

[58] Lachenmann, "On Structuralism," *Contemporary Music Review* 12 (1995), 98.
[59] Lachenmann, "The 'Beautiful' in Music Today," *Tempo* 135 (December 1980), 20–24.
[60] Lachenmann, "The 'Beautiful' in Music Today," 22; Steenhuisen, "Interview," 9.
[61] Lachenmann, "On My Second String Quartet," *Contemporary Music Review* 23 nos. 3/4 (2004), 59.
[62] Steenhuisen, "Interview," 10; Lachenmann, "On Structuralism," 100.
[63] Schaeffer, "Acousmatics," 81.
[64] Viktor Shklovsky, "Art as Technique," 3–18.   [65] Schaeffer, "Acousmatics," 81.
[66] Schaeffer, "Acousmatics," 79.   [67] Steenhuisen, "Interview," 9.
[68] Lachenmann, "On Structuralism," 102.   [69] Lachenmann, "On Structuralism," 100.

made, how they can be presented, where they can be heard – are revealed to be culturally mediated decisions, not given rules. Aware of this, the listener is free to embrace alternatives to those rigid rules, such as the sounds created by *musique concrète instrumentale.*

Having examined Lachenmann's conceptions of sound and perception, we can turn to the opera *Das Mädchen mit den Schwefelhölzern* (*The Little Match Girl*).[70] In a letter from 1975, years before he began even sketching the piece, Lachenmann foresaw it as the "pinnacle" of his oeuvre.[71] Premiered in 1997, the opera in many ways did reach a peak. The work features an unprecedented range of sounds and means of sound production. With his first excursion into the theater, the idea of perception broadens to welcome the visual, a new mode of composing and listening that Lachenmann referred to with the subtitle of the piece: "Musik mit Bildern" (music with images). The theatrical surroundings also bring to the fore a relationship central to this chapter: that between sound and the act of expression.

In the same 1975 letter, Lachenmann claimed that his "music would come through in as popular (!) a manner as possible – without concession, of course – and express something."[72] For many the word "popular" warrants a question mark rather than an exclamation mark when affixed to Lachenmann. Yet in the choice both of genre and of Hans Christian Andersen's well-known story as a narrative, the work did invite a larger audience than that loyal to modern music concerts. And true to his word, the composer did not concede, not that anyone ever expected him to. Andersen's story may be familiar, but Lachenmann's presentation is anything but. There are no singing characters on stage, nor much of any clearly sung text. The title part is played by a dancer/actress and the vocal music associated with her is sung by two soprano soloists in the orchestra pit.[73]

Not much text, though, is needed, as Lachenmann allows the familiar story to tell itself. It is the tale of the girl who sells matches on the cold city streets on New Year's Eve to raise money for her family. To keep warm, she lights matches one by one, the flames of which inspire visions of

---

[70] The score for the opera is not commercially available. I would like to thank Breitkopf & Härtel for providing me with a copy.

[71] Lachenmann, " Musik zum Hören und Sehen: Peter Ruzicka im Gespräch mit Helmut Lachenmann," program book for the premiere at the Hamburg Opera, January 26, 1997, 39.

[72] Lachenmann, "Musik zum Hören und Sehen," 39. Translation taken from Nonnenmann, "Music with Images," 2.

[73] Sketches of the work reveal that Lachenmann had once planned to have several singers perform the part of the girl. There would also be performers on stage for other characters. Dörte Schmidt, "Theater der Wahrnehmbarkeit: Musikalische Dramaturgie, Szene und Text in Helmut Lachenmann's *Das Mädchen mit den Schwefelhölzern*," in *Musiktheater heute: International Symposium der Paul Sacher Stiftung Basel 2001*, ed. Hermann Danuser (Mainz: Schott, 2003), 198–201.

Part I Auf der Strasse
  1. Choralvorspiel "Oh, du frőliche"
  2. "In dieser Kälte"
  3. "Frier-Arie" (1. Teil)
  4. Trio und Reprise ("Frier-Arie," 2. Tiel)
  5. Scherzo I ("Königin der Nacht")
  6. Scherzo II ("Schnalz-Arie" – "Stille Nacht")
  7. "Zwei Wagen"
  8. "Die Jagd"
  9. "Schneeflocken"
10. "Aus allen Fenstern"

Part II An der Hauswand
  1. Hauswand 1 ("In einem Winkel")
  2. Ritsch 1 ("Ofen")
  3. Hauswand 2 ("Da erlosch")
  4. Hauswand 3 ("Litanei")
  5. "Schreibt auf. Unsere Haut"
  6. Ritsch 3
  7. Kaufladen
  8. "Die Weihnachtslieder stiegen höher"
  9. Abendsegen ("Wenn ein Stern fällt")
10. "... zwei Gefühle ..." Musik mit Leonardo
11. Hauswand 4
12. Ritsch 4
13. Die Grossmutter
14. "Nimm mich mit"
15. Himmelfahrt ("In Glanz und Freude")
16. Shô ("Sie waren bei Gott")
17. Epilog ("Aber in der kalten Morgenstunde")

Figure 5.1 Scenes in *Das Mädchen mit den Schwefelhölzern*

burning ovens, Christmas trees, and a holiday meal. She also sees an image of her deceased grandmother, who, after the girl has lit all of her remaining matches at once, takes her up to heaven. On the street the next morning, passers-by find the girl's cold body. In his libretto, Lachenmann divides the narrative into a series of scenes that concentrate on key aspects of the story (Figure 5.1). Some of the scenes present actions in the plot, for example the chase of the boy who stole one of the girl's slippers, the lighting of the matches, and the ascent into heaven with the grandmother. Others are more atmospheric, as they elaborate upon the cold seizing the girl, the noises and activity on the street, and the holiday season in which the story is set (suggested through Lachenmann's oblique handling of such appropriate songs as "Oh, du fröliche" and "Stille Nacht").

Two interlopers into Andersen's tale demand their own scenes. Lachenmann includes excerpts from texts written by Gudrun Ensslin, a member of the Red Army Faction in three scenes ("Aus allen Fenstern," Hauswand 3 ("Litanei"), and "Schreibt auf. Unsere Haut"). Lachenmann considers her to be "something like a deformed variant of [his] little girl."[74] Whereas the latter lights matches on a cold street full of shops to keep warm, Ensslin lit fires in two department stores to attack the "fascist" state of West Germany. The use of Ensslin's texts allowed Lachenmann to contemplate a question that he had long pondered. The two knew each other as children, and with her appearance in the opera alongside the title character, he asks – and has us ask – how did the girl that he knew, or any girl as suggested by the Andersen character, become the woman who committed such desperate acts.[75] The second guest is Leonardo da Vinci. In the " . . . zwei Gefühle . . . " scene, Lachenmann draws upon an excerpt from the artist's writings that describes his feelings upon staring into a dark cave.[76] The text creates links between the girl, Ensslin, and Leonardo. The trio experience the "two feelings" described by the painter, those of "fear and desire." Moreover, all three are "outsiders," the poor, the political radical, and the artist.[77]

The images born from Lachenmann's concept of "music with images" also play a significant, if not altogether clear, role in the operatic realization of Andersen's tale. Music, as described by the composer, evokes various associations, all part of the aura of a work. Now the aura includes images, an ambiguous term that encompasses mental pictures and particular sensations, such as the cold pervading the opera. A new dimension, the visual, has been added to the realm of perception. Not so much added, as merged with, for the lines between listening and seeing become blurred. Taking in a work like the opera, "one looks with one's ears, and listens with one's eyes."[78] With the senses blended, perception becomes a "larger and at once transcendent experience for all."[79]

[74] Lachenmann, "Les sons représentent des événements naturels," program book for the 2001 production at the Opéra National de Paris, 38.
[75] "Radical Experiment and Sensuous Adventure: Helmut Lachenmann about Music after the End of Music," *Friends' Magazine: For Friends and Patrons of the Salzburg Festival* (2001). www.festspielfreunde.at/english/frames/200112/ef 200112`08.
[76] This section of the opera exists as a separate piece entitled . . . *zwei Gefühle . . .*, *Musik mit Leonardo*.
[77] "Radical Experiment and Sensuous Adventure." Kaltenecker argues that all three characters bear suffering and form three layers of suffering. Kaltenecker, *Avec Helmut Lachenmann*, 244.
[78] Quoted in Nonnenmann, "Music with Images," 19.
[79] Lachenmann, "Musik zum Hören und Sehen," 39. Translation taken from Nonnenmann, "Music with Images," 2

That Lachenmann introduced the idea of music with images with a theatrical work seems appropriate. A scenic art demands a "visual" music. The visual elements of the sounds can assemble with the images created by the sets and stage action. Lachenmann, however, maintains that the two are not directly connected; in particular, the musical images do not illustrate the theatrical ones. The "sound events," according to him, are "self-sufficient," operating within a "theatre" and "landscape" of sound.[80] The "consonant," "warm" chords heard during the illusion of the glowing oven, for example, are not "symbolic"; rather, they are part of an "acoustic mise-en-scène" of "harmonic vibrations" that the listener can "feel." The acoustic scene follows more of a compositional than a theatrical logic, as the consonant chords result from a systematic "filtration" of chromatic clusters during the passage.[81] Lachenmann has even gone so far as to suggest that staging is not needed. The opera is "concert music with images and no staging."[82] Indeed, all a director would have to do to mount the work would be to "project the score on stage" and "point visually to the act of listening."[83]

Lachenmann's efforts to keep music with images apart from theatrical images may stem from the unequal terms of the relationship between sound and the visual. As Kahn has pointed out, the latter typically triumphs over the former.[84] Images tend to be more immediately comprehensible and defined than sound. As such, the visual overwhelms the sonic and typically relegates it to some sort of subsidiary role, be it as an accompaniment or as an illustration. Lachenmann uses the idea of music with images to escape such subjugation. The concept acknowledges the visual, as has to be done with a theatrical work, but it insists that music possess its own visual dimension, one separate from and unyielding to that on stage. To counter the unequal relationship, Lachenmann has music supplant the visual. With the score projected on stage, the musical image occupies the space once commanded by the theatrical scene. Music can provide everything needed for opera, both sound and image.

The concept of music with images proves just as unsatisfying as a production featuring a projected score would be. Both leave us wanting more. With the former, we need a clearer idea of what these images are and how they exactly function within the sensory wealth of opera. Lachenmann's appeal to the "self-sufficiency" of music is a surprising and unconvincing stance. Partaking in older modernist rhetoric of autonomy and purity, it comes across as a rearguard defense. It is also especially odd to argue the

---

[80] Ryan, "Composer in Interview," 24.
[81] Lachenmann, "Les sons représentent des événements naturels," 41.
[82] Quoted in Nonnenmann, "Music with Images," 25.
[83] Quoted in Nonnenmann, "Music with Images," 25.   [84] Kahn, *Noise, Water, Meat*, 158.

autonomy of music by describing how it co-opts the visual. Finally, why set music apart in a theatrical work?

We could continue to interrogate the concept of music with images by trying to figure out how it functions within the scenic world of the opera.[85] Such critical thrusts, though, would ultimately sink into the ambiguities of the idea. A more productive approach is to lift the concept momentarily away from the opera and place it into the larger patterns of signification made by sound, that is, what sound can evoke and how it does so. A turn to signification offers a departure point in examining how sound, with or without images, functions in the opera.

As volatile of a realm as sound is, it signifies in one of two directions: the specific and the enigmatic. Sounds typically come from a source, say a brook, a car crash, or a person screaming. Even if we do not see the source produce the sound, we know where it most likely came from, or could have come from. Given our focus on the source, a sound points back to its origins, and turned there, it signifies its origins. It evokes and means a brook, a car crash, a person screaming. This mode of signification is so strong that we tend to link sounds that are not clearly from a source to a source, saying that it *sounds* like a brook, a car crash, a person screaming. Kahn describes the tendency of sound to signify as a powerful force, one that has caused apprehension for musicians. The evocation of the worldly, as he points out, has demoted sound.[86] Nothing so beholden to the noises and associations of the everyday world could be suitable for music. Indeed, it is for this reason that Schaeffer sought to sever ties with the origins of his recorded sounds. He aimed to create "sonorous objects" that would bear no apparent resemblance to a source and would be appreciated "for themselves."[87] In other words, sound would be sound. It would signify itself; that self, though, is not always too clear. If we cannot connect a sound to a particular source, it comes across as an acoustic phenomenon, something with no meaning other than the generality of sound. It becomes an enigma. With no source in sight, we have no ready meaning or role to assign to a sound. Yet we will try to find one, or quickly grab at anything that is given to us. A classic example is Penderecki's *Threnody: To the Victims of Hiroshima.*

---

[85] Nonnenmann and Kaltenecker for large part accept Lachenmann's concept at full value. The former acknowledges Lachenmann's claims of autonomy; however, he sees a natural correlation between the images of the sounds and those on the stage. He also applies the concept retroactively to Lachenmann's works prior to the opera and claims that they create images, most of which are quite apparent according to him. His argument pays little attention to the long-standing debates over the ability of music to signify or even to imitate non-musical events or objects. He also does not consider issues regarding the signification of sound discussed below. Nonnenmann, "Music with Images," 20–26; Kaltenecker, *Avec Helmut Lachenmann*, 245–60.

[86] Kahn, *Noise, Water, Meat,* 69–70.   [87] Schaeffer, "Acousmatics," 78.

Bearing the original title *8′37″*, the piece went relatively unnoticed. When the screeching clusters were associated with screams and anguished cries of sorrow, the work attracted much attention. Wrenching composed sounds could all too easily become the painful noises emerging after an atomic explosion.

Where does music with images fit into this pattern of signification? The name alone points sound toward the specific, the images that music can evoke. The concept as explained by Lachenmann, though, pulls back from the specific. The images are not those of the objects or events that may have produced the sounds but rather the visual displays created by those sounds, whatever they may be. They could be recognizable images connected with a sound or some sort of image that we do not expect, something more at home in the world of sound and perhaps not even all that visual. The contradictions riddling the idea emerge once more. Here is a conception that builds upon the ability of sound to evoke the specific, only to curtail that ability by insisting upon the autonomy of sound and the images it produces. With that final twist, another parallel emerges between the two types of *musique concrète*. Whereas Schaeffer moves from sounds to music and Lachenmann from conventional music to sound, they both avoid the specificity of sound.

The signifying patterns of sound play out more freely in the opera than the idea of music with images would suggest. Even if Lachenmann's concept keeps a distance from the specific, some of the operatic sounds rush toward it. Others move in the opposite direction toward the enigmatic, but they only get so far, as we will see. Regarding the former, it is surprising how illustrative certain passages can be. For example, in the scene where the girl and the grandmother rise to heaven, Lachenmann conveys the growing gulf between heaven and earth by pushing up in range from the already stratospheric heights in the strings and plunging the heavy sonorities in the lower brass further and further down. At one point, he even pulls out ascending chromatic scales. It is hard to imagine a Baroque depiction of the Ascension being any more descriptive.

In some scenes, the sounds are suggestive but not so clearly representational. The opera opens with tableaux of cold, which reinforce the meteorological and social frigidity in which the girl is trapped (scenes 1–4). Cold is admittedly not the easiest condition to capture in music, although Baroque composers again found ways of doing so, as with Vivaldi's "Winter." Lachenmann musters sounds unheard in the eighteenth century: high-pitched "toneless" clusters, the wisp of breath passing through a brass instrument, and bowed bells. The sounds sustain an atmosphere, but one that many listeners may not interpret as cold. Vagueness, though, has no place at the beginning of the work, or elsewhere for that matter. Cold must be perceived, and above all sound must be presented as capable of conveying it and other images. We have to realize early on that sound can claim the specific. To chill the opera house, Lachenmann goes beyond these suggestive sounds and relies on means more obvious and immediate than anything in the Baroque *Imitation-Lehre*. The singers in the orchestral pit make shivering and chattering noises and even rub their hands together. With these parts there can be no ambiguity. We now have a visible source producing the sounds of the image to be conveyed. Specific human sounds and gestures capture the specificity of cold.

Then there are the enigmatic sounds – none perhaps more so than that created by the rubbing together of pieces of Styrofoam in the third scene of Part II (Hauswand 2, "Da erlosch"). It is a unique sound, one created by an everyday object handled in a not-so-everyday manner. It is also an ambiguous sound, assured to inspire as many different images as there are listeners. For Lachenmann, it is a rich sound, one that he turned to in a few works written prior to the opera. In *Kontrakadenz* (1971), the static hiss forms an unsettling sonic backdrop. Piano and wind sounds no sooner pop in front of it than disappear into its hollowness, until there is nothing else than the hiss. The Styrofoam scraping is one of the many striking sounds from earlier works to reappear in the opera. On the sonic ties between the two, Lachenmann commented: "I at least knew that all of the things invoked speechlessly in my previous compositional work had this once been put into words."[88] It is an odd turn of phrase, especially given how the opera makes the few words that are sung unintelligible and how, as we will see, it emphasizes the condition of speechlessness. The remark, though, reveals how the dramatic scenario provides ways to interpret the various sounds, making them as comprehensible as words. Whereas the Styrofoam hiss puzzles in *Kontrakadenz*, it plays a particular dramatic role in the opera.[89] The sound follows the orchestral luminescence suggesting the girl's illusion of a warm oven created when she lights one of her matches. When the match burns out ("erlosch"), she plunges back into the cold, a minute or so of just the Styrofoam noise. An enigmatic sound has been given a specific meaning.

That even Styrofoam rubbing can be rendered in such terms reveals how much the signifying pattern of sound has been skewed to the specific. There

---

[88] Quoted in Nonnenmann, "Music with Images," 24. The concept of speechlessness is discussed below.

[89] Lachenmann had earlier connected the Styrofoam sound with the cold overwhelming the girl in his *Les Consolations* (1977–78). The work also draws upon the text of Andersen's tale. Reinhard Febel, "Zu *Ein Kinderspiel* und *Les Consolations* von Helmut Lachenmann," *Melos* 46 (1984), 95.

is little possibility of the enigmatic in the work. Nor can suggestive sounds, such as the toneless clusters and wind blowing through brass instruments, preserve a degree of ambiguity. They and other evocative sounds become illustrations of cold, as is to be expected given the emphasis on frigid temperatures in Andersen's story and the staging. The story relies upon a small number of obvious and familiar images. With these reference points being so clear and concentrated, it is difficult for sounds to stand apart from them and achieve their own images. It is difficult, but not impossible, as the analysis below of the opening of Part II reveals.

The opera is as equally fascinated by the relationship between sound and language as it is by the relationship between sound and image. Lachenmann notably chose a story that would not overwhelm him with words. The tale is short, and there are few spoken lines, the material that is most likely to make it from page to stage. On top of that, he took less than Andersen gave, using only a few significant words (such as "kalt") here and there.[90] Texts, though, are necessary to introduce the two outsiders, Ensslin and Leonardo. Both are represented by excerpts from their writings. The excerpts along with the bits of prose from the original story supply Lachenmann with material to further his long-standing explorations of how to incorporate language into a musical work. Not surprisingly, he has concentrated on aspects of sound: the sound of words, the interaction between musical sounds and those of language, the extraneous sounds created during the production of words, and the non-sound of words, the "speechlessness" where meaningful words used to be or should be.

Of particular interest is the question of how clearly words can be heard. Lachenmann's previous works feature everything from comprehensible stretches of speech (*Salut für Caldwell*) to obfuscated blocks (*Consolation I*). The opera covers those extremes and points in between. Ensslin's text is first presented by a voice speaking lucidly on tape, made less lucid at times by the crowd of other sounds – bits of radio broadcasts, musical quotations, and orchestral bursts – conveying the fracas of holiday shopping ("Aus allen Fenstern"). The next time we hear the text it is presented in a coarse whisper and rendered unrecognizable ("Litanei"). The Leonardo text ("...zwei Gefühle...") is not so disfigured, but it is still difficult to understand. Lachenmann staggers words and syllables and divides them up between two speakers. Sometimes words and phrases can be made out, sometimes not. One has to persevere to comprehend the language, an effort that enriches the realm of perception. Effort is also required to

---

[90] In the earlier work *Les Consolations*, Lachenmann took the opposite approach to Andersen's text. The work sets extended sections from the story.

grab understandable bits out of the farrago of phonemes, syllables, and words in such early scenes as "In einem Winkel." As these examples show, language is for the most part obscured in the opera, obscured by either being overwhelmed with sound or turned into sound.[91]

What of the voice that delivers the text? For Lachenmann, the conventional lyrical voice used in opera was a "trauma."[92] Earlier works featured singers, but the composer had always drawn out of the performers other types of sounds. *temA*, for instance, isolates the flow of breath (German *Atem*). An opera, though, could not completely sidestep traditional vocal production. It had to be confronted. The conventional vocal sound was especially challenging, as the voice, like any familiar instrumental timbre, possesses what Lachenmann calls "pre-established, standardized magics."[93] Lachenmann uses the word "magics" to refer to the wonder and uniqueness of musical moments and effects, which, though, can lose those qualities by being "standardized" through conventions or even "cheapened" by the mass production of popular music.[94] The "magics" of the operatic voice have become so regulated as to make them especially difficult to change. According to Lachenmann, early modernist composers, namely Schoenberg and Berg, already faced this problem. The traditional lyrical voice did not adapt easily to the angular melodic lines and dissonances of atonal idioms; it always came across as a "quotation" of an earlier musical period. The way of dealing with it was to quote the quotation, to use the more conventional voice when characters sing actual songs, as with Marie's lullaby in *Wozzeck*.[95] The traditional lyricism of the voice could be used for traditionally lyrical moments, whereas the rest of the time the voice would take on newer sounds to suit the atonal surroundings, notably *Sprechstimme* and more declamatory styles.

For Lachenmann, the only way to deal with the magics of the voice was to handle them in the same way that he did those of instrumental timbres: *musique concrète instrumentale*. The voice, though, is the most difficult sound to "dephilharmonicize."[96] As with instruments, he begins not with the conventional tone but with all the sounds involved in the production of that tone and that are considered antithetical to it, for example the noise of

---

[91] The blurring of the lines between language and sound was a key interest in music of the 1950s and 1960s. Lachenmann was undoubtedly aware of and influenced by many of the approaches taken during that time, particularly those of his teacher Nono.

[92] Stephan Mösch, "Die verborgene Schönheit," *Opernwelt* 9 (1997/Yearbook Issue), 47.

[93] Véronique Brindeau, "Entretien avec Helmut Lachenmann," *Accents: Le journal de l'Ensemble Intercontemporain* 10 (January–March 2000), 6.

[94] "Broken, Conjured-Up Magic," *World New Music Magazine* 16 (July 2006), 80–81.

[95] Brindeau, "Entretien," 6 and Lachenmann, "Musik zum Hören und Sehen," 40.

[96] Kaltenecker, *Avec Helmut Lachenmann*, 26–27.

breathing and the movement of the tongue.[97] Lachenmann musters a variety
of vocal noises, but he also draws upon more conventional tones. The latter,
however, are typically used more in sonic ways – bursts of high registers, the
material of crescendos – than in any extended, let alone traditional, melodic
writing. To make the point of how far he has moved from the conventions of
the operatic voice, he plays the quotation game used by Berg, although with
a twist. In the first part of the opera, there are two scenes called "Königin
der Nacht" and "Stille Nacht." We hear bits of the Mozart aria and the carol,
but without the lyrical voice. Two sopranos use *sshh* sounds to hush the
Queen's sprightly coloratura, while the vocal ensemble members perform
the carol melody with tongue clicks. Where there used to be song and the
voice of song now stand the remnants of song and the voice of *musique
concrète instrumentale*.

The disintegration of the operatic voice is one means by which Lachenmann subverts the "aesthetic apparatus" of opera, an effort bolstered by
emphasizing images over text and scattering what little text there is. For him,
the genre of opera was "obsolete" (überalterten), having become nothing
more than an "artistic arrangement of standardized affects."[98] If the genre
was to have a future, it would have to break free from that arrangement. A
composer, according to Lachenmann, cannot simply use familiar materials
or genres; rather, he or she must recognize the apparatus supporting them
and "master it, technically and spiritually." Only then can "self knowledge
and musical expression come about."[99]

Lachenmann has long considered how expression comes about. Over
decades he has elaborated upon the idea of expression as the result of a
compositional engagement with larger, hegemonic concepts and forces.[100]
One such force is the aesthetic apparatus. Another is the established ideas
of how certain musical materials are understood and typically presented.
The composer not only has to challenge those ideas but he or she must
also engage the possibilities and resistance of the material itself. On another
critical front, Lachenmann distinguishes between affect, the gestures used to
produce a specific, and often expected, emotional response, and aspect, the
involvement with the historical and musical dimensions of the material.[101]
The former typically meets skepticism, if not disdain, as in the above comment about opera being clogged with "standardized affects." Affect, though,

---

[97] Mösch, "Die verborgene Schönheit," 47.   [98] Mösch, "Die verborgene Schönheit," 50.
[99] Lachenmann, "The 'Beautiful' in Music Today," 23.
[100] In particular, see his "The 'Beautiful' in Music Today," 21–24 and "Affekt und Aspekt," in *MEE*,
     63–65. In both articles, Lachenmann notably critiques neo-Romantic composers, who he sees
     as presenting superficial displays of expression. They are especially addicted to the notion of
     affect discussed below.
[101] Lachenmann, "Affekt und Aspekt," 64–66.

cannot be so easily dismissed. According to Lachenmann, affect and aspect are tightly intertwined, the two forming a single strand. They also interact; in particular, aspect can be strong enough to purify and revive even the stalest types of affect.[102] Contrary to the approach adopted here, Lachenmann does not view expression as an act. The concept of aspect, though, does refer to the expressive actions of the subject. Aspect, for instance, raises the questions: how does the subject present itself to the world and how does it react to the demands of the material and aesthetic apparatus.[103]

Das Mädchen mit den Schwefelhölzern raises the same questions. To answer them, we must first identify the subject. Whereas Lachenmann typically views the composer as subject, we will look at figures in the opera, namely the title character, Ensslin, and the often unspecified source of a voice. The expressive act of this subject is the assertion of the self through voice. At key moments, the figures present themselves – their presence, their desires – by raising a unique voice, the means by which they assert themselves in the surrounding musical world. In traditional opera, this is the moment when an aria begins. Lachenmann, as to be expected, never gives us an aria, yet there is still the declaration of self through voice. If the act does not take the form of an aria, then what form does it take? Even more pressing is the question of how the act plays out in the compositional state of sonic flux.

The opening five scenes of Part II (Hauswand 1 to "Schreibt auf. Unsere Haut") provide answers to those questions. In terms of Andersen's story, the scenes depict the girl's lighting of the first match, the fantastic illusion of a roaring oven, and the dwindling of the match and the illusion. Lachenmann appends to the tale two scenes ("Litanei" and "Schreibt auf. Unsere Haut") dealing with Ensslin's political ardor, or illusions. Sound adds its own stories to the tale, ones that have been told many times before. Over the course of the five scenes, two related sonic processes unfold. The first involves transformation, as the defining sound of a scene turns into that of the following section. The chain of metamorphoses creates a larger progression from the giant orchestral cluster of Ritsch 1 to the final solo part and silence of "Schreibt auf. Unsere Haut." The movement from fullness to nothingness occurs often in sound-based works; Grisey's *Partiels* being a classic example.[104] The prominence of the progression is hardly surprising given how it highlights the stuff of sound, such parameters as density, texture, and dynamics. Through these parameters, sound lends

---

[102] Lachenmann, "Affekt und Aspekt," 65–66.   [103] Lachenmann, "Affekt und Aspekt," 65.
[104] In his essay "Klangtypen der neuen Musik," Lachenmann evokes this shape in schematic diagrams of sound events in pieces by himself and Stockhausen. *MEE*, 4–6.

itself to creating shapes, like a gradual declining mass. Appearing so often, that particular shape has become an archetypal figure, that of sonic diminishment. With the five scenes, we once again have the act of expression play out in a fundamental sonic form. In Saariaho's . . . *à la fumée*, the soloists occupy the sonic continuum and assume an expressive presence by commanding that space. The girl and Ensslin find themselves in a winnowing world of sound, and their expressive efforts meet a very different fate.

Those efforts begin in the closing scene of Part I, "Aus allen Fenstern," which depicts the various noises, notably radio broadcasts, pouring out of the homes on the street. Although the scene is not part of the sonic shape discussed below, it merits attention because both characters declare their individuality here. Ensslin emerges for the first time in this scene. A female voice on tape clearly reads a passage from one of her prison letters.[105] Lachenmann juxtaposes the political diatribe with a male voice reading excerpts from Andersen's story. Tales of two "girls" who played with fire unfold side by side. The tape recording gives Ensslin a presence, as the female voice suggests the author of the text being read. No sooner is the voice raised and Ensslin's presence established than both are effaced. The woman's voice becomes lost in the din made by blasts of radio shows and unruly chords and glissandi in the orchestra.

"Aus allen Fenstern" is obviously not the first time we encounter the girl. She has been on stage from the beginning of the work. In the initial appearances, she is not so much a willful individual as a body that responds to stimuli, the cold and noises, around it. The onstage being does not even have a voice, any sounds related to her being created by the two soprano soloists in the pit. The only sounds we hear for a long time are those of the body, like shivering. That changes near the end of the "Aus allen Fenstern" scene when the two sopranos make brief cries of "ich." There could be no more elemental form of the expressive act in opera than this, a single word proclaiming "I" sung to a speechlike tone on an approximate pitch. It should be noted that the girl never makes these cries in Andersen's story. Lachenmann added them to his libretto. They not only serve as a way of giving the girl a vocal presence, as rudimentary as it is, but they also transform her from a freezing body to a person struggling to lay claim to her individuality in a world that views her as refuse on the street. The

---

[105] *Briefe der Gefangenen aus der RAF, 1973–1977*, ed. Pieter Bakker Schut (Hamburg, Neuer Malik Verlag, 1987), 14–18. Audio and video recordings of the opera feature different excerpts from the same 1973 letter, which Lachenmann draws upon again in the "Litanei" and "Schreibt auf. Unsere Haut" sections discussed below.

boldness of her struggle is striking. No wonder Lachenmann has referred to the declamations of "ich" as "revolutionary."[106]

The blunt ways in which the act of raising a voice is presented plays into Lachenmann's attack on the aesthetic apparatus of opera. He channels the expressive impetus of an aria into the most non-lyrical statement possible and has the cries reveal the expressive limitations of the lyrical voice as used in an aria. To recall, Lachenmann argued that such a voice when employed in modernist opera comes across as a quotation of past ideals of vocality. Interestingly enough, he surrounds the girl's exclamations with orchestral quotations, altered statements of emphatic chords taken from the works of Beethoven, Mahler, Boulez, and Stockhausen.[107] The interjections not only cut off her cries but they also reveal them to be quotations. The statements of "ich" do not quote the lyrical voice of an aria but rather the dramatic expression of self that precipitates those numbers. Even the act, here in its most basic form, can no longer be presented spontaneously. The cries suggest that the declaration of self through voice in opera amounts to a quotation, as it has been done so many times before. Outside the boundaries of the genre, the orchestral chord borrowings imply that any declaration of "I" that we may make, even a "revolutionary" one, is nothing more than a quotation, in that it relies on conventional ways of doing so and repeats accepted ideas of the self.

Lachenmann surrounds the statements of "ich" with other words, such as "wo" and "wie," and broken parts of words. In this context, the five iterations of "ich" could be nothing more than the debris of language.[108] Five scattered syllables in the rubble suggest otherwise: *Gud, run, en, si, -llin*. A name has been attached to the spoken voice heard earlier, notably at the same time that the cries of "ich" are assigned to the voiceless figure on stage. The fractured name makes another statement about the act of expressing the self through voice. It suggests that not only are the declarations of the self fragmented but so too is the self, a modernist conception of the subject that Lachenmann has upheld in his writings.[109] Ensslin, like her name, exists in pieces, as does the girl who can only sporadically spit out one syllable. Broken and reduced to a quotation, the declaration of the self comes

---

[106] Personal interview, Vancouver, March 31, 2008. Reinhold Brinkmann sees the girl as a Promethean figure. On that figure and the political dimensions of the work, see Brinkmann, "Der Autor als sein Exeget: Fragen an Werk und Ästhetik Helmut Lachenmanns," in *Nachgedachte Musik: Studien zum Werk von Helmut Lachenmann*, ed. Jörn Peter Hiekel and Siegfried Mauser (Saarbrücken: Pfau, 2005), 127.

[107] Nonnenmann, "Music with Images," 20. Some of the quotations have symbolic values, such as the bleak, powerful A minor chord that closes Mahler's Sixth Symphony.

[108] Nonnenmann argues that "ich" is a remnant of the word "Streichhölzer." Nonnenmann, "Music with Images," 20.

[109] Lachenmann, "Affekt und Aspekt," 68.

1. Hauswand 1 ("In einem Winkel")	2. Ritsch 1 ("Ofen")	3. Hauswand 2 ("Da erlosch")	[Ritsch 2]	4. Hauswand 3 ("Litanei")	5. "Schreibt auf. Unsere Haut"	6. Ritsch 3
Cries of "ich" at the end of this section	"Ich" sound taken up by gong. A large cluster grows out of the gong resonance.	Styrofoam sounds mimic cluster	[Lighting of second match; omitted from the opera]	Whispering of Ensslin text	Writing on drum heads; scraping sounds; silence	Return of full orchestra

Figure 5.2 Sonic diminishment figure in *Das Mädchen mit den Schwefelhölzern*, Part II "An der Hauswand"

across as inextricably compromised. Lachenmann, though, holds out that it remains viable and necessary. He ironically makes the point by having the vocal ensemble sing fragments of a quotation from Ernst Toller's 1920 drama *Masse Mensch*: "erkenn dich doch" (recognize yourself). Toller uses the line to evoke the paradox of recognizing oneself as an individual enjoying personal freedoms apart from the masses while at the same time being one person belonging to the masses, the will of which may come before the needs of the individual. In the opera, the paradox is downplayed as the line emerges as an exhortation for the subject to perceive and present the self.

The next time we hear "ich," the declaration of self is more assertive. The girl now backs up the word with a self-serving action. At the end of Hauswand 1 ("In einem Winkel") and the beginning of Ritsch 1, she lights a match, a bold decision in that she has one less match to sell and less of a chance to make money for her family. She gathers the courage to do so with three cries of "ich." The audacity of the act and the declaration of self give her a presence, but it is a presence that fades. The girl disappears into an archetypal scene of sonic diminishment, one initiated by her own voice.

The first two cries of "ich" are just as terse and strained as those heard in "Aus allen Fenstern." The last one, though, hovers, as Lachenmann extends the final *ch* sound with a softly sustained pitch. The isolation of the sound sets off a series of transformations that will unfold over the course of the next four scenes (Figure 5.2). The resonance of the vocal *ch* melds with that of a Japanese temple gong which, in a bit of Eastern *musique concrète instrumentale*, Lachenmann has the performer slowly rub so as to create a nimbus of overtones. The resonance grows richer with the addition of Turkish cymbals and other gongs. The rest of the orchestra soon enters and turns the metallic halo into a large cluster chord. In the world of music with images, the swell captures the frail match flame turning into the girl's vision of a blazing oven. In the world of music as sound, it represents a moment of transformation, as the lone syllable becomes an unsettled cluster. Lachenmann gives us ways of hearing the cluster as a mutating sound. Writing on Ligeti's *Atmosphères*, he describes how the "stationary" cluster chord is transformed more and more through an internal development process.[110] Lachenmann's sonority may not be so stationary, but it fluctuates just as much as Ligeti's. As in *Atmosphères*, the sonority evolves through changes in density, tone color, size, dynamics, internal agitation, and register. Lachenmann also alters the harmonic color. Through the "system of filtration" mentioned earlier, he

---

[110] Lachenmann, "Klangtypen der neuen Musik," 9.

reduces the large chromatic cluster to bring out "consonant" chords based upon thirds, fourths, and fifths.[111]

Not only does a word turn into an orchestral cluster but a girl also becomes sound. Her voice begins the metamorphosis, and it is her voice that joins the cluster. The two solo sopranos who spat out her cries of "ich" now stream radiant tones on top of that mass. The tones are free of words, just two more lines in the sonority. The girl in Andersen's tale is transfixed by the illusion of a glowing oven, the one in Lachenmann's score is transformed into the realm of sonic flux.

Illusion, sound, and subjectivity call to mind the most famous example of operatic fire music, that from *Die Walküre*. Wagner's music is not so much the object of interest as is Adorno's discussion of it, particularly his notion of phantasmagoria.[112] Lachenmann's aesthetics often stick closely to Adorno's, but in his fire music he departs from Adorno's conception of Wagner's scene, differences that say much about how Lachenmann presents both the force of sound and the expressive presence of the subject. Adorno heard orchestral sound in Wagner's scene as creating a "mirage," similar to the illusions in the magic lantern shows called phantasmagoria. The mirage is that of a separate musical realm in which the feeling of time is suspended and that seems to be without origins, existing within itself. The latter point draws upon Marx's appropriation of the idea of phantasmagoria, which he uses to describe how the labor of individual workers is concealed in the final product so as to create the illusion that the product has come into being magically on its own. For Adorno, Wagner's massed sonorities hide the efforts of the individual orchestral musicians, giving the impression of a natural, all-encompassing sound. As the presence of the musicians disappears, Adorno argues, the subjectivity of Wagner increases. He, not the players, has created the glowing sonorities; sound has become "the domain of his subjectivity."[113]

Lachenmann does not conceal the origins of his sound mass – to do so would violate the emphasis placed on the activity and energy of performance crucial to *musique concrète instrumentale*. Instead of Adorno's individual musicians obscured within the mass, Lachenmann's mass begins with the

---

[111] Lachenmann draws attention to these sonorities with an "auszug" line included in the score. Lachenmann, "Les sons représentent des événements naturels," 41.

[112] Adorno, *In Search of Wagner*, trans. Rodney Livingstone (London: NLB, 1981), 63–87. For discussions of Adorno's concept, see Paddison, *Adorno's Aesthetics of Music*, 124; Alastair Williams, "Technology of the Archaic: Wish Image and Phantasmagoria in Wagner," *Cambridge Opera Journal* 9 (1997), 73–87; and Sherry Lee, "A Minstrel in a World Without Minstrels: Adorno and the Case of Schreker," *Journal of the American Musicological Society* 58 (2005), 33–58.

[113] Adorno, *In Search of Wagner*, 72.

individual musician, the lone percussion player rubbing the gong. We can hear and, given the open orchestral pit (*pace* Wagner), most likely see the origins of the sound. We also become aware of the expressive presence of the girl, who also helped to create the sonority with her cries of "ich." Her subjectivity matters, whereas Adorno ignores that of Brünnhilde and Wotan. Lachenmann wants us to observe how her subjectivity is shaped by sound, especially how her presence diminishes as she is transformed into sound. Finally, Lachenmann uses transformation to rob his fire music of the illusion of being a distinct, eternal realm. It is one sound in a larger chain of sounds. It began as one thing and will turn into something else. Sonic fire burns up quickly.

At its climax, the cluster builds up to the largest sonority in the opera. It is the highpoint from which the archetypal figure of sonic reduction begins. The figure starts not with a gradual slope downwards but rather with a startling drop off. Lachenmann follows the loud brass pulses in the mass with very quiet "toneless" sonorities. It seems that we have already hit the bottom of the reduction, but it is from this point that most of the process will unfold. Lachenmann diminishes the already diminished.

The following scene, Hauswand 2 ("Da erlosch"), features the sound of Styrofoam blocks being rubbed together. As mentioned above, the opera relies on Andersen's tale to have us hear the enigmatic sound as evoking the extinguishing of the match. Whereas the Styrofoam noise plays a suggestive role in the drama on stage, it has a more specific part in the sonic drama. It fits into the chain of transformations by being the antithesis of the cluster. Here is a dry, hollow sound with no harmonic or acoustic richness, and no changes in color. To underscore the point, Lachenmann has the Styrofoam ensemble mimic the cluster. It too is made up of many independent parts, which, as in the cluster, differ in terms of rhythm (notated rhythmic figures versus a free "tremolo") and overlapping crescendo–decrescendo patterns. Similar to the preceding sonority, the Styrofoam mass builds to a climax and then breaks off, followed by a more empty sound, if that seems possible. Lachenmann finds something even thinner: barely audible slow glissandi played flautato in the strings.

The glissandi continue on through the next scene, Hauswand 3 ("Litanei"), in which they function as a drone. Above the unending whir, the vocal ensemble (minus the two solo sopranos) makes dry, percussive whispering sounds, which come across as a vocal transformation of the Styrofoam noise. Unlike Styrofoam, voices can say things, here excerpts from one of Ensslin's prison letters. The language of the letter is, Lachenmann admits, "ugly" and "aggressive," but a concluding paragraph has a "poignant beauty." It bears compassion for individuals "broken" by the confrontation with society.[114] Ensslin lines up the criminal, madman, and suicide victim. All three, according to her, are trapped within the cruelty of the "system," left with no choice but to destroy themselves or others. Through their acts, they also rebel against the system, trying to be not merely a "thing," but rather a human being.[115] Ensslin's message, though, is effaced by the means of text setting. The raspy whispering abrades the words and syllables, which, confounding comprehensibility even more, are broken up and divided between the different singers (Ex. 5.6). To reinforce how soundlike the voice has become, Lachenmann has the instruments "talk back" to them. The orchestral musicians play figures that are underlaid with the texts sung by the vocalists. The pianists and percussionists reinforce the rhythms of the enunciated syllables through attacks, and the brass players recite the texts by producing "toneless" pitches while pronouncing particular syllables. The orchestral response recalls early works such as *Consolation I* (1967), which comments on how difficult vocal communication, let alone text setting, has become by having the instrumentalists simulate the largely incomprehensible lines of the singers.[116] Although Lachenmann obscures the text, he still wants us to know that it is by Ensslin. He does so by returning the radio blasts heard in "Aus allen Fenstern," the scene in which the taped female voice clearly reads from her writings. In the previous scene, the radios and Ensslin's voice were outside elements that broke through the soundworld of the opera. When the radios come back, they are still trespassers. Ensslin's text, on the other hand, is now lodged within the sounds central to the scene and made incomprehensible by them.

Ensslin's letter concludes with the injunction "Schreibt auf. Unsere Haut" (write on our skin), which inspires the final scene in the archetypal figure.[117] The phrase becomes a *musique concrète instrumentale* score direction, as Lachenmann has the percussion players make writing motions on the membranes of their instruments. The gesture creates a light friction sound, which is played with short rhythmic patterns. The sound suggests a transformation of the gravelly, rhythmic whispering, a connection reinforced by the

---

[114] Lachenmann, "Les sons représentent des événements naturels," 37–38.

[115] *Briefe der Gefangenen aus der RAF, 1973–1977,* 18.

[116] Trent Leipert, "Sounds of Speechlessness: Helmut Lachenmann's Early Vocal Works," Master's thesis, University of British Columbia, 2007, 23–25.

[117] A brief word about the Ensslin text is in order. I have employed the capitalization and punctuation used by Lachenmann in the score. The original phrase places a period mark after "auf." The punctuation provides two different ways to interpret the line. The first is "Write down. Our skin." The second, employed here, is a more continuous thought: "write on our skin." The difference between the two is a fine one. Lachenmann's use of writing motions on the drum membranes suggests that he was more attuned to the second interpretation. The meaning of the line in Ensslin's letter is not exactly clear. She places it in parentheses and in lower case letters at the end of the letter.

Ex. 5.6 Vocal ensemble passage, "Litanei" from Lachenmann, *Das Mädchen mit den Schwefelhölzern*
© 1996 Breitkopf & Härtel, Wiesbaden

score direction "parlando" and the brief appearance of the vocal ensemble
to deliver the text phrase in a whispery hocket.[118] The scene closes with the
two timpani players making tapping and scraping noises, which become
shorter and shorter and further and further apart. After two brief lines,
there is an extended silence. The process of sonic diminishment has wound
down. Beginning with a massive cluster, it concludes with faint scraping
sounds and the only possible endpoint, quiet.

The true endpoint is not silence but rather the noise that destroys it,
that of the lighting of the next match (Ritsch 3) in the following scene. The
sudden appearance of loud sounds not only cuts off quiet but also puts
into relief the gradual diminishment that has occurred over the last few
scenes. The archetypal figure comes into clearer focus. Standing back from
it, we can ascertain what roles it plays in two central aspects of the opera,
one proposed by Lachenmann, the concept of music with images, and one
presented here, the act of expression.

Music with images, as discussed earlier, is pulled in opposing directions.
Lachenmann has insisted on the autonomy of the music, which produces
its own images. Many of the sounds, though, can be heard as obediently
serving the theatrical images. The stretch of scenes covered by the diminishment figure offers a broader view of the relationship between sound
and image. The relationship is flexible enough to accommodate the two
different directions. There are moments when the sounds conform to the
theatrical image, as with the lighting and burning out of the match. The
sounds can also stand apart. The diminishment figure wins such independence. Consistent with Lachenmann, it does suggest its own images, albeit
vague ones such as depletion. It should be noted, though, that the composer
typically focuses on the images created by individual sounds, such as the
cluster. He does not describe the image, or images, produced by larger sonic
processes.[119]

Instead of conjuring images, the diminishment figure could be viewed as
telling a story. At this moment, there are two stories on stage, Andersen's tale
and Lachenmann's libretto and score. The two usually coincide, but now and
then they part ways. Lachenmann, for example, deletes the episode in the
original dealing with the lighting of the second match and replaces it with
Ensslin's writings (Figure 5.2). The revision adds to the colloquy between

---

[118] Using the instrumental speaking techniques in the previous scenes, one of the pianists "recites"
a line of text by Leonardo, which will be featured in the upcoming "... zwei Gefühle ..." scene.

[119] Lachenmann does write about larger sonic processes but not in terms of the images they
produce. In his discussion of his Second String Quartet, he describes a transformation from
the opening flautato gestures to the closing pizzicato sounds. Lachenmann, "On My Second
String Quartet," 60.

the fairytale character and the political rebel. At the same time, it adds
to the exploration of sound by providing ample room for the archetype
figure to progress. The lighting of another match so soon after the first
would never allow for the slow diminishment of sound. With the second
burst gone, the opera can devote around twelve minutes to the figure. The
addition of Ensslin's text offers material for the sonic withdrawal. Her words
are ground down to nothingness, a means of text setting that furthers the
archetypal process under way. The process creates its own narrative, one
built upon a sequence of sonic events. The events unfold with a sense of
momentum and clear direction that commands attention. What the "story"
means is, of course, open to interpretation. A few of the ideas that come to
mind are decline, barrenness, and inevitability, all of which resonate within
both Andersen's tale and the opera. The diminishment figure, though, is
not a musical device merely used to bring out those themes. It possesses
autonomy, in terms of image and narrative. So independent is the figure
that it encourages us not to lapse into the habit of hearing music illustrate
the drama. Several changes are made to Andersen's story in this passage,
changes necessary to complement the archetype. Indeed, it could be argued
that the fairy tale is made to fit the world of sound rather than sound being
made to fit the tale.

As mentioned above, another change made to Andersen's tale is the addition of the girl's cries of "ich," which play important roles on both the
sonic and expressive fronts of the opera. The cries, for instance, initiate
the sonic diminishment figure. They also play a role in the inquiry into
the act of expression. The opera figures the cries as one particular form
of the act, that of raising a voice. We can approach that act through two
contexts, one provided by Lachenmann and one laid out here. Throughout
his writings, Lachenmann has returned to the concept of speechlessness
(Sprachlosigkeit). It touches upon the crippling difficulties of communication confronting the subject. The loss is not so much that of the physical
ability to speak, although that can happen and nearly does with the girl, but
rather it is the inability of the subject to raise a voice, one that can be heard
and that can express ideas. Lachenmann considers speechlessness to be just
as much of a basic condition of the modern subject as fragmentation.[120]
We, though, have little awareness of the condition. It has been covered up by
the false fluency (Sprachfertigkeit) of the mass media.[121] Amid the hollow
chatter, it is impossible to raise a personal voice, let alone hear one.

---

[120] Lachenmann, "Affekt und Aspekt," 68 and "Musik als Abbild vom Menschen," in *MEE*, 115.
[121] Lachenmann, "Musik als Abbild vom Menschen," 114 and Lachenmann, "Greifen und
Begreifen – Versuch für Kinder," in *MEE*, 162.

Lachenmann has asked how speechlessness can be overcome. The first step, according to him, is to make the posing of the question perceptible.[122] He does so through a depiction of speechlessness. The girl's obstructed attempts to raise a voice and simply say "I" are symptoms of the condition. The blasts of the radio broadcasts, especially those in the "Aus allen Fenstern" scene in which the cries of "ich" are first made, interject the false fluency of the media into the opera. The scenes stretching across the sonic diminishment figure offer a desperate drama of speechlessness. It begins with the choked statements of "ich," which dissolve into the sound of the resplendent cluster. The stifling of speech does not stop there but continues with Ensslin's voice. Lachenmann sets the stretch of "poignant beauty" from her prison letter; however, the raucous whispering in which it is delivered seems more suitable for the "ugly" language he found elsewhere in the text. He renders her words, though, not in an ugly way but rather in the way that they were heard at the time and are probably still heard today. A voice so troubling in its political message and personal story attempts to speak to us. It does so about criminals, madmen, and suicide victims, all of whose voices have been taken away, or made meaningless, by the "system." In her lack of voice and personal fate, Ensslin joined that damned trio: she was a criminal sent to prison, a mad person to many, and, given the mysterious conditions under which she died, a possible suicide victim.[123] The truths in her harsh tract are not, or cannot be, heard, so discordant are they to the general public. Her passionate words become the empty friction between syllables, the sound of speechlessness. In a fitting touch, Lachenmann blocks out the choral whispering now and then by bursts of radio broadcasts, the sound of the media's speechfulness. Ensslin's voice disintegrates further with the injunction "Schreibt auf. Unsere Haut." Except for one brief whispering declamation by the vocal ensemble, the line is taken literally with the writing on the drumheads. Another means of communication – writing – is tried, but it proves just as hopeless as speech. No legible words emerge from the scrawl, only the whirring noises created by the motion of the performers' hands.

The scenes are bleak but at the same time they are hopeful. By depicting speechlessness, Lachenmann makes us aware of both the glibness of the media and the depletion of the personal voice. Music, as crucial to the composer's aesthetics and social views, can lead to perception. And it is perception, the ability to break apart the familiar and to reflect on the world

[122] Lachenmann, "Musik als Abbild vom Menschen," 114.
[123] The official record states that Ensslin hung herself in prison; however, it has been suggested that she was murdered.

around oneself, that gives Lachenmann hope for humankind.[124] In this case, perception can lead to resistance, as the subject recognizes the means and structures of speechlessness. Having detected them, the subject can then intervene and find ways of overcoming the condition.[125]

This study has approached the cries of "ich" as part of the modernist inquiry into the act of expression, in which it joins such disparate works as Saariaho's . . . *à la fumée*. Despite the differences in genre and forces, the two pieces conduct a similar experiment: they highlight the raising of a voice and then see what happens to the voice when it is set free in the world of mutable sound. In Saariaho's work, the concerto soloists spawn elaborate melodic lines. Through the lines, they negotiate the fluid sonic space of the continuum and take on an expressive presence. In the opera, the act of expression musters only a few spoken words, notably "ich." Neither the girl nor Ensslin create an extended melodic line. Their utterances crumble within both the stream of quick metamorphoses and the collapsing space of the diminishment archetype. The two characters take on an expressive presence, but it is one of loss. The opera reaches the grim conclusion that the act of raising a voice, even such a bold, "revolutionary" attempt as the girl's, is doomed. The voice can barely emerge and is most likely never heard before it disappears. In this sense, speechlessness is an apposite way to describe the expressive fate of both the girl and Ensslin, and Lachenmann has found a fitting means to convey the condition through the flux of sound.

Neuwirth

From the early silent period on, film has reached out to opera. Opera, for the large part, has not reciprocated. It is difficult to think of many operas that incorporate film plots. A recent and notable exception is Neuwirth's *Lost Highway* (2003), which is inspired by David Lynch's 1997 film of the same name.[126] The work not only draws upon a particular film but it also uses the medium of film, to the point that there is a video monitor always playing somewhere on stage. The prominence of video comes as no surprise given that Neuwirth studied film making and theory before dedicating herself to composition. Neuwirth the lifelong student of film will never be too far from the discussion of *Lost Highway*, but Neuwirth the composer will, of course, come to the fore. She is a musician with a rich sonic imagination, shaped by

---

[124] Lachenmann, "Musik als Abbild vom Menschen," 115.
[125] Lachenmann, "Musik als Abbild vom Menschen," 114. For a discussion of evocations of speechlessness in earlier works, see Leipert, "Sounds of Speechlessness."
[126] The score for the opera is not commercially available. I would like to thank Boosey & Hawkes for providing me with a copy.

the works of several composers she holds up as influences, including Varèse and her former teacher Murail. To discuss this film-turned-opera, we will ask what does that imagination have to offer Lynch's film and what does the latter have to give to Neuwirth.

Lynch's *Lost Highway*, it goes without saying, is an unusual inspiration for an opera. How odd can be gathered from a synopsis of the movie. But first a proviso: a film that mingles reality and fantasy, as this one incessantly does, escapes the succinctness of a summary. The film opens up in the home of Fred Madison, a jazz musician, and Renée, a couple whose relationship has been sapped by his impotence and not-so-unjustified thoughts of her infidelity. Their domestic torpor is interrupted by a series of dispatches from a remote, disturbing world: a strange message on the front-door intercom, a video of the two of them sleeping together in bed left in a package on their front step, and an encounter with the Mystery Man, a character who can be in two places at once. The appearances of the Mystery Man precipitate violent events, in this case Fred's murder of Renée. Convicted of the crime, Fred is sent to prison. One night in his cell, he is overwhelmed by headaches. The next morning, the guards open the door to find a different man there. The man turns out to be Pete Dayton, a young auto mechanic. With no one knowing how he ended up there or what happened to Fred, Pete is sent home to live with his parents and take up his old job. He soon becomes involved with Alice, played by the same actress who took the part of Renée, now wearing a blond rather than a black wig. She is the girlfriend of Mr. Eddy, the local crime boss. Seduced by Alice, Pete joins her in a scheme to steal money, get away from Mr. Eddy, and skip town. They drive to the desert, and during their escape Alice disappears after making love to Pete, who also disappears when he turns back into Fred. The Mystery Man returns and has Fred kill Mr. Eddy, after which Fred goes back to his house, rings the doorbell, and leaves the same intercom message that began the film: "Dick Laurent is dead." In the closing scene, Fred is being chased by the police and begins to undergo another transformation, the results of which we never see.

What to make of this mix of doubles, transformations, and a Mystery Man? Slavoj Žižek has ventured an answer to that question.[127] As he so often does in his writings on cinema, he has turned to Lacan. For him, the film opposes reality, Fred's domestic life, and the fantasmatic, Pete's sexual triumphs with Alice and other women. In his cell, Fred transports himself into a world of youthful virility and fast cars. This is obviously a fantasy,

---

[127] Slavoj Žižek, *The Art of the Ridiculous Sublime: On David Lynch's "Lost Highway"* (Seattle: University of Washington Press, 2000).

and a rather clichéd one at that, but Žižek has us consider the notion of fantasy in a more specific Lacanian sense.[128] Fantasy, or the fantasmatic, is a realm in which desire is staged so that it can be given form. With that structure, the subject can gain self-knowledge by asking such questions as, How do I know that I long for this? and What does this longing entail? The fantasmatic draws out desire and never completely satisfies it, for fulfillment would end the pleasure created by acting out that longing. The worlds of Fred and Pete could not be more different. The latter, as filmed by Lynch, is dark, claustrophobic, and muted, so much so that we can barely hear the characters speak. The former is vibrant and full of lively sounds. Ironically, it is also more realistic, as we observe Pete's family life and people holding down regular jobs. As Žižek points out, the twist underscores how fantasy sustains reality, serving as a screen through which we can see reality and make it bearable.[129] Here, day-to-day family life and working life, the stuff usually altered or blocked out, form part of the screen to block out an even more tedious reality, Fred's life.

Fantasy not only ameliorates reality but also promises to conceal the horror of the Real, a traumatic and ultimately unknown psychological register. The promise, though, is not kept. If fantasy gives desire form, it also does the same with the Real, what Žižek calls the fantasmatic Real. In the film, that compound involves scenes of pornography and physical and sexual violence, some of the things that appeared in the cryptic dispatches that made it into Fred's life. By turning into Pete, his dreams of available women and fast cars come to life; so too do his repressed fears and desires. The latter emerge in the shots from porn movies, a gruesome murder, and even bits from a snuff film that infiltrate Pete's world.

The fantasmatic, no matter how long the subject attempts to prolong it, will eventually dissolve. The fantasy of Pete's life begins to fall apart due to the same thing that originally created it: sexual failure. It is at the moment that Alice tells Pete that he will never have her that he turns back into Fred, who could never have Renée. The fantasmatic completely dissipates when Fred kills Mr. Eddy, the supposed obstacle to Pete's desire to possess Alice.[130] With him gone, Fred is even less likely to have either Renée or Alice. The last we see of Fred is as a criminal, just as he was before he created his fantasy life.

---

[128] The following observations regarding the fantasmatic are drawn from Žižek, *The Art of the Ridiculous Sublime*, 13–23 and *The Plague of Fantasies* (London and New York: Verso, 1997), 3–10.

[129] Žižek, *The Art of the Ridiculous Sublime*, 21.

[130] Žižek, *The Art of the Ridiculous Sublime*, 16–17. The Mystery Man actually kills Mr. Eddy. He shoots him after Fred has slashed his throat.

According to Žižek, fantasmatic narratives wind around temporal loops.[131] *Lost Highway* is no exception. Not only does Fred reappear as he was, but the film ends as it began with the same intercom message. Lynch has described the film as having a circular structure. He has compared it to a Moebius strip, a curved figure in which two sides of a sheet of paper appear to be one continuous side.[132] The image captures the fact that Fred and Pete's lives, although seemingly polar opposites, are actually one. Instead of them being a single person or two separate characters, the film offers another way of viewing Fred and Pete – as doubles. They are not the only doubles. The film constructs several pairs, none of them in the same way. Fred and Pete are played by two different actors, whereas Renée and Alice are different people played by the same actress. In one eerie moment in the film, the two women appear together in a photograph. Mr. Eddy has a double that goes unseen: Dick Laurent, the man declared dead on the intercom message. The two detectives, Hank and Lou, assigned to watch Pete identify Mr. Eddy as Dick Laurent. The detectives also have doubles, Ed and Al, who come to Fred and Renée's house about the creepy videotapes that they have received. Near the end of the film, all four appear together in the crime scene at Andy's house. Then there are two characters that appear in both the real and fantasy parts of the film: the Mystery Man and Andy. The former not surprisingly can cross the line between the two realms, as he has demonstrated the ability to be in two places at one time. The latter, as we will see, ties us to the fantasmatic Real of violence and porn, a realm that makes its presence felt on both sides. The variations on doubles serve two points. They reveal how unstable and permeable identity can be, and they create links between the worlds of reality and the fantasmatic.

The double characters lead to double scenes. Lynch creates parallels between the lives of Fred and Pete through the use of repeated images, dialogue, and settings. The shared scenes reinforce the idea that Pete's world is a transposition of Fred's. They also give us something to hold on to in moving from reality to the fantasmatic, as not only does the film change drastically in terms of color and sound but it also changes genre. Pete's world, at first so "real," turns into a film noir, settling into characters and plot lines typical of the genre: a young man seduced by a femme fatale and dragged into a world of crime and seedy motels, a thug mobster, and a pair of detectives who observe developments from afar. With the change, it is as

---

[131] Žižek, *The Plague of Fantasies*, 16.
[132] Lynch's observations are discussed in Bernd Herzogenrath, "On the *Lost Highway*: Lynch and Lacan, Cinema and Cultural Pathology," *Other Voices* 1, no. 3 (1999). www.othervoices.org/1.3/bh/highway.html.

if the movie gives in to the fantasmatic, re-creating itself as a new type of film.

Žižek's writings on *Lost Highway* in particular and the fantasmatic in general offer a point of reference in approaching Neuwirth's opera. Indeed, she encourages us to refer to Žižek by including excerpts from his essay on the film in the liner notes of the CD.[133] In her writings on the opera, she evokes the idea of the fantasmatic, or "phantasm" as she calls it. The concept is never clearly defined but, in her hands, it points to a world apart from reality, one that emphasizes aspects of the fantasmatic Real, what Neuwirth calls distant "threats" and "fears."[134]

Turning to the opera, one thing that stands out is how closely Neuwirth and librettist Elfriede Jelinek stick to their source. The libretto incorporates much of the original film dialogue in English.[135] The staging and video imagery also draw upon scenes from the movie. Neuwirth, of course, adds new dimensions to the film. Multidimensional is the best way to describe the world that she has created in the theater. As mentioned above, video monitors constantly play on stage, showing images that comment on the live action or pick up on other narrative threads. The musical setting has numerous dimensions as well. The orchestra is a medium-sized ensemble of a conventional makeup. A prominent group of six soloists is set apart, including such intriguing instruments as the accordion and retuned electric and Hawaiian guitars. There is an electronic sphere as well, made up of recorded real-world sounds, samples, synthesizer, and live electronics.[136]

Neuwirth utilizes her varied resources to create the state of restless, mutable sound, a condition heightened through amplification. She moves live and recorded music through speakers positioned around the hall. Sounds rush upon the audience from different angles. The overall effect, as she puts it, is a "constantly changing space of sound and images."[137] Sounds not only change direction but also identities. One sound event becomes another type of sonority; a recognizable sample can take on a whole new cast. Fascinated by the "theme of transformation," Neuwirth has sought out both dramatic and musical opportunities to "morph" sounds.[138] Her first opera, *Bählamms Fest* (1999), for example, turns a countertenor's voice into the howl of a Canadian wolf. No wonder she was taken by Lynch's film.

---

[133] Neuwirth, *Lost Highway*, Kairos 001254KAI, liner notes, 24–28.
[134] Neuwirth, "Afterthoughts on *Lost Highway*: 'Waiting for Godot' of Passion and Proximity – An Experimental Arrangement of Futility," CD liner notes, 38.
[135] Neuwirth also incorporates some of the popular songs included in the film soundtrack, notably Lou Reed's "This Magic Moment" mentioned below.
[136] On the use of electronics in the work, see Robert Höldrich, "*Lost Highway* – Totally Electronic," CD liner notes, 34–35.
[137] Neuwirth, "Afterthoughts," 38.   [138] Neuwirth, "Afterthoughts," 37.

The change from Fred to Pete, though, is just one transformation in a sonic world breeding numerous, and often fleeting, moments of metamorphosis.

Attuned to the dynamics of sonic flux, we can appreciate why the state serves as such a forceful way to explore the fantasmatic. The relationship between the two is based upon a mutual exchange. On the one hand, the instability and changeableness of sound heighten features of the fantasmatic, a psychological register marked by constant permutations of reality. On the other hand, the fantasmatic provides an opportunity to accentuate those sonic qualities. Here is a realm where voices can become disturbing sounds, where instrumental timbres can blend to create the sound of an unknown instrument. Not only can these things occur, but they seemingly must happen after one person turns into another person.

Sound grows especially unstable when the different psychological lines – those between reality and the fantasmatic and the latter and the fantasmatic Real – begin to waver, or even break. Lacanian interpretations of the film refer to the lines as sutures, a term shared by Neuwirth. For Lacan, a suture acts as a "conjunction between the registers of the symbolic and the imaginary."[139] Writing on the film, Bernd Herzogenrath proposes that the suture could also be viewed as a stitching that "closes off the real from reality," a divide necessary to prevent the subject from "falling into the void of the real."[140] He captures the two opposing ways in which a suture operates: it joins together opposing areas (reality and the fantasmatic) and also separates them (the fantasmatic and the fantasmatic Real). The doubleness suggests that the seam is not a stable junction. It can pop open, as when the fantasmatic Real intrudes upon the lives of Fred and Pete. For Neuwirth, the suture also serves a dual purpose. It separates reality from the fantasmatic, but it can be "bridged" to give access to the other side, as Fred does by entering the world of the fantasmatic.[141]

Neuwirth also applies the idea of suture to image and sound.[142] The seam exists between live action and music and "reproductions," that is, recorded video images and music. It at once demarcates the two realms through juxtaposition and unites them by revealing similarities between them. In a phrase that captures the double logic of the suture, Neuwirth aims to achieve "continuity in heterogeneity."[143] She overlaps the sound/images seams with the psychological ones. What could end up as messy cross-stitching turns

---

[139] Quoted in Herzogenrath, "On the *Lost Highway*."
[140] Herzogenrath, "On the *Lost Highway*."   [141] Neuwirth, "Afterthoughts," 38.
[142] As a student of film theory, Neuwirth has undoubtedly been influenced by the critical concept of suture, which, drawn from psychoanalytical theory, describes how the spectator is drawn in, or "stitched in," to the artificial visual world of the film, a connection that can break.
[143] Neuwirth, "Afterthoughts," 38.

out to be an imaginative way of playing off the different sides – psychological, sonic, and visual – against each other. For example, live actions on stage vie for the spectator's attention with monitors showing obscure imagery or static snow. The contrast suggests that there is some strange and barely recognizable realm beyond the everyday world on stage or, with the static, that there is a void outside of it. As for sound, Neuwirth plays a recorded passage to open the opera, an odd kind of curtain-raiser. The same music, now played live, returns for the final minutes. The recapitulation completes the circular structure of the narrative, but it also has us cross psychological registers. On a recording, the music strikes us as being removed and distant, even when played as loudly as Neuwirth specifies. It is just as strange as the electronically transmitted voice on the intercom message ("Dick Laurent is dead") that follows the music and sets the story in motion. Not just mysterious, the message is also threatening for it is a brief transmission from the fantasmatic Real, a world that we initially experience at a remove, often in the form of reproductions (like the strange videotapes left on the doorstep). At the end of the work, Fred leaves the same intercom message, this time in person on stage. The opening music befittingly returns live. It not only makes a strong impression on the spectator by virtue of being performed at that moment but it also bears the horrors of the fantasmatic Real that have been endured throughout the opera, things that the opening recorded message and music hinted at. We now know where this music leads; we have been there.

As the two examples show, Neuwirth's sonic and formal conceptions of the opera rest upon the line between reality and the fantasmatic. In a sketch for the work, she refers to the scenes of Fred's life as Part I and those of Pete's as Part II. She marks the entrance of the "phantasm" as beginning with Fred's transformation.[144] In a way, we have another diptych; this one, like Saariaho's, defined to a large degree by contrasting approaches to sound. The sonic differences between the two parts are striking. Just as Lynch radiates the shots of Pete's world with bright colors, Neuwirth animates that realm by making it more sonically vivid than the first part. In the domestic life of Fred and Renée, sound resides in the background, particularly electronic timbres that drone on and have little to do with the couple, nor they with them. The second half fills Pete's world with an array of sonorities. They intrude upon the drama, and the characters respond to them.

The line between reality and the fantasmatic disintegrates well before Fred's metamorphosis. The fissures allow the mercurial, disturbing sounds

---

[144] CD liner notes, *Lost Highway*, 32–33.

of the fantasmatic Real to seep in. The biggest break occurs with the arrival of the Mystery Man at a party attended by Fred and Renée. The look of the character alone tells us that he is, as marked in the score, "from a strange world." He wears white makeup, dresses like a 1930s gangster, and appears outside of time and space. The sounds around him, including his own voice, are equally foreign. Cast as a countertenor, his part consists of vermicular, non-pitched lines, an affected delivery that could not be more different than Fred's laconic speech. Fred struggles to make sense of the character's look and voice and, above all, his ability to be in two places at once. The Mystery Man has Fred call him at Fred's house, only to hear the strange character answer at the other end. The Mystery Man's voice on the phone is not the only disembodied voice that we hear. As soon as the Mystery Man addresses Fred, an offstage tenor voice emerges, a part performed by the singer playing the role of Pete. The sound of the voice is eerie enough, and is made more so given that this is the voice that Fred will possess when he turns into Pete. Just as the Mystery Man can be here and there, we listen to the voice of Fred as it is now and in the future. The ghostly vocal lines of the Mystery Man and tenor are accompanied by equally odd sounds in the orchestra, including a high-range muted trombone line with glissandi that imitates and distorts the tenor part, and the string players making amplified *sshh* and *cchh* sounds while executing free glissandi. These are just two lines in an unruly and, appropriate for the star of the scene, mysterious mix. The fantasmatic Real has made itself known.

Neuwirth uses sound in other ways to set apart the fantasmatic. As mentioned above, Lynch connects the stories of Fred and Pete through corresponding scenes. Neuwirth enhances the links by recapitulating the music from a scene in Part I in the corresponding passage in Part II. She usually adds sonic layers to the reprise to enhance the instability of sound and convey the greater presence of the fantasmatic Real in the second half of the opera. An example of these altered parallels can be found in the scenes where Fred and Pete ask their partners where they met Andy. Fred questions Renée after they have left a party at Andy's house, where Fred encountered the Mystery Man.[145] Pete asks Alice after she tells him about her plan to go to Andy's house and steal the large amounts of cash that he keeps there. Both women respond with the same halting, enigmatic tale: "It was a long time ago . . . I met him at this place called Moke's . . . We . . . became friends . . . He told me about a job" (Ex. 5.7).

---

[145] The scene of the phone conversation with the Mystery Man also returns later in the opera when Pete talks with both Mr. Eddy and the Mystery Man over the phone. The music from the original scene comes back in an altered version.

Ex. 5.7 *Sprechstimme* passage from Neuwirth, *Lost Highway*, mm. 237–40
© Copyright 2003 by Boosey & Hawkes/Bote & Bock GmbH & Co. KG. Reprinted
by permission of Boosey & Hawkes, Inc.

* all notes on electric guitar are played quarter-tone flat except for D

The two deliver their tale in *Sprechstimme*. Neuwirth marks the lines "Sprechgesang à la 'Pierrot.'" She builds upon the associations between the vocal style and otherworldly images of sexuality and violence made in Schoenberg's work to evoke the fantasmatic Real. The vocals of Renée and Alice also resemble the lilting delivery of the Mystery Man, the gatekeeper of that world. Moreover, *Sprechstimme* furthers the exploration of sonic flux. Consistent with the qualities of sound cultivated in the opera, it is a transformation of singing, one that constantly moves between speech and song.

The use of *Sprechstimme* allows us to track how far the fantasmatic Real makes it into the lives of the two couples. Responding to Fred's query, Renée mentions a job with Andy but never divulges that it involved making porn films. Her turn "à la 'Pierrot'" belies her evasion, as it suggests that there is something more than what she is telling Fred, who must be especially suspicious of her given the louche company at Andy's party. The strange vocals are one of the few signs of the fantasmatic Real that Renée ever reveals. In the corresponding section in Part II, Alice lets on that she appeared in porn films. The admission is just another sign of how far the fantasmatic Real has infiltrated Pete's life. To reveal its progress, Neuwirth plays up the qualities of sonic flux. She reprises the music of the earlier passage, including the *Sprechstimme*, but adds a new vocal part, a recording of Alice's voice slowed down and altered until it becomes a blur. A vocal distortion joins a vocal distortion. The transformations of her voice not only take us further into the world of sound but also right into the fantasmatic Real. Like the

Ex. 5.8 Melismatic exchange between Pete and Alice, Neuwirth, *Lost Highway*, mm. 826–28

© Copyright 2003 by Boosey & Hawkes/Bote & Bock GmbH & Co. KG. Reprinted by permission of Boosey & Hawkes, Inc.

s.v. = *senza vibrato*; m.v. = *molto vibrato*

Mystery Man, Alice can present two simultaneous voices. As with him, hers is a voice, or voices, of someone marked by the fantasmatic Real, a mark made clearer by the pornographic images of her that follow the conversation with Pete.

Renée's *Sprechstimme* is the exception to another significant difference between the two parts. Fred and Renée speak; Pete and Alice sing. The latter couple do not just sing but they do so in an elaborate manner, often taking things to the point of melismatic exuberance. Neuwirth uses melismas to underscore her view of singing as being "so artificial."[146] As such it thrives in the world of the fantasmatic, where the vocal excess not only comes across as unreal but also complements the sexual excess of Pete and Alice. Indeed, the two are especially "vocal" when seducing each other and making love. Their first sexual encounter, for instance, ends with a florid response to Alice's clichéd parting question (Ex. 5.8). Needless to say, things will only get more "florid" between them.

On a different front, the emergence of such extravagant singing returns our attention to the opposition between sound and voice. The opera foregrounds the pairing through the contrasts between Parts I and II. The opposition plays almost no role in the former, which consists of dry speech and static sound. It, though, dominates Part II, which has elaborate vocal lines unfold within ecstatic sounds. The interaction between the two brings up the questions explored in both Saariaho's and Lachenmann's works: what happens to the voice in a sonic world of constant transformation and what happens to the subject possessing that voice? Neuwirth's opera, though,

[146] Larry Lash, "The Future of Opera – This is It!, Olga Neuwirth's *Lost Highway* Pulls into Graz," *Andante* (29 October 2003). www.andante.com/article/article.cfm?id=22479.

Ex. 5.9 Pete's last vocal statement, Neuwirth, *Lost Highway*, mm. 1180–90
© Copyright 2003 by Boosey & Hawkes/Bote & Bock GmbH & Co. KG. Reprinted
by permission of Boosey & Hawkes, Inc.

has us ask a new question: what happens to sound when it encounters the
voice?

A concluding scene offers much to consider in addressing these points.
In this passage, Pete and Alice have escaped to the desert after killing Andy.
Even on the run and in the desert, they still have sex. At the climax he tells
her "I want you," to which she responds "You will never have me." Alice
walks away offstage (leaving through a slit in one of the projection screens).
We momentarily lose sight of Pete. When he reemerges, he is no longer
Pete but rather Fred. The fantasmatic begins to dissolve. Neuwirth's score
stokes the drama of the scene and vividly suggests the act of transformation.
What may go unnoticed is the varied group of sonic archetypes that she
marshals in such a short passage. The figures serve dramatic and pictorial
ends; they also offer new conceptions of the relationship between sound and
voice.

Neuwirth sets Pete's exclamation in two contrasting ways. The first features quivering half-step descents and wide leaps, signs of his melodic and
sexual prowess. The second is nothing more than a speechlike whisper,
which recalls Fred and points to the transformation to come (Ex. 5.9).
Alice's scornful response makes for a unique moment in the opera, the only
section for solo voice, no accompaniment. As such, it appears that the voice
side of the voice/sound opposition dominates; yet it is the other way around.
There is, it should be mentioned, a forceful melodic line here, one that displays Alice's melismatic boldness (Ex. 5.10). The whole vocal statement
spans the range of an octave (a'-a''). The curvilinear shape of the phrases is
created by the winding around three particular dyads of either the interval
of a fourth (bb'-eb'' and c''-f'') or a tritone (b'-f''). The phrases build to
melodic high points on either f'' or f♯''/gb''. Alice's defiance is conveyed by
her push through those ceiling pitches to the final a''. The concluding leap
of a seventh (b'-a'') echoes and mocks the jump of a seventh on Pete's final
two words, "want you" (e-d').

Ex. 5.10 Alice's last vocal statement, Neuwirth, *Lost Highway*, mm. 1196–1207
© Copyright 2003 by Boosey & Hawkes/Bote & Bock GmbH & Co. KG. Reprinted
by permission of Boosey & Hawkes, Inc.

The melodic lineaments of Alice's vocal statement, however, give way to
sonic effects and types. The singer changes degrees of vibrato, from none to
much, a direction that plays into the sonic identity that Neuwirth has set for
Alice. She wants us to hear Alice's voice at moments throughout the opera
as resembling a sine tone, achieved by the use of no vibrato.[147] We would
expect quite the opposite for a femme fatale. There is, to be sure, seductive
singing elsewhere, but there are also the sine tone vocals, which have us hear
Alice's voice in sonic terms, here an elemental sound. Moreover, for the final
phrase, Neuwirth utilizes a contact microphone to alter the singer's voice
and make it come across as metallic, more of a sonic than a vocal timbre.
Throughout the statement, Alice also indulges in several portamento slides,
ornamental presentiments of an impending large glissando.

The concluding gesture is an archetypal figure, an open-ended crescendo.
Like many of the other figures, it was refined by Varèse. In his works, the
increase in dynamics drives, and draws fuel from, a larger swell made up
of increasingly agitated textures, pushes to extreme registers, and rhythmic
propulsion. When the sound mass reaches a point of maximum volume and
turbulence, it suddenly stops. It is far from finished, though, as the sonority
remains suspended in the pauses and silences with which Varèse typically
concludes the figure. Such figures, according to Varèse, broach a "fourth
dimension" in music, that of "sound projection," the "feeling that sound is
leaving us with no hope of being reflected back, a feeling akin to that aroused
by beams of light sent forth by a powerful searchlight – for the ear as for the

---

[147] Personal interview, New York City, 23 February 2007.

eye, that sense of projection, of a journey into space."[148] Even single lines, as opposed to masses, can make that journey, as heard in Varèse's *Density 21.5* for solo flute and Alice's departing vocal statement. Through amplification and distortion, the latter grows louder and more unstable. When Alice cuts off the last pitch, the amplification keeps her sound alive. As it lingers in the air, she exits the stage and the opera for good. Her own voice has grown into an independent sound, one that takes off from her, as she does from it.

The open-ended crescendo finds a response in another archetypal gesture, a sudden leap between extreme registers, here the plummet from Alice's final a′′ to the electronic "grumbling, trembling" bass sample. Flouting the registral constraints of traditional idioms, such reversals, as once again exemplified in Varèse's works, reveal how vast the realm of sound is and how quickly individual lines and masses can move between remote points in that expanse. Neuwirth's sounds fleetingly cover those distances. No sooner do they hit the "grumbling" sample than they pop back up to an extreme high range, a piano and flute sample. The composer takes the sounds of the two instruments and "morphs" them, combining them with electronic timbres to create a new sound, an appropriate one for the transformation from Pete to Fred. The "morph" becomes the starting point of the last archetypal figure, the glissando. Neuwirth gives us a protracted glissando that descends undisturbed for about a minute. As is typical of the figure, the sound remains in constant motion and gradually changes in pitch and timbre. A very loud cluster chord in the orchestra severs the downward slide, a gesture as surprising as the sudden appearance of Fred.

As a climactic moment in an opera, this passage is strange, in the sense that such moments typically celebrate the voice, not sound. Pete barely sings and does not sing at all during his transformation, whereas Alice's vocal line, as melodic as it is, creates sonic effects. The last we hear of the two characters is as sound. Given the emphasis on transformation, it could be argued that the two characters become sound: Pete a glissando, Alice an open-ended crescendo. The same could be said about two other characters, Mr. Eddy and Fred. His throat cut, the former drags out painful, "airy closed-throat sounds," which conclude with an open-ended crescendo.[149] The last we see of Fred, to recall, is him being chased by the police and beginning another

---

[148] Varèse, "The Liberation of Sound," 197.
[149] Mr. Eddy does not only become violent, tortured sound, but he can use sounds to violent, tortured ends. In an earlier scene, he pummels a character with the force of his voice for disobeying a No Smoking sign.

transformation. Neuwirth brings back the same sound, the "Fred effect," used for the original metamorphosis.[150] It produces "grotesque sounds" by amplifying and distorting the performer's vacillating screams and moans.[151] Typical of the vocals of the fantasmatic Real, it appears as if there is more than one voice, and all anguished voices at that. The effect too concludes with an open-ended crescendo, seemingly the only exit for the volatile, dynamic sounds that were once voices. Sound, it should be added, is the outcome for most of the major characters, as they either disappear into sounds (Alice, Pete) or are reduced to a body that makes sounds (Mr. Eddy and Fred).

The merger with sound makes a larger point about the state of the individual subject. Like sound, the subject in the world of *Lost Highway* proves to be unstable and mutable. As evident in the bizarre roster of doubles, one person can turn into another or the same character can be two different people. The culmination of the characters in sound takes things a step further. In their final moments, the characters lose their vocal identities and, in most cases, their actual selves. They join the unending flux of sound. With Pete, Alice, and Fred, we have no clear idea of what has or will become of them. All we hear of them in their final moments is moving, contorting, changing sound.

There is one more transformation: sound becomes voice. The opposition between the two has hardly been balanced, nor would one expect it to be for a composer who depicts singing as "artificial," looks askance at conventional forms of opera, and has been immersed in the compositional and technological production of sound. Throughout the work, sound has dominated the relationship, but, at the end of the piece, it goes a step further by assuming aspects of voice, further displacing the latter. In the scene between Pete and Alice discussed above, sound takes on a defining characteristic of the voice, that of the single part. The archetypes, although most of them consist of more than one part, come across as single gestures, or voices. They either fall within Alice's vocal line (the open-ended crescendo) or they are the only sound event at a given moment (the registral leaps, morphing, and glissando). They are the sole gestures, or voices, that we hear, just as Alice's voice was the only line that we heard before the figures. They are the voices that follow hers.

---

[150] The "Fred effect" is placed on top of the reprise of the opening music (now played live). The new part is consistent with Neuwirth's practice of adding layers of unstable sounds to the repetitions of music from Part I.

[151] As marked in the score (m. 345).

Neuwirth exploits both the musical and the extra-musical capacities of these sonic voices. The open-ended crescendo and glissando execute a specific structural role, marking the end of a section or passage, such as the one between Pete and Alice. The crescendo performs a similar role in Varèse's music, releasing the sonic energy built up in a section so that a new one can begin. Stefan Drees has discussed how the glissando functions as both an endpoint and a resolution in earlier works by Neuwirth; here, it serves as the culmination of a scene (and of Pete) and the "resolution" of the gap between the extreme ranges in register preceding the figure.[152]

The figures also act as voices by carrying meaning – not words but rather associations and images. Neuwirth has described how sounds possess a "history" and "condense a whole imagination complex" (Vorstellungskomplex). Furthermore, sounds, like the archetypal figures, "work according to a certain logic," a modus operandi that can be "manipulated" to achieve different effects. Neuwirth adds that sounds may also have "something metaphorical about them."[153] As heard in the concluding scene between Pete and Alice, the "logic" and "metaphorical" qualities are handled in ways that comment on the two characters. Neuwirth "manipulates" the logic of the open-ended crescendo, which Varèse manipulated so well. His crescendos build up tension then disperse it, letting the sonic mass scatter where it will. Neuwirth's figure absorbs and magnifies the sound of Alice's voice and then releases it, leaving her to wander off to wherever she goes, perhaps back into the realm of the fantasmatic Real from where she came. With Pete, the flux of both the glissando and the morphing serve as rather direct illustrations of his transformation into Fred.

As mentioned earlier, the idea of metaphorical sound, interpreted broadly as sonorities that point to or illustrate an action or event, has long caused discomfort for many composers. Schaeffer and Lachenmann, as we have seen, have kept a distance from that quality. Neuwirth has taken a more accommodating view. She admits that the metaphorical aspect of sound can be a "problem" but does not shy away from using it, especially for dramatic ends.[154] On the one hand, she exploits the pictorial qualities of the sounds; on the other hand, she "manipulates" the formal "logic" of the figures. The dual approach can be seen in her use of the glissando. The figure suggests Pete's metamorphosis into Fred, while at the same time it plays structural

---

[152] Stefan Drees, "Tonräume und Klangfarben bei Olga Neuwirth," in *Composers in Residence: Lucerne Festival, Summer 2002, Pierre Boulez, Olga Neuwirth* (Frankfurt am Main: Stroemfeld, 2002), 168–70.
[153] Neuwirth, "Afterthoughts," 38.   [154] Neuwirth, "Afterthoughts," 38.

roles as both the endpoint of a section and a means of resolving the extremes in register. Finally, Neuwirth handles the figures in ways that give them an additional dimension, that of voice. They not only become the voices of characters but they also take up the character of voices, single lines or gestures that clearly stand out, demand attention, and have something to communicate. With the last transformation, she broadens our perception of what sound can be.

The transformation of sound into voice also lends itself to the inquiry into the act of expression. The topic has notably been absent from the discussion of Neuwirth's opera, whereas it dominated the analysis of Lachenmann's. The latter called attention to the act by obstructing it. We heard the girl try to raise a distinct voice only to have it erased by forceful sounds and the archetypal diminishment figure. No such blockages occur in *Lost Highway*. Pete and Alice, the one couple who sing, do so often and effortlessly. With the florid writing, their parts call to mind conventional operatic styles, and not surprisingly they possess the spontaneity of vocal expression characteristic of the genre. The expressive force of the characters does not so much result from manipulations of the act as from the characters' growing instability and merger with the world of sound. If the act of expression is foregrounded anywhere it is in the world of sound. The act in its most basic form involves the lifting of a voice. So focused is Neuwirth's *Lost Highway* on the dynamics of sound that it is not so much the characters who raise a voice as it is the archetypal figures that take up qualities of a voice. Accordingly, the emphasis is not on a voice obstructed, as in Lachenmann's opera, but rather on a voice emerging in the sonic figures. The voices that they gain say much about the characters whose voices they become and about the unique qualities of the archetypal figures themselves.

Thanks to *Du cristal* and ... *à la fumée*, the image of a diptych has returned several times throughout this chapter. While floating that image, the chapter has all the time been constructing a triptych, the panels of which include Saariaho's orchestral works and the operas of Lachenmann and Neuwirth. The three composers share a fascination with the flux of sound. In particular, they have used the state to explore the act of expression, homing in on the relationship between voice and sound. Here the image of the triptych becomes compelling, as the three panels present the same topic in contrasting ways. The Saariaho pieces reveal how the voice can control both the flux of sound and the space of the continuum, a mastery that gives the two soloists an expressive presence. In Lachenmann's opera, the figure of sonic diminishment slowly erases the voice and the expressive means of the subject. *Lost Highway* binds the two together in another type of relationship. Voice, along with the characters possessing voices, eventually becomes sound, and sound becomes its own type of voice. Having discussed all the panels in the triptych, we can stand back from the group and gain a new appreciation of sound, experiencing it as a force of motion and transformation as well as a means of expressive power and reflection.

Conclusion

Alex Ross divides the final chapter of his history of twentieth-century music, a chapter appropriately subtitled "At Century's End," into a series of sections: After the End, After Europe, After Minimalism, After Modernism, After the Soviets, After Britten.[1] His rhetorical repetition takes up a historiographical refrain. Poised at "century's end," many studies have opened up a period or a movement that lies "after" some other, and assumed past, period or movement. There could be no "after" larger than the movement, or, for some, era, called postmodernism. The prefix digs a line between a defunct modernism and a vibrant successor. It is a line that crosses several accounts of twentieth-century music, one that inscribes the idea of a significant change in the closing decades of the century.

It is a line that, of course, has been much disputed. To appreciate the challenges, the dissenting views of four critics will be discussed: Peter Bürger, Hans Belting, Albrecht Wellmer, and Jürgen Habermas. Their dissent rests upon the idea that modernism continues on and that, in doing so, it has not been, or cannot be, supplanted. Although sharing a belief in the continuity of modernism, each of the critics offers a unique description of the contemporary artistic scene and the place and role of modernism in it. This study will add another contrasting perspective. It draws a stylistic map of the last thirty years, one that sketches the broad boundaries of modernism and sees no space for the contested border of postmodernism.

Before discussing the above critics, we need to turn briefly to Adorno, who frequently addressed the longevity of modernism and whose views on that topic have been cited by some of those writers. Adorno's predictions about the future of modernist music changed over time. An especially pessimistic forecast appears in *Philosophy of New Music* (1949). Inimical to the platitudes built around the arts, Adorno argued, modernist works can possess only one realistic goal, oblivion. Rejected, they grow increasingly unheard to the point that they will eventually become silent. Ironically, in later years, as modern music seemed to many to be closer to the void, Adorno's assessments became less bleak. In the 1950s, he discussed the "aging" of new music, a

---

[1] Alex Ross, *The Rest is Noise: Listening to the Twentieth Century* (New York: Farrar, Straus and Giroux, 2007), 514–35.

serious diagnosis but not one that ever inspired the pageant of doomed images – the Sphinx, a blind Oedipus, oblivion, and a shipwreck – that closes the chapter on Schoenberg in *Philosophy of New Music*.[2] The essay "Vers une musique informelle" proposes a new structural approach, as vague as it is, to escape the rigidities of a decrepit modernism.[3] In "Music and New Music," Adorno admits that the category of new music has aged, but, contrary to his previous geriatric report, he stills sees it as relevant, even vital. Be it the older "new" music of the Second Viennese School or recent works of Darmstadt composers and Cage, he argues, "new music" aggressively attacks "established norms" and poses a "tone of menace" to listeners with conventional tastes. Possessing "critical and aesthetic self understanding," it "refuses" to be part of the "force feeding" of comforts and familiarity to the public.[4]

It is one thing to say that modernism continues and another to say how it does so. Even Adorno faltered here. Modernism, according to him, is driven by the pursuit of advanced material; however, as mentioned in the Introduction, he, near the end of his career, began to doubt how elite the material could remain and how far the pursuit could go. In his discussion of the continuity of modernism, Bürger dwells upon Adorno's idea of advanced material. According to him, the concept blinded Adorno to the developments that would be most crucial to the future of modernism. In particular, Adorno failed to reckon with the significance of Stravinsky's neoclassicism. Focused on advanced material, Adorno depicted neoclassical music as a regression, whereas, for Bürger, neoclassical styles mark an important change in the focus and means of modernism, one pertinent to the 1980s, the decade in which Bürger was writing. By reaching out to past idioms, Stravinsky's works broadened the materials of modern music beyond the rarefied patch prized by Adorno and revealed how modernist techniques could be applied to "regressive" elements to create new compounds.[5] The neoclassical pieces hold the germ for what Bürger calls a "dialectical continuity." Modernism "must recognize as its own much that it has until now rejected." Once welcomed, the old and the familiar must be treated with modernist means, an application that both enriches the outside materials and affirms the "essential category of modernism." The blending of old and new is "precarious," but it is

---

[2] Adorno, "The Aging of the New Music" and *Philosophy of New Music*, 102.
[3] Adorno, "Vers une musique informelle," in *Quasi una Fantasia*, 269–322.
[4] Adorno, "Music and New Music," in *Quasi una Fantasia*, 255–56.
[5] Peter Bürger, *The Decline of Modernism*, trans. Nicholas Walker (Cambridge: Polity Press, 1992), 34–36.

through that combination and the confrontation with the compositional challenges inherent in mixing the two that modernism will find a way to push on.[6]

Belting places the discussion of old and new on more recognizable critical ground. Instead of a dialectical relationship, he points to the irrevocable tensions between tradition and innovation upon which modernism has long "thrived." Things, though, may not be as tense as they once were, as modernism, by bequeathing a rich body of established styles and revered works, has increasingly become part of a growing tradition. Belting affirms that innovation is still a relevant concept, a belief that departs from the attitude that the possibilities of sheer newness at this historical moment are thin, if not nil. Writing on the visual arts, he points to developments in media and technology, particularly video. Recent technologies can keep "the pace of new artistic invention" "accelerating," but he concedes that "the weight of these innovations has diminished in the same measure as has their ability to shape a new style." Nonetheless, Belting upholds innovation as crucial to modernism. It is the means by which the latter "expands" and keeps ahead of its own developing tradition.[7]

Other critics have looked beyond the newness of materials and idioms to conceptions of modernism as a broad cultural undertaking. Wellmer sees modernism as fueled by the "permanent compulsion to innovation and subversion of form and meaning" but places those impulses within a modernity defined by "the rational, subversive, and experimental spirit of modern democracy, modern art, modern science, and modern individualism."[8] Both Wellmer and Habermas draw a distinction between modernism and modernity; the former being an artistic movement that fits into the cultural period of the latter, which began with the Enlightenment. The hallmark of modernity has been a spirit of critique. Artistic modernism has sharpened that critique, turning it on the means of artistic production as well as ideals such as rationality, unity, and totality. The perspective has kept modernism alert and provided a means of continuation, as it is always ready to home in on some new ideal or artistic possibility.

Habermas presents modernity as a "project" that originated with the Enlightenment separation of the arts, sciences, and morality into autonomous realms. In those spheres, each of the three would develop

---

[6] Bürger, *The Decline of Modernism*, 44–47.
[7] Hans Belting, *Art History after Modernism*, trans. Caroline Saltzwedel, Mitch Cohen, and Kenneth Norcott (Chicago and London: University of Chicago Press, 2003), 3–6.
[8] Albrecht Wellmer, *The Persistence of Modernity: Essays on Aesthetics, Ethics, and Postmodernism*, trans. David Midgley (Cambridge, MA: MIT Press, 1991), viii.

its own logic.[9] The separation, though, went too far, a striking example being the insularity of modernist arts in the period after World War Two, a time in which Habermas, echoing Adorno, claims that modernism "aged."[10] For him, the inward stare must be directed outwards. The original Enlightenment ideal was that the separation of the three realms would release the potential of each, an accumulation of knowledge that could be used to enrich daily life. According to Habermas, avant-garde movements such as Surrealism tried to collapse the wall between art and life only to fail. Modernist arts need to participate in the larger effort to reconnect aesthetic realms and everyday praxis, an endeavor that could give modernism, in its aged state, momentum and purpose.

As long as the gap between aesthetic realms and everyday praxis stands, modernity remains, as Habermas puts it, an "incomplete project."[11] Wellmer refers to modernity as an "unsurpassable horizon."[12] Belting claims that it is "impossible" to "end" modernism.[13] The rhetoric of incompleteness and infinity reveals the extent to which the idea of continuity pervades their accounts. Modernist arts, contrary to Adorno, do not merely struggle to continue in the face of oblivion; rather, they are destined to continue, and could seemingly do so forever, albeit not always under the most welcoming conditions. Not surprisingly, the above three critics and Bürger have used that rhetoric to oppose declarations about the rise of postmodernism. The rejoinder is swift, if not a little broad: how can there be a successor or an end when modernism remains engaged in a long-standing, and possibly unrealizable, project or when it can never be exceeded?

Their arguments are, of course, more substantial than this. Unfortunately, there is not enough space to discuss each critic's views in detail, only space to present their cases in relation to the ideas mentioned above. Habermas places postmodernism, exemplified by historically referential architecture and neoconservatism, in the company of antimodernism, the opposition to modernity, and premodernity, the call for a return to the positions prior to modernity.[14] All three "conservative" movements "appeal" to the "aporias" generated by modernity as a reason to abandon the project of expanding

---

[9] The discussion refers to Habermas's essay "Modernity: An Unfinished Project," which was first given as an acceptance speech upon receiving the Adorno Prize from the city of Frankfurt in 1980. An English translation can be found in *Habermas and the Unfinished Project of Modernity: Critical Essays on "The Philosophical Discourse of Modernity*," ed. Maurizio Passerin d'Entrèves and Seyla Benhabib (Cambridge, MA: MIT Press, 1997), 38–55. This account of Habermas's views draws upon Martin Jay, "Habermas and Modernism," in *Habermas and Modernity*, ed. Richard J. Bernstein (Cambridge: Polity Press, 1985), 132–39.

[10] Habermas, "Modernity: An Unfinished Project," 41.

[11] Habermas, "Modernity: An Unfinished Project," 38.

[12] Wellmer, *The Persistence of Modernity*, vii.   [13] Belting, *Art History after Modernism*, 4.

[14] Habermas, "Modernity: An Unfinished Project," 53–54.

and eventually integrating the three cultural spheres with everyday praxis.[15] Postmodern arts, for example, reject utopian claims, insist on the "fictive character of art," and seek "to confine aesthetic experience to the private sphere."[16] As challenging and remote as the culmination of the modernist project may be, Habermas argues that we should not, and cannot, forsake it, for to do so would be to give up hope in a larger and more integrated aesthetic realm. Wellmer acknowledges the changed emphases in recent artistic production that have been upheld as hallmarks of postmodernism, such positions as pluralism, anti-utopianism, and irony. He, though, considers them to be part of the self-criticism central to modernism. Instead of being a new, subsequent movement, postmodernism amounts to an internal critique that broadens the boundaries of modernism.[17] Belting claims that there can be no end to modernism because there is no alternative to it, let alone a successor.[18] New developments in media and technology have expanded modernism to the point that it has evolved into a new form of itself, what he, drawing upon the work of the anthropologist Marc Augé, refers to as "hypermodernity."[19] Finally, Bürger contends that the modernist period can never be completed let alone trumped, as all new styles, be they post- or anti-modern, refer to it.[20] Moreover, the means of modernism are germane to the dialectical engagement between the past and the present so crucial to contemporary arts.

This study easily enters the conversation sustained by Habermas, Wellmer, Belting, and Bürger. It agrees on the general terms of the discussion, those being the continuity of modernism and the opposition to notions of postmodernism. The case made to support the two points, however, contrasts with those put forward by the four critics. The differences result in part from the means and scope of the argument taken up here. The means have largely been analytical, a discussion of compositional elements to bolster larger points about approaches to material and expression in late modernist music. Through analysis, this study looks outward from the individual work, and not that far outward at that. Habermas and Wellmer open up large cultural vistas stretching across centuries. Bürger and Belting too follow distant historical and cultural lines. Not much beyond the musical realm has been charted here. Moreover, just roughly thirty years of that realm have been discussed in any sort of detail. Artistic modernism, as described by Habermas and Wellmer, is a single component of a larger modernity. Dealing with

---

15 Habermas, "Modernity: An Unfinished Project," 44.
16 Habermas, "Modernity: An Unfinished Project," 54.
17 Wellmer, *The Persistence of Modernity*, vii, 88–89.
18 Belting, *Art History after Modernism*, 4–6.
19 Belting, *Art History after Modernism*, 4.   20 Bürger, *The Decline of Modernism*, 44–45.

only recent musical manifestations of artistic modernism, this study has, in comparison, labored over a sliver.

The sliver, though, has its rewards. A tighter focus yields more specific accounts of how modernism has been extended, accounts rich in compositional detail. The grand theories of an "incomplete project" or an "unsurpassable horizon," as valuable as they are, never entertain such fine points. The details, it should be noted, can inspire broad, if not grand, theories. The analyses undertaken here have inspired one such theory – that of a modernism based upon lines of inquiry. It is along those lines that modernism has continued. So strong have they been that they have kept modernist idioms going on into a new century.

As the four critics have each maintained, the continuity of modernism precludes the possibility of a postmodernism. In a study of competing ways in which postmodernism has been defined, Helga de la Motte-Haber argues that the longevity of modernist idioms complicates efforts "to speak of the threshold of a new age."[21] Not so for many champions of postmodernism. Jencks, for example, acknowledges the role of modernist techniques in postmodern architecture, but he holds that their appearance is ultimately a sign of obsolescence, not vitality. According to him, the techniques become "double coded," speaking at once to their modernist origins and to the new postmodern aesthetics to which they hew. Through the coding, the origins and aesthetics of the techniques are transcended.[22] Wellmer's notion of an internal critique reverses Jencks's concept. Modernist works absorb, or transcend, the new aesthetic stances associated with postmodernism, thereby expanding the field of the former. The two arguments reveal how much an either/or logic rules the critical debate. Elements of both periods may be present but one will ultimately dominate. The result is curious visions of cultural mergers. A new aesthetic field can already be broad enough to take in and transcend modernism, or modernism can be big enough to absorb new challenging aesthetic fields.

Instead of the either/or settings of Jencks and Wellmer, this study looks out to a pluralistic realm. The notion of pluralism, it goes without saying, is crucial to the arts since World War Two (and to the decades before). Pluralism, modernism, and postmodernism form a critical trinity, so closely have they been connected to each other in the discussion of contemporary

---

[21] Helga de la Motte-Haber, "Postmodernism in Music: Retrospection as Reassessment," *Contemporary Music Review* 12 (1995), 78. For a discussion of the different approaches to postmodernism in German scholarship, see Joakim Tillman, "Postmodernism and Art Music in the German Debate," in *Postmodern Music/Postmodern Thought*, ed. Judy Lochhead and Joseph Auner (New York and London: Routledge, 2002), 75–91.

[22] Charles Jencks, *What is Postmodernism?* 15.

arts. The three have been arranged in different ways, depending on the view being proposed. The most common combination is the tight connection, almost overlap, between pluralism and postmodernism. The typical post-modern work blends styles and periods. Beyond the single composition, the pluralism of the artistic realm is considered to be a manifestation of the postmodern worldview. The third part of the trinity, modernism, is placed at a distance, consigned to the fading past.

This study presents another configuration. There is no overlap between pluralism and postmodernism or between pluralism and modernism for that matter. The broader artistic field is considered to be pluralistic, not the exclusive terrain of either one of the *isms*. The question then becomes where do modernism and postmodernism fit into that realm. Danuser has offered some points to consider. Writing in 1988, he observed that it was no longer possible to speak of a single cultural epoch because of the deep pluralism in the arts, a comment as valid then as now. Modernism, as Danuser put it, is one part of the larger cultural sphere (Teilkultur).[23] For Danuser, there are several such parts. In the early 1980s, for example, he described the interlocking of modernism, postmodernism, and neomodernism.[24]

Two of the three parts, modernism and postmodernism, will be taken up here; neomodernism, Danuser's term for the return to the mixture of Romanticism and early modernist idioms that shaped music around 1900, is his rather short-lived critical invention and will be dismissed. As for modernism, the crucial question is, what kind of part is it? Within the pluralistic scene, modernism plays two significant roles. First, it is a point of reference. "Relevant art today," according to Bürger, "must define itself in relation to modernism."[25] Through the process of self-definition, "relevant" works give modernism a ubiquitous presence, as something either to be supported or rejected. Second, modernism functions as a source of ideas and impulses, a role evident in the modernist lines of inquiry. The different lines have provided musicians with energies that they can tap into, including the flux of sound, breakage of the fragmentary, and tensions of silence. They also reveal ways to approach those impulses. Building upon a century of challenging composition, modernism offers a repository of demanding materials and ideals.

As both a constant point of reference and a source of compositional impulses, modernism has a broad reach across the pluralistic realm. Even movements and lone works that disavow modernist aesthetics cannot help

---

[23] Hermann Danuser, "Zur Kritik der musikalischen Postmoderne," *Neue Zeitschrift für Musik* 149, no. 12 (1988), 5.
[24] Hermann Danuser, *Die Musik des 20. Jahrhunderts*, 406.
[25] Bürger, *The Decline of Modernism*, 44.

but evoke those aesthetics through denial. Moreover, many types of music, including disavowing movements and works, draw upon the impulses cultivated in lines of inquiry. Neo-Romantic idioms, for example, have rejected modernist tenets through the recourse to tonality and older expressive ideals, yet they have kept company with modernism in various ways, including the use of the dissonant fibers of modernist idioms and the shared interest in securing more direct means of expression. So far-reaching have the modernist inquiries been that they have been taken up in musical realms well beyond the concert hall. The diaspora of modernist elements (a topic for another book) can be heard in the fragmentation and layering in hip-hop; mobile, mutable sound in electronic dance music; dissonances and odd noises in film music; and stillness in ambient idioms.

Postmodernism, as held here, has no presence in the pluralistic realm. Instead of the trinity of pluralism, modernism, and postmodernism, this study holds up the pair of pluralism and modernism. Two arguments against the rise of a postmodern movement or period will be succinctly presented, each of which grows out of points raised earlier. The first joins the consensus among the above four critics: there can be no postmodernism as long as modernism continues, or, for some, remains open-ended. The continuity of modernism, as explored here, results from ongoing lines of inquiry. A successor to modernism would supposedly stanch the lines or, at least, initiate new ones. If anything, so-called postmodern works have continued the lines, some of which, like the fragmentary, are aesthetic positions that have been viewed as characteristic of postmodernism but are actually long-standing modernist interests. The second argument is premised on the breadth of modernism as both a point of reference and a source of ideals in the contemporary scene. With modernism so extensive, it becomes difficult to conceive of a movement that could stand in opposition to it, let alone supplant it. Moreover, works considered to be postmodern typically evoke the presence of modernism and partake of its ideals.

The two arguments may seem to suggest that modernism is so far-reaching that there is no alternative to it. Or, to put it another way, all works are modernist, at least to some degree. The either/or logic of Jencks's double coding and Wellmer's internal critique would seem to be insinuating itself into this study. One way to check that logic is to measure the range of modernism. To this end, a map of the contemporary scene needs to be drawn. The map, in the cursory sketch offered here, shows a group of works deeply rooted in modernist traditions, a modernist continent, as it were. The pieces analyzed in the preceding chapters populate that land. On separate continents or remote islands are other types of pieces. Whereas they have all been touched by modernist aesthetics to a different extent, they have managed to stand apart from them and claim a largely independent stylistic ground. These removed lands include such styles as neo-Romanticism, the new simplicity, and minimalism.

The map is admittedly superficial, but the idea of a map points to the crucial critical task that needs to be undertaken. We need to come to terms with the pluralism of the contemporary scene, to understand what is going on within that dense mass of works. A map forces us to think along lines of range, distance, and connections. This study has charted the range of modernism in music of the last thirty years. As shown here, modernist idioms cover a lot of ground. They have been pushed both onwards by the various inquiries and outwards to the extent that they have interacted with other styles. Even with the broad reach of modernism, there is still distance between some styles and pieces and that modernist "continent." It is important to measure the distance and to see how remote some works have managed to be and how close others can get while standing apart. We need to ask through what stylistic and aesthetic positions that distance is created. Another step is to perceive the connections between pieces. Across great or small distances, there are usually affinities between works, especially ties with modernist ideals. For instance, Chapter 3 showed how compositions of all different stripes, those called modernist and those called postmodernist, share an interest in the fragmentary.

In many ways, it comes down to lines on a map. The map inferred from some accounts of music since World War Two is marked by a single line, that between modernism and postmodernism. That line does not appear on the map sketched here. There is instead a web of thin lines between individual compositions. The lines reveal the connections that exist between pieces, the distances between them, and the stylistic groupings within the contemporary pluralistic realm. Through these lines we can get our bearings within that realm and gain a clearer idea of the larger tensions, dynamics, and patterns shaping it. Such reconnaissance is necessary if we are ever to make sense of the extensive pluralism in which contemporary arts are created.

In her book on the "new" modernist poetics, Marjorie Perloff observes that "as we move into the twenty first century, the modern/postmodern divide has emerged as more apparent than real."[26] Surprisingly for a scholar who has seen an endless horizon of "afters," Ross too has questioned the rise of a postmodern period.[27] If there is an "after modernism," as he suggests, it

---

[26] Perloff, *21st-century Modernism*, 164.

[27] Ross, *The Rest is Noise*, 515. Ross's reasons for questioning the concept of postmodernism are very different from those advanced here: "Some have tried to call the era postmodern, but 'modernism' is already so equivocal a term that to affix 'post' pushes it over the edge into meaninglessness." Nonetheless, he does not claim that contemporary arts fit within an encompassing era, no matter what it is called.

is not what has been called postmodernism. Nor does he claim that we have moved completely beyond modernism, which, he admits, perseveres, albeit in the shelter provided by government funding and coteries.[28] As Perloff and Ross make clear, the beginning of the twenty-first century has inspired scholars to redraw the map of contemporary arts. Much of their efforts have focused on the once seemingly inevitable line between modernism and postmodernism. With that line fading away, we can recognize the ongoing vitality of modernist styles at the turn of a new century, a music that continues to expand upon the imaginative explorations that it began around the turn of the last century.

[28] Ross, *The Rest is Noise*, 523–27.

Select bibliography

Adorno, Theodor. *Quasi una Fantasia: Essays on Modern Music.* Trans. Rodney Livingstone. London and New York: Verso, 1992.

Aesthetic Theory. Trans. and ed. Robert Hullot-Kentor. Minneapolis: University of Minnesota Press, 1997.

Essays on Music. Ed. Richard Leppert. Berkeley: University of California Press, 2002.

Philosophy of New Music. Trans. and ed. Robert Hullot-Kentor. Minneapolis: University of Minnesota Press, 2006.

Belting, Hans. *Art History after Modernism.* Trans. Caroline Saltzwedel, Mitch Cohen, and Kenneth Norcott. Chicago and London: University of Chicago Press, 2003.

Blanchot, Maurice. *The Writing of the Disaster.* Trans. Ann Smock. Lincoln: University of Nebraska Press, 1986.

The Infinite Conversation. Trans. Susan Howard. Minneapolis: University of Minnesota Press, 1993.

Bürger, Peter. *The Decline of Modernism.* Trans. Nicholas Walker. Cambridge: Polity Press, 1992.

Clark, T. J. *Farewell to an Idea: Episodes from a History of Modernism.* New Haven and London: Yale University Press, 1999.

Clarke, Michael. "Jonathan Harvey's *Mortuos plango, vivos voco.*" In *Analytical Methods of Electroacoustic Music.* Ed. Mary Simoni, 111–43. New York and London: Routledge, 2006.

Cox, Christopher and Daniel Warner, eds. *Audio Cultures: Readings in Modern Music.* New York: Continuum, 2005.

Dahlhaus, Carl. *Schönberg und andere.* Mainz: Schott, 1978.

Schoenberg and the New Music: Essays. Trans. Derrick Puffett and Alfred Clayton. Cambridge University Press, 1987.

Danuser, Hermann. *Die Musik des 20. Jahrhunderts.* Laaber: Laaber-Verlag, 1984.

Davies, Stephen. *Themes in the Philosophy of Music.* Oxford University Press, 2003.

Decroupet, Pascal and Elena Ungeheuer. "Through the Sensory Looking-glass: The Aesthetic and Serial Foundation of *Gesang der Jünglinge.*" *Perspectives of New Music* 36 (1998): 97–142.

Douglas, Mary. *Purity and Danger: An Analysis of Concepts of Pollution and Taboo.* 2nd edn. London: Routledge & Kegan Paul, 1969.

Frey, Hans-Jost. *Interruptions.* Trans. Georgia Albert. Albany: State University of New York Press, 1996.

Goldman, Jonathan. "Exploding/Fixed: Form as Opposition in the Writings and Late Works of Pierre Boulez." Ph.D. thesis, Université de Montréal, 2006.

Habermas, Jürgen. "Modernity: An Unfinished Project." In *Habermas and the Unfinished Project of Modernity: Critical Essays on "The Philosophical Discourse of Modernity."* Eds. Passerin d'Entrèves, Maurizio and Seyla Benhabib. Cambridge, MA: MIT Press, 1997.

Harvey, Jonathan. "The Mirror of Ambiguity." In *The Language of Electroacoustic Music.* Ed. Simon Emerson, 175–90. London: Macmillan, 1986.

In Quest of Spirit: Thoughts on Music. Berkeley: University of California Press, 1999.

Hoeckner, Berthold, ed. *Apparitions: New Perspectives on Adorno and Twentieth-century Music.* New York: Routledge, 2006.

Hospers, John, ed. *Artistic Expression.* New York: Meredith Corporation, 1971.

Jameson, Fredric. *Postmodernism or the Cultural Logic of Capitalism.* Durham: Duke University Press, 1991.

A Singular Modernity: Essay on the Ontology of the Present. London and New York: Verso, 2002.

Jencks, Charles. *What is Postmodernism?* New York and London: St. Martin's Press, 1986.

The New Moderns: From Late to Neo-modernism. London: Academy Editions, 1990.

Johnson, Julian. *Webern and the Transformation of Nature.* Cambridge University Press, 1999.

Kahn, Douglas. *Noise, Water, Meat: A History of Sound in the Arts.* Cambridge, MA: MIT Press, 1999.

Kaija Saariaho. Paris: IRCAM, 1994.

Kaltenecker, Martin. *Avec Helmut Lachenmann.* Paris: Van Dieren, 2002.

Lachenmann, Helmut. *Musik als existentielle Erfahrung.* Ed. Joseph Häusler. Wiesbaden: Breitkopf & Härtel, 1996.

Linden, Werner. *Luigi Nonos Weg zum Streichquartett.* Kassel: Bärenreiter, 1989.

Mahnkopf, Claus-Steffen. "Neue Musik am Beginn der Zweiten Moderne." *Merkur* 594/595 (1998), 864–75.

Mahnkopf, Claus-Steffen, Frank Cox, and Wolfram Schurig, eds. *Polyphony and Complexity.* Hofheim: Wolke Verlag, 2002.

Metzer, David. *Quotation and Cultural Meaning in Twentieth-century Music.* Cambridge University Press, 2003.

Meyer, Felix and Anne C. Shreffler. "Webern's Revisions: Some Analytical Implications." *Music Analysis* 12 (1993): 355–79.

Nonnenmann, Rainer. "Music with Images – The Development of Helmut Lachenmann's Sound Composition between Concretion and Transcendence." *Contemporary Music Review* 24, no. 1 (2005): 1–29.

O'Brien, John, ed. *Clement Greenberg: The Collected Essays and Criticism.* 4 vols. University of Chicago Press, 1986–1993.

Paddison, Max. *Adorno's Aesthetics of Music.* Cambridge University Press, 1993.

Perloff, Marjorie. *21st-century Modernism: The "New" Poetics*. Oxford: Blackwell, 2002.

Pousset, Damien. "The Works of Kaija Saariaho, Philippe Hurel, and Marc-André Dalbavie – Stile Concertato, Stile Concitato, Stile Rappresentativo." *Contemporary Music Review* 19, no. 3 (2000): 67–100.

Saariaho, Kaija. "Timbre and Harmony: Interpolations of Timbral Structures." *Contemporary Music Review* 2 (1987): 93–133.

Spree, Herman. *"Fragmente-Stille, An Diotima": Ein analytischer Versuch zu Luigi Nonos Streichquartett*. Saarbrücken: Pfau, 1992.

Wellmer, Albrecht. *The Persistence of Modernity: Essays on Aesthetics, Ethics, and Postmodernism*. Trans. David Midgley. Cambridge, MA: MIT Press, 1991.

Whittall, Arnold. *Exploring Twentieth-century Music: Tradition and Innovation*. Cambridge University Press, 2003.

Williams, Alastair. *New Music and the Claims of Modernity*. Hants: Ashgate, 1997.
  "Ageing of the New: The Museum of Musical Modernism." In *The Cambridge History of Twentieth-century Music*. Ed. Nicholas Cook and Anthony Pople, 506–38. Cambridge University Press, 2004.
  "Swaying with Schumann: Subjectivity and Tradition in Wolfgang Rihm's 'Fremde Szenen' I–III and Related Scores." *Music and Letters* 87 (2006): 379–97.

Žižek, Slavoj. *The Art of the Ridiculous Sublime: On David Lynch's "Lost Highway."* Seattle: University of Washington, 2000.

Index